Hill Station Teacher

A Life with India in It

by Ruth Unrau

KIDRON CREEK PUBLISHERS
North Newton, Kansas

For Paula and Susan,

our fellow Talented Travelers.

Hill Station Teacher

Printed in the United States of America.

Library of Congress Number 97-72288

International Standard Book Number 0-9657489-0-1

Design by John Hiebert. Printing by Mennonite Press, Inc., Newton, Kansas 67114

Cover Photo: Seth Mark (left), former buyer and liaison officer; Ron Kapadia, former director of plant services. Photo by Walt Unrau.

Contents

I. The Writer's Journal 1
*The process of putting together the book; our six visits
to India and Woodstock School over thirty years*

II. **Hill Station**
1. Mussoorie, Queen of the Hills 7
The town, with a short history of its development
2. The Bazaars 19
A walk through the several bazaars
3. The Road 29
*Following the road east or west from the town and down
to Dehra Dun*
4. The Hillside 39
The homes on the Hillside above Woodstock School
5. The Christian Communities 47

III. **Woodstock School**
6. Woodstock School: Traditions 55
The history of Woodstock and traditions that have survived
7. Life in a Boarding School 67
The unique problems of living at a boarding school
8. Academe 77
The academic program
9. The Ladies' Staff Room 85
The teaching staff and personal relationships
10. The Great Rhododendron Hike and Other Sporting Events . 93
The athletic program, with hiking as a major sport

IV. **As We Live and Breathe**
11. The Flora and the Fauna 103

12. Weather Report 113
13. Coping 125
   Dealing with water, electricity, and telephone shortages
14. Food 135
15. Clothing 143
16. Shelter 151
17. The Support System 157
   Appreciating and getting along with our helpers
18. The Society Page 167
   Our social life, celebrating holidays
19. Wordwise 177
   A look at the various languages, books, newspapers

V. The World Beyond our Hill
20. The Villages 185
21. British India: The Raj and the Rajahs 191
   The inheritance from the British Raj
22. The Wider World 203
   The sacred cow, the caste system, poverty
23. Religions of the Hill Station 211
   Hindus, Buddhists, Muslims, others
24. Missionary Life and Good Times 221
   Visiting the mission stations

VI. Travel Guide
25. Going Places 233
26. Other Hill Stations 243

End Notes 253

The Writer's Journal

NOVEMBER 1964. When the principal of Woodstock School, Canon Samuel R. Burgoyne, and his wife, Mary Esther, visited in our home in North Newton, Kansas, Walt and I made inquiries about spending a sabbatical year at Woodstock School in North India. However, the school was asking for a three-year commitment and we could not leave our jobs for that long. And then somehow we had the invitation for Walt to come as business manager and for me to teach English for the school year of 1965-66. We packed our barrels and our children, then sixteen and ten years old, for a once-in-a-lifetime experience abroad.

JUNE 1965. While we were flying to India, Paula made friends with some of the other passengers and learned that we were sharing the plane with about seventy Presbyterians who were visiting South Asian church centers. They knew all about Woodstock School. Of course they did; they had owned it at one time.

Where and what was this place we were going to? Woodstock School is an international, non-denominational, Christian school that includes kindergarten through twelfth year, teaching an American curriculum as well as a stream for the English General Certificate of Education, both O and A levels. The school is accredited by the Middle States Association of Colleges and Secondary Schools. It strives for a mix of students, one third each of North American, Indian, and other international students. The enrollment averages 450 students, with the larger classes in the higher grades. Usually over sixty seniors graduate each year. Woodstock is about 175 miles north of Delhi in the foothills of the Himalayas. The environment is six directional, all the points of the compass as well as up and down. A map of our neighborhood should be sculpted to show not only where north is, but how the paths rise and fall, how they go in and out of the embracing folds of the hills.

We enjoyed a year of getting to know another culture and a look at another part of the world. We were in India during a short war with Pakistan. I think the culture shock we experienced came after returning home to realize how affluent we were, how many options we had, from choosing a breakfast cereal to choosing a college.

We left Woodstock with the casual comment: "If you ever need us again, let us know."

SEPTEMBER 1969. A letter from Woodstock came reminding us of that half-promise that we would come back if needed. Could we come for a three-year term starting in July 1970

This time we paused. We had just begun building a new house. Paula would be a high-school sophomore and would have to finish school at Woodstock. Susan would be a college senior, but she could arrange for a semester of independent study in India. They both urged us to go. It seemed that our daughters had built up a good deal of nostalgia for India. When we pointed out the financial damage, they suggested that we were being materialistic. They were willing for us to limit our retirement reserve so that they could go to India and be non-materialistic. With their encouragement and the support of the Commission on Overseas Mission of our denomination, Walt resigned from his work as business manager of our church press and I from my teaching at Bethel College. We put the last coat of varnish on our new house, rented it to a college couple, and flew off.

I took along a manuscript I had started about our experience at Woodstock, thinking it needed more pith. I was glad for the opportunity to finish it in the land of its conception.

JULY 1970. In the four years since we had left, much of what we had known as Woodstock had changed. About half the staff were new faces for us, but the principal, Robert Alter, we had known earlier. The challenge this time was to help direct the school as it changed from one primarily for missionary children, most of them from North America, to a school that served the needs of Asian and European children. Many of the missionary children had gone home with their parents as mission boards turned over the administration of churches, schools, and hospitals to Indian administrators.

The country survived another short war with Pakistan, culminating in the formation of the country of Bangladesh from what had been East Pakistan. We received an education in the economics of the green revolution, as well as the hard realities of famine and flood.

JULY 1973. We came home after three years knowing we had had our experience abroad and would from there on be quiet stay-at-homes, content to pursue our jobs until retirement. The culture shock this time was the shocking price of orange juice at home and the fact that every family now owned two cars. We settled comfortably into our "new" house, grateful that we had not sold it before going overseas, for it had increased dramatically in value. Walt found an accounting job and I went back to teaching at Bethel College. I had my unfinished manuscript, along with lots of notes written on the backs of typing exercises, and fresh resolutions about finishing the book. This was to be my third book, following the two books for children that had previously been published.

A study of India should touch many fields: psychology, sociology, politics, art, music, architecture, dance, cooking, sport. It is the equivalent of a liberal arts education. All I wanted to do, I protested, was to tell the story of our experience in India. But I was challenged to read all I could find about India, and that study was rewarding enough, even if I never finished my book.

JULY 1975. I was spending summers on my India book, but it was not going well. Using the book as an excuse, I returned to India by myself for five weeks. I borrowed a typewriter and holed up in a guestroom at the school to write, interviewing friends and meeting new people.

FEBRUARY 1981. Union Biblical Seminary at Yavatmal, India, asked Walt to come for two years as business manager. They would be moving the seminary to the large city of Pune. Both daughters were pursuing advanced academic degrees by that time and we were free to go. Again we resigned out jobs, rented our house, attended mission orientation conference, packed our suitcases, and waited for visas. The visas were refused. Since we were ready to go *someplace*, we were soon on our way to Botswana in Southern Africa, again to work at activities related to business and English.

By now the India manuscript was heavier, dog-eared, and nearly finished. I took it to Botswana, thinking I would spend my afternoons on it, since I was officially classified as "an unassigned spouse." However, I found Southern African distractions for my afternoons.

SEPTEMBER 1983. At the end of our two-year term, we decided to go home by way of India. Our reasoning was that we would never be in that part of the world again. We would touch base with Wood-

stock School one more time. Our friends, the Kapadias, who were in
the U.S. at the time, loaned us the use of their house for ten days, and
we settled in with their cook and caretaker to look after us. We were
with Carl and Sally Lehman, another couple who had served in
Botswana. We had the fun of showing them our Mussoorie and making comparisons with the then and now, Africa and India, samp and
rice. In spite of the daily rain, the experience was exhilarating.

Mussoorie had changed in the eighteen years since we had first
come.

"It has changed only for the worse," the retired principal of Oak
Grove said. He was returning to visit after seventeen years.

We had to agree to some extent, but not totally. There were
signs of improved housing; people were better dressed and better fed.
But Mussoorie had become more congested, and the slums of Landour were still depressing, especially the building at the top of
Mullingar Hill.

OCTOBER 1983. By now we were in our wrinkled age and old
enough to sit still. Walt was called back to his old accounting job and
I decided to write full time. A commission to write a book of biographies of Mennonite women persuaded me to buy a magical word
processor. Reluctantly I put my seventeen-year-old India manuscript
on a top shelf, resigned to another distraction.

SEPTEMBER 1984. A cable came for Walt to come back to
Woodstock as a volunteer for a semester to assist the new business
manager for a few months. We would also go to the mission field in
central India and to Bangladesh for auditing duties. I packed both
the book of biographies and the India manuscript, parting regretful-
ly with my word processor.

Politically, this was the most traumatic of any time we had
spent in India. Indira Gandhi was assassinated on October 31 and
the Union Carbide gas leak at Bhopal caused thousands of deaths
and an international furor. Bill Jones was principal during this visit.

FEBRUARY 1985. Back home again, to finish the book of biographies by summer. Then back to the India book, now with the working
title of *Hill Station*. I wished I could, by some miracle of computer-screen
patching, present all the information simultaneously—the five-thou-
sand-year history of India; its religions, art, geography, biology, and languages—as I introduced my readers to Woodstock School and its place
in the Indian setting. I settled for a history that disposed of millenniums
in a few paragraphs, setting a record for short histories of India.

FEBRUARY 1986. Once more a cable asked us to come to Woodstock for a short visit. And once more we responded. Again, a new principal, Hugh Bradby from England, and a new group of staff members, all looking incredibly young to be responsible for this prestigious institution. We returned home in July, agreeing that this would be our last flight. These visits to India had been exclamation points in the story of our lives, marking enriching passages, but it was time to close that chapter.

APRIL 1993. But one more time. A new building, the Media Center, funded by American Schools and Hospitals Abroad, needed a short-term accountant and the Middle School needed an English teacher to fill in for one on maternity leave. At the time I was working on a book on the history of the General Conference mission in India. I gave it to a committee of readers, and we left for our sixth sojourn in India. Ron Flaming, a former Bethel colleague, was principal. Another Woodstock, very different, very challenging. Paula visited for the celebration of our fortieth wedding anniversary, for which our Koinonia group sang together the old hymn "Great is Thy Faithfulness." Shortly after that a Bangladeshi student fell from the road near his hostel to a tragic death, and the community sang the same hymn at his memorial service. We said our reluctant goodbyes in December.

SEPTEMBER 1995. Having finished the book about the Mennonite mission in India, I got back to *Hill Station*. There is so much more to say about India, but my inner voice says, "Focus, keep your mind on the subject, why are you wandering all over India?"

We had been in and out of India during a thirty-year period. For six of those years, India was our world and Mussoorie was its center. When Peter Jennings reported that Sikh terrorists had been driven from the Golden Temple, we listened and mourned for that conflicted country. We had been in that temple when it was serene and mystical. We listened appalled to the report of the assassination of Rajiv Gandhi. We had our television memory of him lighting the fire of his mother's pyre.

Indira Gandhi once said, "No statement about India is wholly true." With this as my disclaimer, I can present this report of our experiences there and the paths of inquiry that led off from them.

Chapter 1

Mussoorie, Queen of the Hills

In July 1970, Walt, Susan, Paula, and I arrived in New Delhi for a second term, a half day behind schedule because of an airline mechanics' strike. The taxi driver who had been sent by the travel agency to meet us had not waited; he could not forego a half day of fares. As Talented Travelers, we were not upset.

An hour passed and no one appeared from the usually dependable travel agent. With many misgivings we accepted the services of a driver who had been hovering about insisting that he could take us to Mussoorie. We paid his agent in advance. Our taxi was an Ambassador, a vehicle that surely had never been new; and the driver was an unkempt, uncommunicative Hindu. Our destination was a hill station on the first ridge of the Himalaya Mountains in North India, six hours away.

The taxi coughed out of the YMCA driveway into the street. We knew then that we were in trouble. Our taxi had no brakes, and we came within inches of hitting a bus. We insisted that he stop at a garage, and we paid to have the brakes repaired before proceeding toward the Mussoorie foothills. Halfway to our destination, the driver told us that we would spend the night at Roorkee, but we reminded him that he had promised to deposit us in Mussoorie that night. Unfortunately, we persuaded him to continue, and we arrived in Dehra Dun by nine o'clock.

Mussoorie lies 3,000 feet up, twenty-two miles and forty-five minutes by zigzag road north from the valley town of Dehra Dun. Our good humor increased as we thought of arriving within an hour at Woodstock School. Looking up to the top of the horseshoe ridge, we understood why Mussoorie has been called "Queen of the Hills."

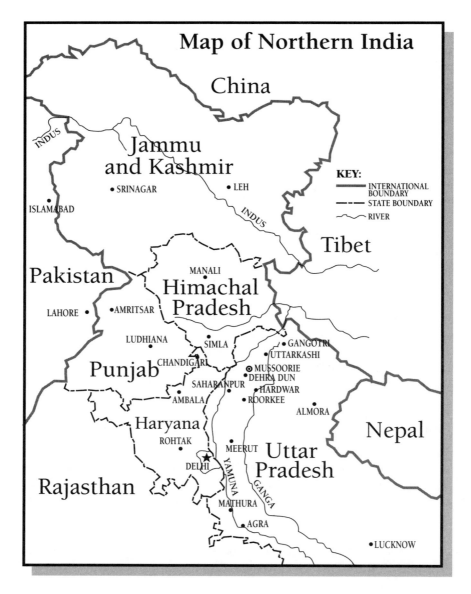

Map of Northern India

The Queen that night was decorated with the jewels of her electric lights. They glittered along the six miles of the ridge, west to east, from Library Bazaar, though the Mall, Landour Bazaar, and finally Mullingar Hill. Beyond Mullingar, out of sight beyond a fold in the hills, was Woodstock School.

The best approach to Mussoorie, except by helicopter or elephant, is by the snaking road that slithers up the walls of the mountains. The trip might include encounters with monkeys, cows, and goats; salutes from herdsmen, holy men, and milkmen; and nausea for those of us who become carsick on U turns. The signs along the road caution: "SLOW has four letters, so had LIFE. SPEED has five letters, so has DEATH."

But we should have listened to our driver back there in Roorkee. Neither the taxi nor the driver was meant for the hills, and certainly not for the climb from Dehra Dun to Mussoorie. Five miles from the top, he wore out the last of his gears and coasted to a stop at the freight depot below Mussoorie. At that point, our overwhelmed driver stepped out of his taxi and disappeared into the night. Walt caught a ride with a friendly driver of a jeep and continued to Mussoorie.

"He is leaving us unprotected women to the dangers of the sinister Indian night," Susan said cheerfully. Paula moaned. Since Hong Kong she had developed an infection on her cheek, another discomfort on her list of woes.

Actually, we were safe enough. The coolies peering through the car windows were only curious. In half an hour, Robert Alter, principal of Woodstock School, rescued us in his jeep.

Since then, we have watched scores of travelers tumble out of taxis in the Quad at Woodstock School. Although they are exhausted by jetlag and altitude, still they must immediately describe to the welcoming committee how terrified they had been of the twists and turns of the mountain road, how awed by the taxi driver's confidence as he drove on the "wrong" side of the road, how the radiator boiled over, how the scenery was breathtaking. Some travelers arrive already ill of "Delhi belly" or a form of dysentery. Some are already depressed by the change of culture and sight and smell of poverty.

North India has perhaps a dozen towns called hill stations. Srinagar, the capital of the state of Kashmir and Jammu with its spectacular "Indian Alps," is the northernmost. From there, Simla, Mussoorie, Naini Tal, and Darjeeling angle southeast through the foothills, touchdowns on the crow's flyway. Simla (the newer spelling is Shimla) was the summer capital during the British Raj, luring government officials and their families as well as Indian princely rulers. The schools of Naini Tal attracted missionaries and government employees. Darjeeling is still the jumping-off place for famous mountain climbers on their way to Mount Everest.

And then there is Mussoorie at 6,580 feet, somewhat less famous than Srinagar and Simla, attracting fewer trekkers than Darjeeling, but at one time patronized by thousands of middle-class Britishers, a few maharajahs, and the Nehru family. Many Westerners working in North India sent their children to Mussoorie schools and then came up to spend the hot season with them.

"Gay, friendly, cosmopolitan," according to Fodor's travel guide. "Gayest of the U.P. hill stations," says a local pundit. Understandably, a minister in 1884 preached against "the highly immoral tone of society [in Mussoorie], that it surpassed any other hill station in the scales of its morals."[1]

Hill stations have a different atmosphere from other Indian towns, and each hill station is different from every other. Yet they have much in common: the holiday mood of the visitors, the obsequious merchants, the quaint facades of the Victorian hotels. However, the real charms of all hill stations are scenery and mountain air.

Fanny Parks, the intrepid traveler of the early 1800s who was fascinated by all of India, on her first visit was ecstatic about the delicious air.[2]

Mussoorie's additional claims to hill station fame are a cable car going up the top of Gun Hill; Kempti Falls; and the nearby source of the Jumna River, one of the famous five that water the plains of North India. A hill station usually has a lake. Mussoorie's is a pond in the Municipal Gardens that is large enough for one rowboat and two goldfish.

Like all other hill stations, Mussoorie has a Mall for promenading, an atmosphere of fading English elegance and respectability, and a number of "seasons" with imported entertainers. Above all, it has those spectacular views: a 200-mile panorama of snow-capped mountains, many over 20,000 feet. Tourists swarm out of their hotels to look at the snow peaks to the north or the Doon Valley to the south. And like other hill stations, Mussoorie has a winter that seems dreary to a tourist; but winter is the time for the permanent residents to reclaim ownership.

How does a remote hilltop become a hill station? In 1811 the area was included in a purchase from the local rajah by a Captain Hearsey. It was sold a year later to the East India Company. In 1823, F. J. Shore, the English superintendent of the Doon, and Captain Young, commander of the Ghurka corps stationed there, discovered that this hill area abounded in game. They built a shooting box on the north side of Camel's Back Hill, then thickly covered with live oak forest. Captain Young built the first house on Mullingar Hill in 1826, his hilltop to be known as the Potato Garden.[3]

In 1828, the British Station Hospital and Landour Depot for troops was established in Landour, the eastern section of the settlement. English soldiers were busy during that period defending the rights of the East India Company against the local princes. Many of those who came to Landour during those early years were the officers and privates of the Bengal army who had lost their health in the plains. Much of this history can be read from the acres of marble in the two hillside cemeteries.

The Survey of India office opened in 1832 with Colonel George Richard Everest as Surveyor General. The Colonel fixed the position and altitude of Mount Everest and it was named in his honor.

Saharanpur was the gateway to the hill district. Some archaeologist had already found fossil remains in the Siwalik hills, and the jungles were described as pestiferous. A hundred years ago, visitors traveled by horse from Rajpur at the foot of the range to Mussoorie; or they were carried in *palanquins*, hammocks on poles shouldered by four men. This tortuous, torturous seven-mile journey did not discourage visitors.

The hill station gradually took on the accouterments of civilization. Englishmen built houses along the ridge from Cloud's End at the west to Oakville Estate at the east, a twelve-mile span. In Mussoorie, an excellent family hotel run by Mr. Webb boasted a ballroom and five billiard tables. The first brewery in India was built here in 1830. Its cheap beer contributed to the deaths of a number of pedestrians who fell off the mountain.

An incident at Gun Hill deserves a short footnote in Indian history. The gun was procured shortly after the Mutiny of 1857, and for a time it was fired each noon from the top of the hill. The firing caused considerable controversy, for townspeople complained that it was more of a nuisance than a help. No matter which way the gun was turned, someone objected. When it faced east, the proprietors of the Grey Castle Nursing Home reported that it loosened the plaster and patients were unnerved when chunks fell on their beds. Facing north, the cannon pointed directly at a private residence. Facing south, it performed as guns were intended until the man in charge forgot to remove the ramrod and sent it through the tin roof of Stella Cottage.

Finally the decision was made to aim the cannon at the Mall, which seemed a safe distance away. Ruskin Bond, a local writer, describes the discharge as a ball of moist grass and cotton waste. One day the gunner used an overcharge of powder and the cannon ball landed with some force in the lap of a proper English lady who was departing from the Mall by palanquin. The frightened coolies dropped her with a jolt. "It was the last straw," Bond quips, "—or to be exact, the last straw cannon ball." Since 1919 there has been no gun on Gun Hill to announce the noon hour.[4]

Schools flourished. The Church of England and other denominations joined the Muslim, Jain, and Hindu groups in providing religion and culture. When the railroad came to Dehra Dun in 1901, the journey from the plains became more comfortable. A hydro-electric power generator sent electricity up to the town as early as 1909 (thirty years before Rural Electrification reached my family's Indiana farm). In 1919 "the evening wink" was introduced: the lights were dimmed briefly sometime between four minutes to nine and three minutes past to let the Mussoorie residents know that it was exactly nine o'clock, bedtime. The companionable wink was discontinued when it was found to be illegal. And then in 1930 the motor road from Dehra Dun was completed, making Mussoorie one of the more accessible hill stations. One authority says that road was an accommodation to McKinnon Brewery for transporting beer barrels, beer a patriotic necessity for the troops in Mussoorie.

Dehra Dun is now listed on Air India flight schedules, and helicopters occasionally bring distinguished visitors to the top of the hill. Since 1979, a television satellite tower on Lal Tiba, the highest point in Landour at 8,000 feet, relays programs from New Delhi.

Some fifty years ago, writing in the *Mussoorie Times*, the Rambler asked, "For who now remembers that practically the whole station once belonged to only the three families of Hearseys, Powells, and

Skinners?" We met progeny of the Powells and Skinners, but none of the Hearseys.

The tourists come up from the plains, particularly from April through June, to escape the heat. Honeymoon couples arrive in October after the monsoon passes. The well-to-do settle in at the Savoy or other "4-star" accommodations, but hundreds of middle-class shopkeepers and office workers stay in little hotels back on the hillsides. They stroll along the roads, the Indian men in their dark business suits and their wives in stylish saris and shoes with little heels, visiting the hundreds of tiny shops. They ride the Ropeway cable car to Gun Hill to look back toward Delhi. (Probably some of the women limping in their little heels think wistfully of the comfort they left behind.)

From roadside pavilions the visitors view the Doon Valley and the great plains to the south. Turning to the north they are awed by the Himalayas that form the barrier to an invisible China. The children play in the Municipal Gardens or ride horseback through the bazaars; the smaller ones ride in baskets on the shoulders of coolies. The whole family takes tea at Kwality's, sitting at tables by the second-floor windows to watch the color and movement below.

The larger hotels promote floor shows and beauty contests, but for the most part, the crowds of visitors amuse themselves in the mornings with mountain views and in the afternoons with Indian movies at the Rialto Theater and Picture Palace. The Shakespearean Theater up near Sister's Bazaar has long ago crumbled down to its slanting stage. (Studying it taught me the real meaning of upstage and downstage.)

During the season when the population expands from 20,000 to 100,000, we Unraus enjoy walking through the bazaars and joining the tourists in people-watching at Kwality's windows. As we eat our *samosas* and drink our tea we look out over the square below and into the shops that surround it. Well-dressed shoppers stroll through, followed by ragged coolies pushing rented baby carriages full of purchases or sleeping children. Tibetan refugees in heavy woolen skirts and boots tromp by. A proper English couple, shapeless in shabby tweeds, saunter through on their daily stroll. Muslim women scurry along, imprisoned in their *burkhas*, those tent-like

robes with little gauze grills through which they view life outside the
zenana. We are inclined to think of the burkhas as hollow shells, but
occasionally we see the flash of a neat foot, a jeweled hand, or a
bright sari, and we know that there is a sister hidden there.

We watch a Sikh wind yards of fuchsia turban around his head.
Merchants in leisure suits of white pyjamas escort plump wives in
bright satin Punjabi tunics over full trousers. Widows in white saris
sail through the bazaar, tacking across the square from one shop to
another. (The sailing metaphor is completely inappropriate in this
hill-locked town except during the monsoon season. Then there is
enough water for the believing to walk on.)

School children abound, students at the ten English as well as
numerous Hindi medium schools in the area. Children dismissed
after a day in Mussoorie schools have the same enthusiasm for freedom as do children in North America. We saw them in troops coming and going, and those in like uniforms make up their own charg-
ing battalions.

In was easy in our first days in India to see people as scenery
and to take pictures of them as they made colorful compositions. We
sought out "the typical Indian scene" to send home to our families.
It took some time to overcome this compulsion and to learn again
that probably nowhere in the world, and particularly not in India, is
anything typical. A knowledge of even a few of the communities
made one wary of generalizing about any aspect of India.

Mussoorie is composed of many minority groups. In addition to its
Hindu majority, the town has a large group of Sikhs, the religious cult
that dominates the Punjab, that vast Kansas-like breadbasket to the west.
They and the Jains established reform movements with Hinduism. Not
so many Muslims live in Mussoorie now as before the bloodbath of the
Partition, but the veiled women are evidence that a congregation still
exists. A remnant from the British past, mostly descendants of military
or government officials, is now living out a retirement of nostalgia in the
only home they have known except for time spent in England for their
education. Both Indian and Western school communities are prominent.
Closely linked to the Western schools are the missionaries, now few in
number, who either work at the schools or come up from the plains to
visit their children during the hot season.

Indian government and military personnel are employed by the cantonment, by the Survey of India, by various mining operations in the mountains, or by the Indian Administrative Service with its school on the west side.

The Tibetan refugees have become a large and industrious minority who operate businesses and schools as well as work on construction crews. They consider themselves temporary inhabitants because they plan eventually, hopefully tomorrow, to return to Tibet. Their return will come about when China gives up its claim to their motherland.

Somewhere in the warrens of the slums live the Nepalese coolies. At the other end of the social spectrum, a few maharajahs or their descendants maintain their antiquated palaces.

Looking on at all of us are the hill villagers. They come into town to deliver milk and produce, but they traditionally have been observers rather than participants of town life. They belong to these hills. They do not know when their Rajput ancestors drifted here from the west, but they are Pahari (mountain) people, speaking the Pahari dialects and wearing the Pahari style of clothing common across the foothills of the Himalayas. Our main contact was with the *dudh wallahs* who brought their cans of buffalo milk and baskets of wild fruit to our kitchen.

At the east edge of this community of diverse cultures, religions, and economic levels, Woodstock School adds it own piece to this mosaic.

The idea for such a school began in 1845 when Waverley, a Catholic school for girls, was established in Mussoorie as its first academy. Protestant military and missionary parents promptly planned a school for their daughters. They appealed for teachers to the London Society for Promoting Female Education in the East. (Try making an acronym for that title.) Of the four respondents who reached India in 1854, one received a proposal of marriage before she arrived at the school, two returned to England within two years, and the fourth married and opened a school in Simla. But the Protestant Girls School survived. In 1856 it moved across town from Library Bazaar to Woodstock House, its present location.

A succession of both young and elderly ladies ran the school, but difficulties in finding staff prompted the sale of the school in 1872. At that point the Presbyterian women entered the picture. Groups of them in Philadelphia and Chicago pledged to share the support of Woodstock. Through the years, mission boards joined to provide management and staff. The school is now under a self-perpetuating board.

During its long history, many dramatic, in-house incidents have affected the school as well as external events such as wars, the Mutiny of 1857, the Partition of 1947, famine, and weather. For Woodstock the events ranged from the inconvenient to the tragic. In 1884 just a few minutes before a visit from the Duke and Duchess of Connaught (he was the favorite son of Queen Victoria), the thatched roof on the south verandah collapsed. Every man was called to lend a hand, and just in the nick of time supports were put in place and the debris was deposited in the ravine below. A fire in the carpenter's shop in 1941 was bad enough, but it could have been totally disastrous. Water from the garden tap was thrown on the fire, and banks of potted plants in the garden were sacrificed to save the building.

This is the appropriate place to put Mussoorie into the context of Indian geography and history.

India is the seventh largest country in the world, as large as Europe outside of Russia, a natural geographic area with something of the outline of Texas. It stretches 2,250 miles north and south and 1,000 miles from Bombay to Calcutta. It is two-thirds the size of the United States with just as much variation in climate. Geologists speculate that the Himalayas were once on the bottom of the ocean. Now they exist as three parallel ranges with wide plateaus and Shangri-la valleys such as in Kashmir and Kulu. The mountain wall is 1,500 miles long with a width between 150 and 200 miles. Its high mountains form the ridgepole of the world.

There are many long histories of India; the short histories of India are also long. Evidence exists that India, along with the Nile Valley, Mesopotamia, and the Hwang-Ho Valley in China, is one of the "mothers of civilization." Archaeologist have found traces of an advanced civilization of the Dravidians during the period from 4000 to 2500 B.C. They have uncovered pillared palaces, modest brick skyscrapers, and evidence of city planning. Drainage systems existed, and that forerunner of the hot tub, the municipal bath. Artists worked with copper, bronze, and gold to turn out lovely figurines and jewelry.[5]

But something happened to wipe out those thriving cities and bring an end to this era. During a 1,000-year period beginning about 2500 B.C., Aryan hordes of nomads swept down from the north. Greeks, Persians, and Romans imposed their pale skins on those of the dark Dravidians, but driving many of them south. Writers suggest that India has seldom fought a successful war, but it has never lost one because each invader horde coming in to conquer stayed to be absorbed as Indian subjects. The British who refused to be absorbed had to retreat.

Only a few remnants of these cultures are still visible. Greek pillars decorated with vines and bunches of grapes, the Muslim tradition of purdah, the Mogal (Turkish) gardens, and polo fields remind us of earlier occupants. The Mogul court introduced the formal wear of today's Indian men, the close-fitting jacket reaching just above the knees, worn over narrow jodphurs.

All these cycles of victory and defeat, greatness and decline, growth and decay, grandeur and squalor left imprints on India's history. One can see a golden age in whatever culture is studied.

Our friend, Mr. Abhinandan, the cloth merchant, ponders India's past and future with us.

"You have a long history," we say.

"Yes, a long history. We are a big country, a big population, and we have many problems at the same time. Refugees from the Punjab, Tibet, Bangladesh."

"Do you think India can control its population so that everybody can have enough to eat?"

"I am quite sure. The day will come when everybody will eat. That means smaller families and raising more food, both. Everybody thinks, even the villagers who are not educated, that they must have smaller families and grow more food. If the country succeeds, it will be a nice country. Yes, I am optimistic. A country is a big family. China has also a big family and they are managing."

"Where would you like to live when you retire?" I thought he might want to move to Dehra Dun or to be nearer his daughter.

He had never thought of retiring. "Retire? No, this is a quiet place. I don't want to live any place other."

What did we Unraus, who lived in one Indian community for six or seven years, hardly a moment in India's history, learn from the centuries of Indian culture? We saw the excesses: the plenty of the rich and the famine of the poor; the beggars and the maharajahs; the well-fed cows and the skinny coolies; the goatherds and the goddesses. Geography and climate surely must have something to do with history, we concluded. Religion, insofar as it makes people moral or immoral, just or cruel, has something to do with history.

To everyone his own India. Ours was the India of the hill station with the vitality of its bazaars and peacefulness of its valley, the decadence of its buildings and the poverty of so many of its villagers. Ours was also an India of fascinating history and generous-spirited people.

Chapter 2

The Bazaars

The only sensible way to explore Mussoorie is on foot. We liked to go once a week, whether we needed to shop or not, just to stay in touch with the streets, the shopkeepers, and the scenery. In some respects we led a very provincial "western" life on the school campus. We visited the bazaar to remind ourselves that we were on the other side of the world from Kansas.

So on Saturdays, joining the exodus of students from their dormitories, we marched the mile west toward town where the action was supposed to be. The students loped along the relatively level stretch of

Paula Unrau and Carla and Wendy Reimer at Northern Stores. Photo by Vic Reimer

Tehri Road with their distinctive Woodstock hill-climbing gait, leaning into the wind at ten degrees from vertical. Although we stormed the city together, we were conquered individually. The students had their favorite tea shops and other hangouts, and we had ours.

The bazaars begin at the top of Mullingar Hill. Landour Bazaar, with its own ambiance, extends from Northern Stores to the Clock Tower. We liked it for its lack of elegance, its look of authenticity. Northern Stores is typical of the many small shops that we pass. It is a narrow store, probably eight by eight feet, open at the front with shelves to the ceiling. Since the Northern Stores' man comes to our door for grocery orders, we do not spend much time there.

We start down the hill, passing a *derzi* who is sewing an electric blue satin dress, and a *moochi* cobbling desert boots. We greet the egg man who keeps his eggs in mounds behind him. We will buy six when we return and stow them carefully among the purchases in our shoulder bag. We pass the barbershops and tea stalls, second-hand shops and cloth shops, most of them mean, dark little places. Wives and children of the proprietors drift in and out, for many shopkeepers live in rooms back, above, or under their places of business. People use the street for work and play. A shoe repairman spreads out his tools, and card players squat around a jute sack on the ground. A derzi spreads a large bedcover on the roadside to fill with cotton.

After a sharp turn in the road, we start a long descent toward a small level square. When we hear a truck or a jeep coming, we flatten ourselves against a wall, for a vehicle that starts up or down the hill roars along, carried by the blast of its horn. Throughout the bazaar are places wide enough for cars and trucks to pass, but this road is by no means a two-way street. A stalled car has to be pushed to a place wide enough for traffic to pass.

Landour Bazaar would be a wonderful setting for a movie chase: an Ambassador taxi hurtles through the bazaar pursued by the bad guys in a jeep. The taxi starts up Mullingar Hill, stopping for the bull on the corner, stopping for the baby playing in the middle of the road, stopping to back up to maneuver around a corner at Northern Stores where the Chukkar goes to the top of the ridge. The jeep doesn't see them turn and takes off on Tehri Road. It misses the corner and leaps off into the blue, rolling over and over in slow motion to the bottom of the cliff. Probably it lands in a tree top and the bad guys live to shake their fists at the Ambassador as it zigzags up the road above them.

But I digress; they are going east and we are going west. At the bottom of Mullingar, the character of the bazaar changes. Living back of these shops is a Tibetan community, and along with the little hotels, restaurants, temples, and cloth shops we find Tibetan displays of jewelry and decorative items. The babies playing in the street are more round-faced than Indian babies; some of the mothers wear the Tibetan *chupa*, an ankle-length, full-skirted jumper, but many of the younger women wear saris.

We come to an antiquated structure that Mr. Abhinandan, the cloth merchant, calls the Diamond House. It is a huge old building, its front facing the bazaar and its back rising above the road below. Once it had been a bank, but it had long ago been condemned. Small-time entrepreneurs still sell their wares from baskets on the front steps and live in its lower regions. We would have signed a petition to keep it from being torn down. The fixtures for the thousands of light bulbs that were once lit for holy-day celebrations are part of its decoration. Although decrepit now, it still has the proud bearing of an old dowager with a ruined face and infirm support, who remembers when she wore large pearls across a broad bosom. Susan, Paula, and I—never Walt—used to speculate about how much fun it would be to restore it and live in it. We have delusions of grandeur.

Mr. Abhinandan was our friend as well as the school supplier. He sat cross-legged on a low platform covered in white sheeting. Bolts of cloth were arranged horizontally from floor to ceiling, leaving just enough space for us to sit on a bench in front of him while he spun the cloth off the bolt for us to admire, covering one offering with another. Walt chose cloth for the servants' uniforms and winter coats, and Abhinandan's derzis made them up. We Unraus bought material for sheets and curtains. I was attracted to every new type of bedcover that came in, for they were unique and decorative.

Continuing on our way through Landour, we come to an area with a more modern appearance. Ram Chandar's store was our supermarket. It looked somewhat like an American grocery store of the 1930s when shopping was a one-to-one encounter. We could also give orders to his man who came to our door. Because Ram Chandar owned a refrigerator stocked with cold Fantas and Cokes, he attracted the tired and thirsty.

Other noteworthy businessmen along that bazaar road are the cotton fluffer, the peanut man, and the carver of walking sticks. The cotton fluffer took cotton out of mattresses, fluffed it, and stuffed it back into the ticking. The plucking of the taut string of his fluffing contraption made a pleasant little twanging sound with the rhythm of a metronome. Old students (alumni) remember that sound with nostalgia, but nowadays most dormitories have foam mattresses. The peanut man looked age-worn, part of the antiquity of Landour Bazaar. He squatted day after day, his peanuts roasting in hot sand over a bucket of glowing charcoal. We thought he would live forever, but he was gone by the time of our last visit. In 1905 an early carver of walking sticks sold one to the Princess of Wales, when she was visiting, for the collection of her husband who was to be King George V. The biggest bargain in the bazaar is labor. The derzi could make a skirt for Paula for 25 cents (that was in 1970; inflation has hit there, too). We could have new shoes made from a picture in Sears catalog, including the intricate decorations. But what were bargain prices for us were often unaffordable for the villager and the coolie, although they might be charged even less than we were.

Anything essential could be bought in the bazaar. Although we found little ready-made clothing, no chocolate chips, only two kinds of cold cereal, everything we really needed was available: a warm bedcover, cloth, charcoal, a heating stick (an electric coil) that could heat a pail of water in fifteen minutes. Tobacco wallahs sat cross-legged on shelves above the street and on demand made up leaf bundles of pan, that combination of spices, betel, and tobacco that many people were addicted to. Grains and spices were heaped in open bins, attractive to beasts and birds. Glass bangles of all colors shimmered in piles, essential to the properly dressed Indian female. Children's clothing swung from shop doorways.

The smells of the bazaar became so familiar that we came to take them for granted; onions cooking in mustard oil from the food shops; sewage from the latrines just below the road; all the spices that go into curry powder, including ginger, cloves, mustard, tumeric; chilis piled in boxes in an open-fronted store; horse sweat as we passed a string of ponies; bubbling sugar and ghee (clarified butter) from the sweet shop; and sandal wood incense from anywhere.

My professional curiosity was piqued by the sign "Typing College." Inside a narrow shop were four or five standard typewriters on ledges along the sides. Students were learning to type from a book. There was no sign of a teacher.

Two hundred sixty cell-sized shops occupied the half-mile between Mullingar and the Clock Tower. During my first few trips to

The clock tower.
Photo by Marion
Deckert

the bazaar, I had kept my eyes at street level, overwhelmed by the variety, but one day I looked up and realized that people lived on the shelves above the shops. Leaning from open windows or frail balconies, women and children watched the street. Often the fronts of those second- and third-story apartments were bandaged with laundry. Saris fluttered from railings in six-yard rainbows.

In 1935 the townspeople collected money to build the Clock Tower to celebrate the Jubilee year of King George V. When we first arrived in Landour, we laughed at the gaudiness of the tower, painted every few years in another coat of pink and green glory. We complained that it never had the correct time. We demanded Greenwich mean time, an unrealistic expectation, and as we settled in, unimportant. The Clock Tower was a landmark that we learned to tolerate, then apologize for ("the pink and green really doesn't seem out of place in Landour"), and then admire as a symbol of the community we had come to appreciate. When we last visited, we were offended that the color had been changed to pink and maroon.

The Clock Tower marks the end of Landour. Three roads merge there. A lower road comes up from the back of the bazaar with a sharp twist. In our time, a jeep had to back up to get around it. Another road from the schools across the narrow valley to the south meets the bazaar road at this point.

For the next half mile after the Clock Tower, a stretch of schools, shops, and homes rise on the left or descend on the right. And then we come to Union Church and Picture Palace, a movie theater. Here the road stops, and the left arm of the T goes down to the bus and taxi stands, the point where travelers from Delhi and Wichita disembark. The right arm takes us into Kulri Bazaar, another center of activity with shops that are bigger and offer more variety than Landour's. In the last few years, video games have been added for the amusement of students and tourists.

The Mall is the road from Kulri Bazaar to Library Bazaar. After Kulri, the main road begins to climb, and we pass numerous little shops on the right. On the left, amid the palm trees, stands the Methodist Church, color-washed in buff. A few years ago a sign was tacked to one of the trees, "Religious Place, Do Not Spit." We pass Kwality's which is a *pukka* restaurant (to use the term loosely, the real thing), and then the archway that invites us to the Rialto Theater, showing Hindi and, occasionally, Western movies. Then the Allahabad Bank and Postal and Telegraph building usually mark the end of our Saturday excursion.

But there is more. A road meanders from this area around Camel's Back Hill and rejoins the bazaar road after two kilometers. It offers a breathtaking 200-mile panorama of the Himalayas. The main road goes on through an open area, a saddle between two valleys. The Tibetans had set up small stalls there, each about eight feet wide and four feet deep, with flimsy plastic roofs. When I walked past in the mid 1970s, I counted forty-one stalls, all selling the same type of merchandise, stacks of shawls and cloth pieces. Every merchant would have unfolded every one of the items for my inspection. When we returned some years later, we found that the Tibetans had expanded their territory and the variety of their wares, displayed on folding cots set end to end. The line extended down a long concrete ramp that led to homes in the valley below.

Eventually, we come to Library Bazaar (or Gandhi Chowk) with its statue of a benevolent Mahatma Gandhi. Shops surround the square. A motor road connecting Library to Picture Palace comes up from below.

During "the season," on the road between the Allahabad Bank and Library Bazaar, one sees the hill-station face of Mussoorie. Women show off their best saris, little girls flutter in party dresses, and boys sport new jeans and T-shirts. The Punjabi outfits are creative and coordinated, with intricate tucks, buttons, and pleats, in contrast to the almost uniform patterns of a few years ago. A Tibetan mother in the traditional chupa is accompanied by her daughter in jeans.

Cars with special permits, horses, and ponies nose their way through. Cotton candy, roasted corn, coconut slices, soft ice creams and the usual Indian *gulab jamans*, *jelabies*, and *samosas* are offered for nourishment. The monkey man puts his pets through their paces and then picks up the coins tossed by the tourists.

Comparing the crush of tourists in 1993 with that of previous years, we noted a definite increase. Private cars, taxis, and buses were parked in every available space. We understand the anguish in the editorial of the Dehra Dun *Himachal Times* of July1987 that complained about the exorbitant charges and lack of amenities for tourists in the crowded hotels; the nuisance of motor vehicles filling up and polluting the roadside; and the "spurious" goods offered. Hotels were being built on every available square foot. With their "homely comforts," hotels range from the ratty to the acceptable. Hakman's and the Savoy are the old established names, but there have been hundreds built since they appeared. Proprietors go in for regal names: Imperial Hotel, Prince Hotel, Nabha Place, Moti Palace, Connaught Castle. We did not have the experience of staying in any of them, but we wondered what it would be like to spend the night at Heavens Club. We suspected that the facilities might not rise to the promise of the name.

Scattered throughout the different bazaars are the shops of the *kabardi wallahs*. The junk shops of Landour are a tumble of very used merchandise. One could buy a toaster that would never work, a two-year-old *Time* magazine, or a yellowed book of Dwight L. Moody's sermons. (Old books on theology were rife on the Hillside.) One knows that in the back of every kabardi shop there will be some treasure: a porcelain figurine, a rare book, a silver filigree comb. A sign on one of the shops proclaimed, "Second hand goods and rear books, buy and sale." (We rearly read rear books, even when they are on sale.) When the kabardi wallah hears that a Westerner is leaving the Hillside, he comes by to dicker for what can be resold to new arrivals or to townspeople. India is a country where sealed units of refrigerators are rebuilt, the broken handle of an iron is bolted together, uppers of shoes are patched, school papers are folded into sacks for holding rice or sugar.

The most sought-after objects by our family were arts and crafts that we thought would be useful or decorative if transferred to Kansas. The craft shops sometimes displayed a combination of trash and treasure, and we had trouble telling one from the other. Vinod's was a high-class shop (speaking of items for sale but not appearance) near the Clock Tower. We looked at but did not buy a very regal maharajah's folding chair, the one he took on safaris, ornamented with brass inlays. We once bargained for a pair of fragile crystal lamps that we fortunately did not win.

Walt found a huge brass bowl hidden in the back of the shop. The lid was decorated with jewel-toned enamel inlays and perforations in a pattern of flowers. Vinod thought it might be Persian. We bought it for our anniversary, Christmas, and Mother's Day present. Walt polished it to a thing of beauty. We enjoyed it, but could never explain its use until we read that in the Middle East after an elaborate dinner in the Muslim harem, the ladies wash out their mouths and spit into a large bowl with a perforated top. Our beautiful bowl is a wash basin.

In some shops a sign announces "fixed price," and even though one desires the merchandise to the point of tears, the heart of the merchant refuses to reduce the price. But one can, indeed one is expected to, bargain with many of the merchants. Walt is rather skilled at the bargaining table. The merchant offers, Walt counters; the merchant comes down, Walt comes up; the merchant responds with a story about how his children need shoes; Walt starts to walk off; the merchant calls him back and offers the goods at Walt's price as a special favor in recognition of the great friendship he has for him. Both have enjoyed the encounter.

For the serious shopper, to hurry is fatal; you must adapt yourself to the merchant's pace. In the cloth shops in Dehra Dun you take off your shoes and fold yourself onto the sheet-covered floor. The merchant sends a boy for a cup of tea made with sugar and milk, or a warm Coke if you prefer. You have a polite conversation about who you are, where you came from, and the size of your family. He offers condolences because you have only daughters. Then the merchant spins out yard after yard of exquisite silk and brocade, and your protests that you want only to look at the cloth on the bolt are unavailing.

The Kashmiri shops display walnut carvings, papier-mache' bowls and boxes, embroidered shawls and rugs. The more expensive are masterpieces and the least expensive are underpriced by Western standards. In some village a family was producing them to sell to tourists like us, making a bare living at the trade. Should we buy these things and exploit the poverty or not buy them and ignore the need? We realized eventually that we were not responsible for supporting every craftsman in India. But with a sense of righteousness we did what we could.

In our inexperience, we laughed at those shopkeepers who turned on the light only when the customer came into the shop, and then turned the light off again before he was out the door. That, we thought, was no way to run a shop. We knew from our marketing textbook that a brightly lighted store attracts customers. Now we know better, and applaud them for practicing survival skills and saving energy.

At the top of Mullingar Hill is a pavilion housing several rickshaws with eight or twelve coolies sitting around ready to man them. We never required their services. Tourists and elderly ladies or patients on the way to the hospital use them. A rickshaw will hold two small people comfortably, but two large Delhi wallahs will crowd into one, holding their three children on their laps. The perspiring coolies will strain up a hill, then try to hold back the rickshaw as it gathers speed on its descent.

Western students have had great fun with rickshaws, sometimes giving the coolies a ride in their own vehicles. When two teachers once helped push the rickshaw to get two older Woodstock women up Mullingar, the coolies's sense of propriety was offended. It is inappropriate for anyone but a coolie or a silly student to push a rickshaw. Fewer rickshaws jingle through the bazaars nowadays, but the number of taxis has multiplied.

Chapter 3

The Road

For two years we lived at Palisades, a wonderful house in a curve just below Tehri Road. As we sat reading in our front yard, we often heard flute music coming from the distance and then nearer, wreathing the road above us. A string of horses appeared followed by a young boy playing a wooden flute. He came from some village back in the hills, but we were never to know the young Pan except for his music.

Tehri Road was our link to other communities and the rest of India. The road going east through the bazaar becomes unraveled at Mullingar Hill. The skein known as the Chukkar goes up the hill as a concrete motor road. Little foot paths lead off from it to houses that have discovered flat spots to crouch on. The Chukkar, however, is merely a distraction from the main skein of Tehri Road that leaves Mullingar to go east past Woodstock School.

The first building of note as we walk toward school is the Landour Community Hospital, which you miss unless you look up. A small bazaar has sprung up where the hospital drive joins Tehri. Those too ill to walk can be taken up by dandy or stretcher. The drive with its one sharp hairpin turn is wide enough for an ambulance. I was astonished to see the white van zooming up the drive backwards. The driver expertly backed into the turn, then shot forward for the final lap. Our pregnant friend, Margaret Toews, said she took the ambulance and forgot about her labor pains during that part of the ride.

No houses have been built along Tehri at road level, for it has been carved from the hillside. Retaining walls, *pushtas*, rise above the road on the north, and they support it on the cliff side as it crosses

ravines. Houses above and below the road are built on rock outcrop-
pings. British names of the houses have the sound of home:
Mullingar and Tipperary for the Irish; Redburn and Albergeldie for
the Scots; Woodstock, Rokeby, and Waverly for readers of Sir Walter
Scott; and all kinds of castles and courts for the English..

Ten minutes further from the hospital drive is Cozy Corner, a
tea stall. A path goes down at this point to join a "new" motor road
below, then diverts to the dormitories and Dhobi Ghat, the village of
the washermen.

But we do not take that path. We continue on Tehri a short distance until we find a broad path that leads to an archway with a bold
"Woodstock." Above us we see the massive buildings that make up
the school. Tehri Road continues around the Woodstock hill, cutting
though the campus. About a mile further is a tea stall and the tollgate, Jabarkhet. The dudh wallahs and other villagers, including our
flute player, find their way home by paths that branch off Tehri Road
which continues for forty miles to Tehri City.

Of course, we are not the only foot travelers on our road. Early
in the day we meet children going to the elementary school just
below the road at Cozy Corner. When they see us, they whisper and
giggle. Then a little boy is pushed forward to say impertinently,
"Guda morning, Memsahibji, OK." Then he runs off, intimidated by
his own rashness, followed by giggles from the other children. I am
told that hill children are less inhibited than children of the plains
who come from school quietly and soberly. Ours are the well-
combed but drably dressed children of the workers in the community. I think they must always have been late for school. They loiter and
tease each other, and some of them cry at being teased. A few of them
ride homemade skateboards in the tiny schoolyard.

We meet workmen carrying charcoal, timber, stacked tins of
kerosene, great bags of rice, and an occasional piano. Hill people
come up from the crooks and creases of the valley with their milk or
vegetables. The men wear jodphurs and the women the full skirts of
the Pahari tradition. Usually they were walking, but over the years
more and more of them have acquired horses or mules and even
jeeps. The animals have close-woven panniers balanced on each side,
filled with gravel or produce. We meet an occasional jeep belonging
to one of the mining operations from somewhere in the hills. The
jeeps, motorcycles, and scooters send us scurrying to the safe side of
the road. In the last few years taxis have become more numerous.

Building the road

For a time students hired taxis to drive themselves back from the bazaar, but such indulgences were ruled out by an unfeeling administration who thinks that students need the exercise.

Sometimes a big powerful car comes up from Delhi and manages to bend its way through the bazaar and around the sharp corners of the Hillside. We laugh at its length, and then we notice that it is the same model as our middle-income, middle-sized vehicle back home. In India we admire Land Rovers, jeeps, Maruti vans, and even Ambassador taxis.

"I would like to have a little scooter," I said wishfully to Walt when we decided to go back to India, but he shook his head. Scooters were considered dangerous, as were motorcycles. We had a number of scarred friends who owned them. Accidents happen often on Tehri Road, particularly to buses and potato trucks. The driver of the potato jeep drove over the *khud* (face of the cliff) three times in one year. On the first occasion, he arrived at the bottom of the abyss limp and unharmed.

"Too drunk to get hurt," the admiring students reported.

The next time he broke his leg but was back on the job in a few days. The third time he killed himself, and a more sober driver took over.

The bus that goes to Tehri City in the morning and returns in
the evening gives its passengers a scenic ride. The streaks down the
side of a bus from each window are evidence of the nausea of riders,
not a good advertisement.

In the 1970s we watched the Department of Public Roads
"paving" the stretch of road above our house. First a wall of large
rocks was dumped along the outer edge, making the narrow road
narrower. A man sat above our house every day, hammering rocks
the size of basketballs into duck eggs. Sometimes he missed when he
threw his rocks back onto the pile, and one would come tumbling
down to put a dent in our tin roof. The damage would not show up
until the next rain. Further up the road another solitary man worked
at the same tedious task. They were paid by the job and not by the
hour, and they worked steadily.

The smaller rocks were spread over the road. Then a steam
roller was brought in to press them into the dirt. More dirt was
spread over the rocks, making a passably smooth surface, and then
the process was repeated. Is this paving? we asked. Later a layer of
tar, cooked along the roadside, was added, and we had good stretches of "metalled" road.

The "new" road was built in the 1970s, following the inside of
the hill just below Tehri Road. Trucks can now drive out into the
Tehri Hills without going through the bazaar. Food can be delivered
to the school kitchen at dormitory level rather than being carried
through the bazaar on the backs of coolies. The road is an engineering miracle. For the most part, the builders had to lay a new roadbed,
blasting off mountainsides and filling in deep ravines. In roadbuild-
ing, the string used to form the perimeters of the pushtas look like
colossal cats' cradles strung by children.

One Sunday afternoon as we returned from a picnic tea, we came
upon a colony of Rajasthani families who had been brought in to work
on the new road. They were camping along the roadside in makeshift
shelters. Cooking fires glowed; children ran about while their parents
waited for their tea water to boil. The brightness of the twilight scene
surprised us. The April wind was still cool, but the workers were
dressed only in the thin cotton skirts and *dhotis* of desert Rajasthan. The

women wore gorgeous tatters of vermilion and gladiolus, colors not often seen on the village hill women. But still there was something familiar about this attire. These were the long full skirts that hill women wear in darker, heavier materials. And the colors were those worn by the women when they dressed for holy days. Many Paharis claim that in their very distant past they came via Rajasthan to the Tehri Hills.

Occasionally a group of dark-skinned gypsies from Gujarat set up camp below the hospital. They sleep under plastic sheets strung over a tent pole. The men make tools and sharpen knives and the women, dressed in silver-trimmed tatters, cook, tend their babies, comb lice from each other's hair, and look sullenly bored. They work for a few weeks and then move on.

Each time we came to Mussoorie, we trekked at least once to Happy Valley to visit the Tibetan School, located north and west on the road from Library Bazaar. In 1959 when the Dalai Lama fled from the Chinese take-over of his government in Lhasa, Mussoorie was one of the hill towns that welcomed him and his people. Coming from the highest country in the world, they preferred the hill towns of India: Darjeeling, Mussoorie, Rajpur, Dharamsala, Simla, and Kulu. In 1965, the school in Happy Valley accommodated 1,200 students, 600 of them in dormitories and the others in homes in the area.

The Dalai Lama enjoyed attending occasional concerts at Woodstock School, when he would slip in after the lights went down and slip out before they went up. Woodstock Staff would sometimes be invited to Happy Valley for auspicious events. Walt and Paula met the Dalai Lama at an audience and tea when the Tibetan religious and political leader made one of his frequent visits to Happy Valley. I stayed home with a bug and missed my only opportunity to shake hands with a head of state.

Dhanaulti lies fourteen miles east of Woodstock on Tehri Road. One spring, we adults planned an Easter weekend trip for the children of our mission. Dhanautli is a favorite destination for hikers, a birdwatcher's paradise set in a deodar forest. India's tourism department has since made it a tourist attraction, but when we went it was pretty much undiscovered. We thought.

We rented the school jeep weeks ahead, reserved the forest bungalow from the District Forest Office in Dehra Dun, and made elaborate plans for four meals. We were eight adults and ten children.

The bane of my traveling experience has been the Early Start. Years ago when my parents tried to gather the four of us children into the car for a "trip," the Early Start was the first commandment. Naturally we planned an Early Start for Dhanautli that Friday morning so that we could travel in the cool of the day. Eighteen bodies were too many for the jeep, whose legal limit was eleven. Besides, we had all those sleeping bags, cooking pots, food, drinking water, and goodies for tea time. Two of the men went off to arrange for a small trailer, and two went back to the bus stand to take a bus. The rest of us sat down on our sleeping bags to exercise patience. The bus takers came panting back to report that the bus happened not to be going that day.

We had intended to leave the Woodstock gate at eight. Promptly at ten we got away, the Early Start foiled again. But never mind. We stopped along the way for all the scenic views. We plowed up a drift of suffocating dust, but we knew we would soon find the cool and clean space of Dhanaulti.

When we arrived at our forest bungalow, we found that in spite of our pukka reservations, we had been bumped by a government party. There are places in India where a light skin and a foreign look can send us to the head of the line, but Dhanaulti is not one of them. The bungalows are for government use, a fact well understood by Indians even while they chafe at the injustice of it all.

The men in our party dickered with the decision makers of the usurping party. (Never send a woman to do a man's work; Susan once tried to negotiate for train reservations because she knew more Hindi only to have the ticket agent ask what was wrong with her husband.) Our negotiators triumphantly got the use of the kitchen house, which consisted of two bare rooms and a verandah, and a half-time use of one of the bathrooms. Next they had to negotiate for water from the village spring. After some discussion, we were allowed to fill our buckets for cooking and bathing.

After a cold lunch, half of us returned to the jeep to follow the road to Tehri City. We drove through spectacular mountains with picturesque villages caught in their crevices, with terraced fields of wheat, potatoes, and green beans. ("Picturesque" describes the view from the road. To maintain a romantic view of most Indian villages, one should keep at a distance.)

About twelve miles before reaching Tehri City, we entered the village of Chamba. A *mela* was in progress, and the streets were so packed with people that we stopped the jeep at the outskirts to join them. People were standing on rooftops of homes and shops, and peddlers displayed balloons, cloth pieces, little tinsely ornaments, anything that would draw a few paisa from the pockets. The "over and over," a crude Ferris wheel with four boxes, was popular with the children. The cameramen took pictures from the jeep, discreetly with a telephoto lens, good portraits of women dressed in their bright saris and elaborate jewelry, including silver nose rings six inches in diameter.

The next day at camp was spent eating, socializing, and hiking. We left for home at mid-afternoon, stopping for the inevitable tea on a saddle of a ridge with two fine views. When we were within three miles of Woodstock, we found the road blocked by boulders. We hiked home, leaving two of the men with the jeep to wait several hours until the road was cleared.

The road that goes down from Mussoorie to Dehra Dun is a cliffhanger, a scratch on the walls of the hills, but well engineered for vehicles that have passed their safety inspection tests and for drivers who are not in a hurry.

We Unraus tended to attract taxis that had never taken a safety inspection test. And every driver was in a hurry. Where was that Indian disregard for time that is so widely admired by Westerners? Possibly all those taxis rushing up the hill to Mussoorie are carrying pilgrims avid for meditation. More likely, each driver hopes to get in as many trips as possible during daylight hours.

Many adventurous people are intimidated by that road. Pearl Buck was often quoted concerning the terror she felt when coming up to speak to Woodstock students. My own fear was of the forty-five minutes of nausea from which I recovered five minutes after the road flattened out.

"If I ever get back to Mussoorie, I will stay on my own mountain until we go home to the States," I would moan from the corner of the taxi where I was trying to enter a state of Nirvana.

"Oh, Mother, you always say that," an unfeeling member of the family would reply.

One sunny December day we took a more direct route to Dehra Dun by hiking to Rajpur, which lies seven miles just below the school. Rajpur had been a way station, supplying ponies, coolies, dandies, and rations for the last leg of the trip to Mussoorie. In the early 1800s Fanny Parks and many undaunted British men and women had come this way. On the bridle path, the less valiant were intimidated by tales of mad elephants and hungry tigers. By elephant, camel, or oxcart they brought everything they needed to make life comfortable and elegant. Annie Steel gave advice on what to take up to Mussoorie for a woman with her children and nanny. She listed what would go into each of eleven camel loads, such as portable bathtubs, china dishes, sterling flatware, and costumes for social and ceremonial functions. A piano would not fit on a camel's back and would have to have its own cart.[6]

Susan and I joined a small party guided by Diana Biswas, coordinator of the music department, taking a strenuous path, crossing creek beds and following quarry roads. The day was made pleasant by bird song and little flowers, and a stop to drink authentic Hindustani tea, a potion boiled with milk and sugar and tasting strongly of buffalo. We trekkers arrived at the back door of Rajpur while the morning was still fresh, to be greeted by rosy-cheeked Tibetan refugees busy at morning tasks.

Nineteen years later we took the same walk. The path by then had become more of an obstacle course. Not only had our hiking muscles aged, but the old route was more difficult to find. New quarry roads with large rocks made walking painful, and landslides left some paths almost impassable. The greatest contrast between the then and now had occurred because of cement factories that sent tons of pollutants into the air that dimmed the once sparkling beauty of the valley. By our next visit nine years later, the situation had improved somewhat.

Our destination in Rajpur on that trek was the Tibetan Center where we could buy carpets. And I admit that we always returned to Mussoorie by taxi.

Many retired people live in the area, for they appreciate the peace and beauty of the valley and its accessibility to Mussoorie and Dehra Dun. From the taxi we had glimpses of neat white-washed

Indian style houses set in English gardens. Madam Vijaya Lakshmi Pandit, Indira Gandhi's aunt and Nehru's sister, lived on an estate near Rajpur. A gracious and intelligent woman, she had invited her Parent-Teacher audience to visit her, but I had never found the appropriate occasion to knock on her door.

Our valley, our doon, is considered by historian Ramesh Berry to be second in beauty to none, unless it is Kashmir. The Himalayas rise to form its northern wall and curve around it, and the Siwaliks form a gentle southern boundary. Dehra Dun is flanked by the dry rivers of Bindal and Rispana, then by the rivulets, the Tons and the Song, and finally by the Jumna and the Ganges. These last two rivers, which meet at Allahabad, are some forty miles apart in our scope. They embrace one of the most productive areas in India.

Berry, in his pamphlet *The Story of the Doon Valley*,[7] says that once it was a lake with dinosaurs and mastodons, and elephants with tusks fifteen feet long. They have left their bones in the Siwalik Range and inspired legends in which prehistoric monsters cavorted with the gods and titans. Only Lord Shiva survived, and the area was named Siwalik, the abode of Lord Shiva.

Recorded history indicates that the Doon came under the control of Ashoka the Great in the third century B.C. Ashoka, as ambitious as Alexander the Great, determined to conquer the whole world. Later, sickened by the bloodshed, he embraced Buddhism with the vow to lay aside the sword. He was the example of the benevolent ruler who became the servant of his people. The first builder to use stone in India, he inscribed on pillars his life philosophy, as well as edicts to his ambassadors. One of the fourteen pillars still standing in India, the Kalsi stone is located near Dehra Dun at the confluence of the Tons and the Jumna rivers. It was discovered in 1860, and when the moss of centuries was cleaned off, the inscription from 253 B. C. was readable on a white background. The languages used on the pillars in India were Kharoshthi and Brahmi, languages less durable than the stone on which they were written.[8]

After Ashoka, the valley was invaded by the Sikhs, Rajputs, Gujars, and Marahthas. Finally the land became the property of squatters, *dacoits* (bandits), and blackmailers. In 1803 the Gurkhas came down from Nepal to put an end to the rule of the decoits. Next came the British, defeating the Gurkhas and reinstating the Rajah of Garhwal. To maintain law and order, they sent F. J. Shore and Colonel Young, who built a hunting box on the site now occupied by Mussoorie, and we have come full circle.

Chapter 4

The Hillside

Most of the homes are accessible only by narrow lanes, inviting, shaded tunnels that wander over the heavily wooded hillside. While there are many paths, one does not become lost, for they lead into each other, and sooner or later, probably in not more than ten minutes, a path brings the wanderer to a familiar house or up onto the Chukkar, or down again to Tehri Road. Some of the paths are broad and well-swept; some are narrow and intended only for goats; but there is no path on the Hillside, no matter how perpendicular, that a Woodstock child has not attempted.

The common trees are ban and Moru oak (which we compared to live oak in the U.S.), rhododendron, pine, and cedar. Many of the oak trees have been twisted by the wind into surrealist shapes, their elbows jutting at surprising angles. The trees around Hillside homes are green the year round. The new pink leaves push the old ones off, and the wind or the sweeper brush them over the khud. Mussoorie is one of the few places in the world where deodars grow, those Biblical cedars of Lebanon.

When dresses were long and men's collars higher, when people perspired less and did not understand the benefits of strenuous exercise, the school principal commuted by dandy from a residence above or below the school. A dandy is a hammock-like sling carried on the shoulders of coolies. Today, only the halt and the broken-legged consider traveling by dandy. Living on the vertical demands exercise, and we were in excellent health while we lived in India.

On our first climb from the school to the top of the hill via Zigzag, an intoxicated path that staggers through live oak forest and Himayalan strata, we climbed slowly, but even so we were breathless at every turn. The last one hundred feet were easier, and then the Chukkar bent down a bit to meet the path, and unexpectedly we emerged onto a horizontal road. We felt that we had arrived in Beulah Land, that we had walked on the upward way and reached new heights of glory. (This is a metaphor only readers who have been brought up on gospel songs will understand.)

Unless we had to hurry, we enjoyed those walks to the top of the hill, but we always seemed to have started too late. In a country where time is avowedly not of the essence, we were forever trying to get somewhere on time, or I was trying to keep up with a better walker.

We were expected to be sure-footed. We were reminded that an exuberant schoolboy had jumped off the path to swing on an inviting tree limb, missed, and fallen ten feet before a bush caught him in time to save him from real harm. And there was Fritz, coming home one night from seeing Ellie at Ashton Court, surprised by the blackout of the September war. He missed one of the curves of Tehri Road, suffering conspicuous scratches. The humiliation of it outweighed the sympathy he received.

But during our last visit we were devastated by the death of a ninth-grade student who fell from the road, a sober reminder that our environment was perilous.

Few places are naturally wide enough to hold a house. Small places are extended by fortress-like pushtas. In an effort to reduce erosion, elaborate masonry drains are built to divert the rushing torrents of monsoon rains. In the 1960s we noticed a very nice plateau over on the next hill and asked why no one had built a house there.

"That's Baptist's Folly." (Or it may have been the folly of some other denomination.) "They spent all their mission allowance building the pushtas and had nothing left for the house." By now, even Baptist's Folly is covered by a house.

The advantages of living on the Hillside? The Community Center retreats and programs and Wednesday teas, church services in English, school concerts and plays, mountain trekking. Such physical and spiritual renewal! And with all this the pleasant temperature. Even during the monsoon, life was agreeable.

Mrs. Leonard Waldo, who grew up in the house called Upper Woodstock, wrote:

I wonder if there ever could have been a happier childhood or a grander home than ours. . . . [A friend said],
"Buried to the knees in a snow-drift, I looked upon a palm
tree, and could almost smell the blossoms of the orange
bowers in a valley where frost never fell. It was like sitting
at the North Pole and looking down on the Equator. . . ."
[While sitting under the oaks of Upper Woodstock], we
loved to hear of the wonderful America, the land that
some day we might see. Would the oaks be as grand as
ours? Would the mountains be so blue and high?[9]

The summer hub of Hillside activity was the Community Center, a two-story building located above the school on a small plateau
that included a tennis court and a library, great assets to the Hillside.
Hillside residents were homogeneous. Most of them attended Kellogg
Church, belonged to Community Center, had some connection to
Landour Community Hospital, sent children to Woodstock School,
and belonged to the Parent Teachers Association. Probably in earlier
days, Naini Tal and other hill stations had a church- and school-cen-
tered missionary group. Although the British military officers had
been the first to acquire estates and build summer homes, gradually
many of these were sold to mission boards. The military formed its
own enclave apart from the transient missionary community.

The Landour Hillside has changed, fewer missionaries, fewer
Westerners; the hospital and school are used and administered more
by Indians, as they should be. But one can understand with sympathy the nostalgia of the British couple for their Raj when one remembers the vitality of the Hillside in its heyday.

"The Kingdom of Bengal has a hundred gates open for entrance,
but not one for departure." This quotation refers to the life span of
British soldiers in Calcutta. Death was such a common feature of life
in early British India that there was an almost callous disregard for it.
"It was not unusual to have been breakfasting with a man in the
morning and to be burying him at sunset."[10]

The threat of death was constant. The climate and epidemics,
accidents and military skirmishes conspired against both the frail and
the strong. For the lower military classes, even the discipline (flog-

ging) could be the cause of death. Lady Canning, wife of a viceroy, died of jungle fever, probably malaria. Sister Mary at the Mission School in Sinka was killed by a beam falling on her head; it had been eaten through by white ants. Major General Henry Marion Durand fell from a howdah while riding an elephant. Infants often could not survive the heat of India's plains. The opium pill was the ayah's answer for a restless child, and death could occur before an unobservant mother would intervene. The British paid a high price for its Indian empire with the lives of its men, women, and children.[11]

On the Hillside, to find the cemetery, start from Kellogg Church up on the Chukkar. Take a road that circles the hill and comes back to the Chukkar at St. Paul's Church. On the hill side of this road you will find the main gate to the Landour Cemetery. A bronze plaque is attached to a tall deodar at the entrance with an inscription that gives credit to His Royal Highness, the Duke of Edinburgh, for planting it in 1870. The gate to the cemetery is locked and the wall is high. You can, however, ask for the key at the Parsonage up the road, or find a narrow footpath a bit further on and climb in.

The graves are laid in tiers on the hillside that faces north to other hills across the valley. Back of Kellogg Church a road, now private property, takes you to the top of the cemetery. From there you can wind your way down through the ruins of old graves, learning the history of the community, especially of the military presence as it was during the British Raj. A friend said that the earliest grave she found is dated 1833, but the Woodstock School history records that the first grave was prepared for a Captain Bolton of the Honourable East India Company in 1828, the year the British Station Hospital and Landour Depot was completed.

For a military funeral, the band usually played the "Dead March" from *Saul* on the way to the cemetery. But for the return to the barracks, it broke into dance hall music. In 1833 the commandant in Calcutta was requested not to use the "Dead March," that burials take place without music or the firing of cannon, since the daily sound had a depressing effect on the ill.[12]

Mrs. Waldo wrote of an experience on the Hillside:

As I stood watching [a rainbow], suddenly we heard the mournful music of the "Dead March" from Saul come throbbing down the glen, and looking up the mountain beyond Wolf's Crag, we saw the red uniforms of English soldiers carrying a comrade to this "long home." It was our first idea of Death, but it did not seem very terrible to lie under the heather on that old mountain top.[13]

In hill stations where the ground is rocky, two days are needed to prepare a grave. Since burial often took place even the same day as the death, two spare graves were dug ahead to await the next burial.

In spite of the beauty of the burial ground, the visitor is saddened to read the inscriptions of so many young people and children who succumbed to rampant epidemics that today are subdued. We mourn, too, for all those young men in other parts of India who died for causes that historical perspective has made to seem insignificant. The eulogies, flowery and formal, are full of grief. We can accept the death of a venerable missionary after a fruitful ministry. But an elaborate tombstone reminds us that here was a young person once full of vitality and grace; remember him, they say, we loved him.

The Raikes memorial was a marble stone with a canopy built over it so that one could walk into the little structure. The dome was split and falling in, and the grass grew between the cracks. The inscription dated 1835 was readable in 1987, but is no longer.

> Sacred to the memory of Sophia Mary Raikes, the fondly beloved wife of Charles Raikes of the Bengal Civil Service who departed this life on the 16th of April 1835 in the 19th year of her age. Those who in agony but in humility deplore her loss will deem not her death premature, but through the mercies of that Savior in whom she trusted, she was already meet for immortality; her rare personal and mental endowments were but the blossoms of the tree whose fruits were Christian purity and holiness. May those who now mourn her on earth be made partakers with her in the resurrection of the blessed.

Another grave dates back to 1843. Lieutenant-Colonel Thomas Skinner was buried at the age of forty-four. The inscription, "This tomb is erected by his brother officers to mark their esteem," is typical of the many eulogies inscribed by military friends.

A study of the registers of burials reveals that few of the deaths were the result of battle wounds. There were six cases of hepatitis in 1858. Children died of teething. Consumption and ague (malaria) struck down

The snows, Bandur Panch (monkey's tale)

men and women in their twenties, and dysentery was a common killer. Syphilis was given as the cause of death a number of times.

Some of the graves have significance for Woodstock School. The cholera epidemic of 1910, before inoculation was available, took the life of Miss Williamson. Her friend Miss Kendig, the school nurse, grieved not only for the loss of her friend but also for the lonely funeral which no one but the padre was allowed to attend. A few days later Miss Kendig succumbed.

By our time, many of the marble stones had been removed for their market value, some to be put to practical use as grinding stones for spices. Many of the graves had been taken over by grass and bushes. We were reminded that we cannot be expected to be remembered forever, even when our passing is marked by an impressive eulogy in marble.

Nowadays, most of the deaths in the Landour-Mussoorie community are from accidents, or from "civilized" diseases such as heart attacks and cancer. There is no longer a British Station Hospital and Landour Depot.

Over on another hillside off Camel's Back Road is the civil cemetery, larger, not as grown over, and just as full of the history of Mussoorie's diseases and tribulations. Bones of the former residents lie under tall evergreens, their tombstones, like their bones, crumbling to dust.

On a Sunday afternoon in late August during a break in the monsoon, Walt and I were having tea at the school. A teacher stopped by to report, "The snows are out." We hurried to the top of the hill to see the spectacle.

Near Kellogg Church we stood by the parapet and looked toward Nag Tiba, the snake mountain, almost 10,000 feet up and nine miles from us. Forty-six miles away and 20,000 feet high was Bandarpanch, the monkey's tail, so named for one of the Hindu legends. Far, far to the east was the grandest of them all, Nanda Devi, at 25,600 feet.

"The snows are out," suggests the anthropomorphic, as though the snows decide that this is the time to take the air and reveal themselves. The sun, of course, is the one who makes the decision, or if not the sun, the wind, so that the mist and clouds that usually cover the peaks dissipate. Then the snow crowns are outlined against the intense blue of the sky.

Our family went up to the Chukkur one November day to see the snows, and then as the day pivoted to dusk, our pleasure was climaxed by a sunset that was extravagant even in a land famous for its sunsets. We stood on a promontory to watch the melting of colors on the rose-tipped snow peaks to the north, and the rose-tipped clouds to the south, and the rose, blue, and golden horizon to the west. At the top of our world we were surrounded by sunset .

Afterward we crept down the path in the dusk, as usual having forgotten to bring a flashlight. The shadow of the winter line still hovered, a blue band on the southern and western horizon behind which the sun sets. The winter line is said to be caused by the condition of the atmosphere, perhaps from the dust and smoke of thousands of cow-dung fires in thousands of Indian villages. Whatever the cause, the result is dramatic; and surely, from September to March, one of the seven wonders of our Indian Hillside.

Chapter 5

The Christian Communities

St. Paul's Church at the top of our hill, on the same road as Kellogg Church, had been built in 1840 as the Anglican Church for the cantonment. Mrs. Waldo wrote of St. Paul's as she remembered it in the late 1850s.

> Outside of the church on the smooth gravelled front were gathered the servants, with different conveyances of their masters. Soldiers in red uniforms chatted here and there, solemn white-turbaned grooms held mountain ponies, fair faced delicate ladies stepped from jhampans, gay young officers bowed and smiled everywhere—altogether it was a bright picture against the green hillside beyond. After everyone else had gone into the church, the soldiers marched into the gallery, their swords clattering valiantly at their sides, firing the hearts of the boys below with ambition.[14]

Although the plaster was stained by mildew and the carpet threadbare, St. Paul's had a well-cared-for look. A group of Hillside church members cherished the building and its history, for they had long memories of its place in Landour.

The altar glowed with color. The brass candelabra and the reader's stand, with its symbolic vines and leaves, gathered the gold of the light. The carpet and pew cushions of muted rose, the embroidered altar cloth, and the stained-glass windows spoke of a more opulent time. The church was beamed and pillared with Gothic arches, and the mullioned windows had a nice proportion.

We usually sat in one of the front rows, still reserved by brass plates for "officers" long departed. The rail in front of us was notched at each place. In Mrs. Waldo's day the officers' swords (or rifles?) stood upright with the tips latched into the notches so they would not clatter when the soldiers knelt on the padded prie-dieu. (After the Mutiny of 1857, British soldiers were ordered to carry live ammunition even to church.) Some of the history of the church is written on the marble and brass plaques commemorating the majors and major-generals who had fallen in battle somewhere in India defending Indian territory and English privilege.

In 1970 St. Paul's became one of the congregations of the Church of North India (CNI), a union of Anglican, Presbyterian, British Methodist, Church of the Brethren, and Disciples. It now holds regular Sunday services in English, serving Hillside residents and many Woodstock staff members.

We also visited Christ Church on the other side of town near Library Bazaar. Built in 1836, it was the first church to be organized, and it had served the civilian British parishioners with all the symbolism and liturgy of the Mother Church of England. Christ Church stands on a dignified elevation above the busy road in an atmosphere of English peace and quiet. Its claim to fame is a deodar in the yard planted in 1906 by Mary, Princess of Wales.

The furnishings still reflect vestiges of beauty. The carvings on the altar and pulpit are of white Belgian marble. The enormous Bible on the reader's lectern rests on the outstretched wings of a walnut eagle. The organ pipes with their blue, red, and gold enamel are still resplendent, but no music accompanied our service, for the hand-pumped bellows of the organ had long ago been eaten by rats.

Padre Das, the CNI presbyter for the diocese, informed us that Christ Church and St. Paul's were known as garrison churches, built by the British government with British money. Clergymen were sent from London by the Clergy Department of the government to serve these churches.

Once Christ Church was filled with children and staff from two English schools, as well as with local English and Anglo-Indian residents. With the demise of the Raj, the congregation became so small that services were discontinued. In the 1970s, rather than allowing the property to revert to the state, a remnant of the congregation started holding monthly services, and they are still meeting as of this writing. There is no money now to restore this once vital church, to replace broken window panes, to paint walls, or to fix the roof. It is sad to see a church die. But it is heartening to remember that for over one hundred years this church served a vital community who received the Word, lived it as best they knew, and passed it on.

Most vacationing missionaries on the Hillside attended Kellogg Church, established in 1903 by the American Presbyterian Mission. During the season from April through September, the congregation expanded with the newly appointed missionaries studying Hindi and Urdu at the language school. Almost all missionaries who served in North India had the common bond of having at one time been a part of the Hillside community. This bond continued as they went to their work on their mission fields, no matter what their denominations.

The Kellogg Church building might be the replica of a small-town Midwest church, except that it sits on a knoll above the street with a long flight of steps leading to its front door. For a five-month season, Kellogg Church offered a complete program with a full-time minister, a choir, a pipe organ, and Sunday school classes, with a service *in English*, respite from the Indian village church where missionaries preached in a language other than their mother tongue.

The era of the Western missionary-in-charge is over. The long-sought indigenization of the church happened. Now Kellogg Church serves an Indian congregation with an Indian pastor preaching in Hindi.

Union Church was built in 1874 near Picture Palace in the Mussoorie Bazaar. The pillared porch gives it the look of a Greek temple. During our time, a large congregation of Indians, Anglo-Indians, and Westerners attended. Wynberg-Allen students in their green and gray school uniforms filed in to occupy the front section of the church. We saw the congregation build a balcony to accommodate the standing-room-only assembly. Congregational health changes with the times and the personnel involved. When church attendance of students was no longer compulsory and a popular pastor retired, attendance dwindled, but now the congregation is again vital with an Indian pastor and a strong program.

Many of the Indian office staff at Woodstock attended the Methodist Church in Kulri Bazaar, but our cook and many other Hillside Christian workers attended the Hindustani Church on the campus. This church is a memorial to Miss Edith Jones, a former

Woodstock principal who had an affectionate concern for the welfare of Woodstock employees.

The church is an attractive, white-washed building with a red corrugated roof, furnished with plain benches in a pleasing meeting-house style. The service, held on Sunday afternoons, begins with Hindi hymns which are usually adaptations of Western gospel songs of many verses sung slowly, slowly.

The Catholic Church was highly visible across the valley, along with St. George's College. On the western side of Mussoorie were the Convent of Jesus and Mary and Waverley School. The Seventh Day Adventist Mission ran Vincent Hill School beyond Library Bazaar, but it was closed down in the late 1960s.

British residents remaining after the days of the British Raj are part of the Christian community. They or their forebears had come to join the army or go into civil service, business, or the church. Certain families followed a tradition of serving in India to the sixth and seventh generations, and then widows and daughters stayed on after the deaths of their husbands and fathers. After Independence in 1947, a number of British ex-patriates retired to hill stations. Officers of the Indian army often chose to retire here among people with whom they could reminisce instead of going back to an unfamiliar town in England. The exile was self-imposed and not unpleasant.[15]

As an example of the British remnant I think of Alfred and Muriel Turn-Duff Powell, she a proper English lady and he a military man of the world. Muriel Tern-Duff taught piano at Woodstock in the 1930s and then went to live with her parents in South Africa. After her return to Woodstock and a seventeen-year courtship, she married Alfred in 1956. The ceremony was celebrated in Christ Church, decorated for the occasion with scarlet rhododendron and white banksia roses.

Alfred Powell's grandfather had been one of the founders of Wynberg-Allen, the Anglo-Indian school that had originally been established for the domiciled children of European businessmen. Alfred had attended school there until he was thirteen and was sent to England where designated English schools catered to those children who were sent "home" by their parents. After his schooling, Alfred joined the army in India.

We knew the Powells through their sixties, seventies, and eighties. I assumed they would live forever, he busy with his investments and she teaching private piano. One day when I took tea with them, they explained that they were going to volunteer at Landour Community Hospital to be what we Americans call "pink ladies."

"My dear, we don't want to show up the nurses, they might resent us if we did that, but we do hope to improve the nursing service."

We enjoyed talking to the Powells, listening to their proper British tones, pouncing on fascinating historical references, and trying not to react to Alfred's bawdy remarks. They seemed to have the ideal retirement plan, living on the Hillside in summer and in Dehra Dun in winter. They never spoke of returning "home" to England. By the time of our last visit, they had both died.

When Muriel Powell asked Vera Marley, Woodstock's most famous Anglo-Indian, "Are you coming to the Indian music concert?" Miss Marley answered, tongue in cheek, "My dear Muriel, the British in me cannot stand that type of music."

The term Anglo-Indian originally referred to Europeans domiciled in India, while those of mixed British and Indian blood were called Eurasians. Gradually the Eurasians adopted the Anglo-Indian title for themselves.

The first Englishmen to come to India were for the most part adventurers, debtors, derelicts, criminals, and convicts. When in the late seventeenth century merchants, soldiers, and civil servants, without wives, came into this land of promise, the men were encouraged to marry Indian women and produce children. In fact, they were encouraged to the extent of five rupees a month for each child. In those early years, it was acceptable for Europeans to marry Indians.[16] These native sons cost nothing to bring out from England, were already used to the climate, knew the language, and made good soldiers.[17] Until 1833, the East India Company did not approve of nonofficials, such as missionaries, businessmen, and indigo planters, entering the country.

These early binational families became English, since it was considered easier to teach Indians the language and customs of the father than for the father to learn the language of the mother. The Indian mother was usually ostracized by her own family, so the children depended completely on the father and the success of the East India Company.

The necessity for intermarriage with Indian women disappeared when the route through the Suez Canal was opened in 1869, shortening the time of passage. English wives accompanied their husbands, and English unmarried women, known as the Fishing Fleet, came out to visit aunts and to find mates. A strong color bar was created that discriminated against Anglo-Indians. This prejudice became one of the least attractive imports of British India.

Anglo-Indians were necessary to the British in running the country. They were looked upon with favor when English became the official language of the government. Though they wanted little to do with them socially, the British felt responsible for their employment and offered A-I's good positions in the railroad and postal systems.

In earlier times, many Anglo-Indians regarded their English-ness as a cut above their Indianness. But Indians looked with some disdain on children of mixed marriages, calling them "kutcha butcha," half-baked bread. Rejecting and rejected by both Hindus and Muslims, Anglo-Indians usually became Christians. They formed their own communities, married among themselves, wore Western clothes, and spoke of "home" in England, although they might never have seen English soil.

Certain names are prevalent. A group called "aristocratic Eurasians" included Colonel James Skinner, the son of a Scots father and a Rajput mother. He was part of Delhi society until his death in 1841. A man of intellectual accomplishments, Skinner wrote his memoirs in Persian, but he is remembered in history books as the commander of Skinner's Horse, the famous cavalry regiment that he founded. He was buried in Delhi in St. James' Church which he had built near his house. Close by is a mosque for the benefit of his Muslim wife and relatives. A branch of Skinner's progeny is well known in the Mussoorie community and they deserve their own biographies.

Some of the families like the Gardners and the Hearseys were descendants of noble families on both sides, but even they felt discrimination. General Sir John Bennett Hearsey, the son of an English army captain and a Jat princess, was one of the great figures of the Mutiny. He showed more sense than most British authorities by advising them to let the sepoys (Indian soldiers) provide their own grease for the cartridges.[18]

When the British withdrew after 1947, Anglo-Indian prestige
again diminished and A-I positions were open to Indians. Many A-I's
emigrated to other Commonwealth countries. Others, though, have
become reconciled to their Indianness and have found a place for
themselves at one social level or another. On our later visits to India,
we were not nearly so aware of the Anglo-Indian as separated from
the mainstream of Indian nationals as we had been some twenty
years earlier.[19]

Chapter 6

Woodstock School: Traditions

A long procession of dedicated, unique administrators and teachers have served the school for varying lengths of time. The faculty often worked under handicaps, even in our time, when death, problems of obtaining visas, or bad weather caused delays in assembling a full quota for the opening of school. The most difficult year must have been in 1940 when Dr. D.E. Alter took over from Mr. Parker, who assured him that every post was filled.

The path up to the school buildings

But in January during the winter break, one teacher died suddenly while on vacation, one young man resigned to return to the U.S., taking with him another of the high school teachers as his bride, and the math teacher took a year's leave for the sake of his health. Dr. Alter did what every principal before and since has done: he prayed, he reassigned current staff to new positions, he asked a mother to fill in, and he tapped the shoulder of a traveler enroute to somewhere else to stay to teach languages.

And so it still goes. A recent principal wrote: "Every staff member is busy, and some overburdened, in the great Woodstock tradition."

So that the reader will have some idea of the layout of the school and the terrain, I will describe the path we took when we lived in the College Duplex, the lowest housing on the campus.

We left our back door to take a flight of steps up to a path that runs below Midlands, the high school girls' dormitory. It goes around the hill and past Ridgewood, the home of the younger boys. Alter Ridge, the circular building that houses the dining hall, kitchen, and younger girls' dorm, has since been built on that level. The path then joins the Dhobie Ghat road and we pass Clifton Hostel for high school boys, which has a swimming pool of sorts. Our road climbs until it joins the "new" road that parallels Tehri Road above it, and we take a flight of steps and an upward path to Tehri, which we cross to take an exhausting ramp to the school. We are now 6,500 feet above sea level, ready for a day's work, having climbed, by our estimate, the height of Niagara Falls.

The Quad is a court paved with flagstones and surrounded by a building that houses offices, schoolrooms, the infirmary, apartments, a carpenter's shop, and the dining room and kitchen. Verandahs on both second- and third-floor levels are attractive with ivy and geranium trailing over the rails.

Walt enters the Quad to go to his office, but the girls and I pass the Music Building to go up a covered ramp to the high school and its wing, Parker Hall. From this ramp, steps lead up to a playground and open gymnasium. The verandahs and covered ramp make it possible to go to any class without getting unreasonably wet during a monsoon.

The high school building is without external charm, built of brown cement blocks and covered by the typical red corrugated roof. The spacious entrance hall has a view of the bazaar a mile away. This building has six levels, and all but the topmost have access to a ground level. The terrain is an architect's challenge. My first impression was of regimented bleakness: slick concrete floors, high ceilings, "missionary buff" walls in the classrooms, and gray enamel in the hallways. Later we were given a budget to brighten the rooms with paint and drapes. Chalkboards were a problem; we endured plaster covered with green paint until we discovered that glass with the underside painted is an improvement. (Subject to breakage by wooden-backed erasers thrown carelessly.) But the last time I taught, I found no improvement in the gritty chalk.

The back door which opens out from the lobby of Parker Hall, the auditorium, leads to the new Media Center. It sits on a newly leveled area and includes classrooms for computer science, English, art, and journalism and also has a small stage and auditorium. The story of clearing the space, engineering the drains, controlling the rock slides, getting permits for water, and auditing the accounts would make a long chapter. Now that the building is in use, it is much appreciated, and thanks can be given for the grant from ASHA, American Schools and Hospitals Abroad, a division of U.S. Agency for International Development.

These are the facilities. Some of them date back to 1854, others are new. Even some of the newer ones are not adequate, but good teachers make the most of what is available. We are reminded that Adam lived in Paradise before the Fall, so we know that perfect facilities do not guarantee success.

One year my eighth grade students came from Thailand, India, Bhutan, Nepal, the Philippines, Bangladesh, Japan, Korea, Australia, New Zealand, Germany, Ethiopia, England, Canada, the United States, and other countries that I can't remember. Some of the girls' names were Minam, Sangeeta, Namrata, Sarena, Meetu, Chukie-Om, Rochita, and Julia. Some of the boys' names were Sonam, Tairon, Jade, Vikesh, Abhishek, Koang Jin, and Ben. Their parents worked at such jobs as manufacturing, engineering, teaching, piloting, doctoring, preaching, banking, translating, tea planting, and exporting of teakwood, silk, and sheep intestines.

During our sporadic visits, we watched as the school changed its reason for existence from serving predominately missionary children to serving students from all parts of the world and from all religions. Indian nationals from other countries, notably Africa, came back to India to learn to know their mother country and to Woodstock because they desired a more international education than they would have received in an Indian school. For several years a group of Canadian students attended Woodstock while their parents worked on the atomic reactor plant in the deserts of Rajasthan. A number of children and grandchildren of Woodstock alumni come from North America to experience a year of high school abroad. Woodstock is one of the few schools in that part of the world with an American curriculum. It has a reputation for high academic standards and at the same time gives special emphasis to the interaction of Indian and Western cultural experiences. There are North American students who never cease to yearn for home and McDonald's, but most are eager to adapt, learn, and appreciate.

We met only a few people whose names we could drop in order to impress our Kansas friends. Unfortunately, we Unraus were too late for royalty, the dukes and duchesses who came through before the Partition, and we missed Pearl Buck, the author. But we met a couple of talented movie makers, one of whom had been a student in my tenth grade English class. We tried to bring in parents of students to speak at PTA meetings and graduations, and that list was impressive. What tradition are we talking about here? The one that says that Woodstock School uses all resources at hand, and if they are mothers, fathers, or aunts, all the better. Sir Edmund Hillary, the conqueror of Mt. Everest, was asked every year, so we heard, but he could never make it. Too short notice, he said. And now he is gone.

Another group of people, ubiquitous but important to our lifestyle, was the army of workers who made the place habitable. Families from the Tehri Hills have been employed as workers from generation to generation, and their relationships are known to staff members who cross these generations.

Sweepers, bearers, *chaprassis* (clerks), *malis* (gardeners), *dhobis* (laundry men), carpenters, more than eighty were on the payroll, besides the *khansamas* and *ayahs* (cooks and nursemaids) who were hired privately by the staff. More is paid to the workers in the way of tribute than in money, although we did not feel that the administration exploited its helpers. They were paid as well as or better than those employed by surrounding schools. Walt spent considerable effort in improving housing and pension plans.

We lived with contrasts, and we on the staff provided contrasts. We came from all over the world and we benefited because of this diversity. With our common needs and common likable traits, we all had different stories to tell and different goals and attitudes, some of which seemed unreconcilable. But the better we understood one another, the better we understood ourselves.

In our isolated, insulated community, we looked for opportunities to give variety to living and to "make" news.

The Hobby Show, originally called the Beetle Show, was a monsoon event and a very big deal. Collecting beetles, collecting anything, was an activity that could be pursued in spite of rain. Beetle collections were rampant, and awards were distributed for big, rare, fast, and en masse. One award winner was labeled "The Beatles" and featured beetles playing paper instruments.

Talent shows, scheduled at least once a semester, ranged from the hilarious to the somewhat funny, from sophisticated subtle humor to slapstick and bathroom jokes; from first tries on the violin to highly polished musical performances. We never attended a student talent show that did not include comments about the dining hall food. The most appreciated skits were those of students poking fun at the staff, making teachers squirm with imitations of voice, walk, and mannerisms.

A magician came to the high school office, a small man in khaki who looked more like a sweeper than an artist. He wanted to give an evening performance for the student body for a reasonable fee. He crouched there on the floor of the office and performed a few tricks for the little crowd that gathered. He was quick and clever, and we all voted for him except the Bender of Budgets.

"There is no line item for him."

Sale Day in the Quad. Bill Starr is auctioning off a puppy

But somehow, probably with bargaining and compromise, the performance happened, another bright spot in the monsoon grayness.

May Day with its May queen and maypole are now a memory, but Sale Day survives. The Parent Teachers Association sale was a celebrative, money-raising event. This one took a year of planning, and it seemed that every parent, staff member, and friend of the school was on a committee. At one time our Mennonite group was responsible for the doughnut sales and the country store. They got up very early, both men and women, to make raised doughnuts. During my tenure as doughnut chairperson, the school kitchen crew got up early to make doughnuts from a Mennonite recipe. We went in at the sensible hour of eight o'clock to ice the 130 dozen and see that they were sold. How soft we grow. I commandeered the seventh graders to hawk them to the doughnut-devouring hordes, and by noon I had discharged my responsibility, having sold the last two dozen to myself.

Members of other denominations manned stalls for Indian dolls, candy, toys, and artwork; or they were involved with the lunchroom or the carnival. Parents on the plains brought up tin trunks full of arts and crafts from their areas: basketry, chikan embroidery work, Tibetan rugs. The goal was always to sell more of everything than was sold the year before, but eventually expectations had to be lowered. I wondered while dripping pink, white, and brown icing on the doughnuts, why we all just didn't give one hundred rupees to the cause and be done with it. But the PTA was something of a family reunion. Parents came for the event, and Indian friends from Dehra Dun and Mussoorie. We all profited from the school improvements that the money made possible, such as playground equipment, better classroom lighting, and drapes for Parker Hall. As fewer parents came up to live on the Hillside, the activities of the PTA were curtailed. But the PTA sale is still a major event in the spring.

On Nehru's birthday, November 14, Woodstock celebrates with Employees' Day. Students take over the chores of the chaprassis, bearers, and janitors while the workers participate in their own Sports Day, special tea, and a movie.

Church going and religious education have always been a part of the Woodstock program. In those early days (1910) when Woodstock was a school for girls, a procession of dandies carrying the staff and the less able-bodied snaked through the bazaar, followed by a crocodile of little girls going two by two. The destination was Union Church in the bazaar. The boys from Philander Smith Institute on Mullingar Hill systematically timed their migration so that they could pass the long line of Woodstock girls.

The students made elaborate preparations for church going. Dressing was a worrisome process.

Now many of the girls appear on the Long Dormitory balcony [in the Quad] and throw down their rugs and cushions for the coolies to arrange in different dandies. The hat bell rings and again there is a scurry to put on hats and find all the little etceteras needed. The bell to assemble in line downstairs rings, cubicles are hastily locked and by

the time everyone is down in line, it is time to start. Some
look quite anxious and worried after the struggle for part-
ners, umbrellas, and finishing their toilet. The signal is
given to start and the girls walk in two's. There is nothing
worth mentioning except the beautiful scenery which surrounds us. . . . The hills around us are very pretty. Everything looks green and with the few houses dotted here and
there, the scene is glorious to anyone who sees this kind
of scene once in a while. An artist might go into raptures
over this view. We are used to this every Sunday and perhaps do not appreciate it as we should.

When they come to the top of Mullingar Hill, the girls who
share a dandy exchange places. Then comes "the dirty and detestable
place known as Landour Bazar." Still they are interested in what is
for sale and wish it were not Sunday so they could buy sweets.

We arrive at our destination hot and tired, longing to drop
into the first possible seat, after handing our umbrellas to
the bearer and of course having our shoes dusted perfectly by a jhampani. This is a most necessary item in our toilet and is a very amusing spectacle. We form a line again
and go into church.[20]

At evening devotions, children found ways to relieve the
monotony of long prayers. Some pranks went down in the history
books. Delphine hid pepper in her handkerchief and then scattered
it about during the middle of the prayer. "First one and then another and still another took to sneezing violently, singly, together and in
chorus." A small boy was removed by the seat of his pants for talking during prayers. The toy pistol of another went off in his pocket.
For punishment he had to fire all the caps in the presence of the
whole school.

Some of the traditions that formed bonds in the classes were
unique to Woodstock. The class symbol and the class word became
important in ways not realized by most U.S. high school graduates.
Each Woodstock class had an unpronounceable class word. In 1966

it was Chpbeuh. For some classes, the name became a rallying cry all over the world. Names like Fundoshi, Zmbxa, Uhuru not only have echoed over the blue Tehri Hills but have also been inscribed in wet cement from Mussoorie to Paris, from Madhya Pradesh to Pennsylvania. Sometimes the word was kept secret for years, sometimes broadcast with abandon.

There were also controversies that divided the students. One year the senior class symbol caused a furor. Some students wanted to include in the class flag the Hindu symbol for OM, the sacred sound of the universe. Since the class flag was traditionally displayed at the graduation ceremony, the Christian students and parents objected. The impasse was resolved, as I remember, by the administration declaring that class flags were not really suitable decorations for Parker Hall, and they were removed to a less conspicuous place.

The argument over the use of OM is understandable, since it is so uniquely Hindu. But almost everything in India has some religious significance. Monkeys and peacocks are sacred, as is *tulsi* (basil). Even the use of marigolds in decorating for commencement brought the comment that those flowers were a prominent part of Hindu worship and their use was questionable. For us, a marigold is an ecumenical flower.

Sometimes the issue was over what the graduating seniors would wear: formal gowns and tuxedoes? jeans? caps and gowns? The most satisfactory solution came when the girls wore saris and the boys some type of Indian suit. This gave students the opportunity to state a lifestyle, since girls could wear either the village hand-woven cotton or Benares silk, and the men could wear simple white pyjama outfits or Nehru jackets.

Paula's class was a congenial group, although the theological differences of their parents extended from conservative fundamentalism to radical atheism. The only cloud over their graduation day was the absence of a classmate who, after frequent escapades, was suspended. But graduation week was usually a special time, for parents as well as students.

Even with those classes who have had a hard time conforming to rules, the long entry hall will be awash with a monsoon of tears as we proceed through the reception line to shake hands and bid the graduates goodbye. Many of the students have gone through an emotional trauma, beginning in their first year with "How much longer can I endure this torture?" to "How can I leave this place?" Somehow

Panorama of Woodstock buildings: the school at upper left, Hostel, Ridgewood, and Midland dormitories

they have survived the food, the monsoons, the academic workload, the walks up and down hill, and living away from their parents.

Paula proclaimed with theatrical regret, "This will be the last time for me" to attend Sports Day, to see a film at the Rialto, to walk to the top of the hill, to go to Sindhi's Sweet Shop. Someone said, "The Woodstock experience is like malaria—once you've had it, it's always going to be a part of you."

The usual graduation cliche' that "nothing will ever be the same" is especially true for Woodstock students. Some of them will never see their best friends again, and the life they go forward to is one they cannot even imagine.

Many Western children born in India have attended only one school, Woodstock, except during one or two furlough years. The boarding school was home base, the unmoving center of their lives. They had studied in small classes, lived together in the dormitory, eaten together three meals a day, participated in class parties and church services, been inspired by literal mountain-top experiences. Leaving to go to their own countries wrenched them from the only life they knew.

These are highly intelligent young people, winners of awards, world travelers. Why then can they not, when they enter good colleges, adapt to new situations and make new lives? Many do, but a significant number find the move difficult. They know more about India than they do about their own country, but they are at a loss for small talk in a society that takes for granted a certain knowledge of current slang, local customs, and style.

In a North American college, the Woodstock students identify best with students from other foreign countries, Peace Corps workers, or students who have spent a year abroad. For months, Woodstock graduates might be lonely people, counting time from one Woodstock reunion to the next. The children of several generations of missionaries had an additional problem. The life they had known as mish kids had disappeared; the "mission station" where they had spent so many happy holidays is now inhabited by nationals, and they can't go home.

Chapter 7

Boarding School

A missionary made this typical comment on the subject of sacrifices: "Our experience in India has been so rewarding that we cannot think of our work as a sacrifice—except for one aspect: it is hard to send our children 1,100 miles away from home to a boarding school."

I suspect that the separation is usually more heart-rending for the parents than it is for the children. The blithe spirit with which some students abandon their parents to rush into the arms of their friends makes one wonder if parents need children more than children need parents.

A few of the younger students cannot adjust to boarding school, are unhappy during every minute of the first year, but these are the exceptions. Most children soon adapt to dorm life, find a circle of friends, and settle into an apparently happy existence. Nevertheless, parents are right to be concerned about their children's schooling.

Why don't Westerners in India send their children to Indian schools where they would receive a better understanding of the culture in which they are growing up? Some parents go to India resolved to send their children to local schools taught in the Hindi medium, but I do not know any who followed through on this good intention. In New Delhi, Cynthia Bowles, the ambassador's daughter, did attend an English medium Indian school for a short time. Some missionary parents successfully home schooled for the first few years.

Most of the missionaries we know worked in villages or small cities. The Indian system of rote memorization, the limited education of village teachers, the absence of teaching aids (in earlier years even paper and pencils), and the narrow curriculum are hazards to learning. But the paramount handicap that Western students encounter, no matter how well intentioned they may be to use the resources of India, is that such an education does not prepare them to enter colleges in their own country.

Our own children attended Woodstock but lived at home. We could get into lively arguments about the pros and cons of boarding school. The pro parents point out that boarding schools have had a long and respected history in the education of English children and thousands of others throughout the world; that students learn discipline, self-reliance, and Christian virtues from the boarding-school experience. The con argument is that parents are responsible for teaching their children discipline, self-reliance, and the Christian virtues and should not hand over their children to an institution for moral training.

The desire for good moral training seemed to be the basis for much of the parent-school tension in the 1960s and 1970s.

"The English teacher is a bad influence on my child."

"The chaplain is teaching non-Biblical theology."

"The dorm mother is too demanding and narrow with her Bible doctrine."

Parents expected teachers to combine high professional standards with humaneness, stability, and an understanding of young people. Other influences affect students besides course content and the expectations of teachers. The peer group for a student at Woodstock exerts more influence than it might in a non-boarding school, and this fact is frightening for some parents.

Some boarding schools allow only limited visitation by parents, but Woodstock School expected the parents to visit when they could. Mothers often left their husbands on the plains to come up as early as April to take their children out of boarding. Morale improved when students moved in with parents, for mothers doted on cooking up good food for their manna-deprived offspring who suffered from institutional sustenance. Since parents saw so little of their children, they rationalized that the time they did spend together should be full of happy experiences, such as good eating and weekend excursions. Some students got better grades while out of boarding, but others—students and parents—lacked the discipline to do homework in a home setting.

Students going into boarding receive a list of what they need to survive. At one time the list included eighteen sets of underwear and socks, all with name tapes sewn in. Wardrobes had to provide for warm, cold, and rainy weather. Those items can be collected and sent in the trunk with the child, but special needs must be provided by the school. The food supervisor sees that the vegetarians are fed. The ayah helps the younger children select their clothes and comb their long hair. Even a few boys need help with hair, and the ayah ties the top knot of a little Sikh into a white handkerchief.

Some of the children have to be taught to take care of themselves, those both Western and Indian who have grown up tied to their ayah's apron strings. While dorm parents supervise mundane matters such as cleanliness and housekeeping, they are also masters of the art of arranging for picnics, trips to the bazaar, craft activities, and treks. They help manage spending money, and they keep the key to the candy cupboard where the children store the goodies sent by parents.

Good houseparents are as important as good teachers in the smooth running of a boarding school. My experience of dorm duty came one day a week substituting for Sheila, matron in the junior high girls' dorm. I was there for the girl who dropped an iron on her foot, and when an eighth grader returned late from a movie. After leading devotions, I stayed around until I thought they were all asleep and then I retired to the dorm matron's bed. I always hoped they would save their midnight parties for Sheila to handle.

On occasion I accompanied groups on Saturday excursions. We once took forty-one boarders, grades one through four, on an outing to the bazaar. They were to form that traditional crocodile line and march two by two. But such a frazzled crocodile. By the time we got them to the municipal playground, one tyke had spent her allowance on candy and then did not have two rupees to pay the attendant on the Ferris wheel after her ride. He had to be paid, for he had put considerable effort into walking the struts to make the wheel go around. So one of us paid, about ten cents.

We all had tickets for the Ropeway, the cable car. On top of Gun Hill, we ate our packed lunches and had our picture taken. Picture taking is the chief business up there. Nineteen "studios" all displayed hill dresses of velvet trimmed with yards of tinsel for the tourist who wanted to be photographed wearing the glamorous Pahari hill costume.

I preferred chaperoning trips to chaperoning some of the other activities. After one experience at a high school dance, we begged off.

Somehow this isolated school had obtained enough high-tech. equipment to raise the sound to brain-damage level, and we valued our hearing too much to risk it again.

Pranks are the pepper for the bland menu of the boarding school, and they provide the subject for alumni get-togethers: the fun of wearing a bear costume from the drama department and scaring the girls coming back to the dorm after a concert; of playing a ghost in the eerie basement music cells; of rearranging the little boys who were sleeping out on the playground and then watching as they awoke startled by their new surroundings.

"In Hostel," one alumnus wrote, "we would slowly roll the shot-put down the top level cement-floored hall. Underneath it sounded like a B-29."

One Halloween, in an effort to even the score with a pettish disciplinarian, the boys filled the padlocks to the classrooms with wax. Pandemonium prevailed when none of the keys worked.

Our own daughters were eager to try boarding. After the careful filling out of forms, Susan went into Midlands for a month. She loved boarding and tried to put a distance between herself and her parents, ignoring us at school as though she were truly independent. She suffered some snide comments from her friends about the way the school was run, the impossible food, the scarcity of hot water, and even the demands of the English department where her mother taught.

She made her own contribution to the betterment of dorm life, for Walt was moved by her outrage to go down to eat breakfast at Midlands, to see why the shower water was always cold and why the girls got such a skimpy amount of peanut butter when the boys got all they wanted. (Peanut butter was the staff of life at Woodstock.) Later he helped improve the system so that hot water became more plentiful, at least when water was available from the pumps. Also, discrimination against girls was discontinued in the peanut butter allotments.

Paula tried the boarding experience twice. The first time she found her roommates uncongenial. The second time she enjoyed boarding and brought her friends to our apartment for lunch before and after having lunch in the bazaar.

We were introduced to boarding food the first day we arrived at Woodstock. Our first meal ended with mangoes, which we did not know how to eat. Furthermore, we had neglected to teach our daughters how to use the fingerbowls that were served with the mangoes. We were lucky none of us drank from them. We did not know how to manage food that is served by a bearer offering a platter. (You help yourself with the serving fork and spoon rather than trying to wrest the platter from his hand to pass around the table.) We were awed by the bearers with their maroon cummerbunds and Nehru caps, and by the little crocheted doilies that covered the milk pitcher and sugar bowl. At the same time, we were dismayed by the poor quality of the Western food that went with this formal setting. Dining was a combination of British elegance and camping out. Luckily, the menu included Indian food every other day. Most missionary children liked curries, and Indian children preferred them to spaghetti and potatoes.

Various strategies were used to call attention to the "inedible" food. Fred Downs, class of '49, wrote, "I can still remember [Bob Alter's] benevolent smile when, as part of the never-ending Woodstock student protest against the quality of the food, I ran around the Hostel playground with a couple of *chapattis* tied to my shoes to demonstrate their durability. So durable were they, in fact, that the string holding them in place wore through before the *chapattis* did." (He was referring to unleavened bread about the size of a pancake.)[21]

One year a high school student representing a group of hungry friends decided to take steps. He wrote to the U.S. Embassy asking them to do something to improve the food situation at Woodstock. This card was referred back to Woodstock by the Embassy. A second card was intercepted and the handwriting recognized. The writer apologized to the food manager.

As a footnote to the episode, I quote from John Kenneth Galbraith, ambassador to India. He tells of going to high-protocol length to honor an admiral with a dinner on the terrace of the impressive new U.S. Embassy in New Delhi. His comment: "The food, as always, was inedible."[22] Perhaps the Embassy officials were sympathetic to the plight of Woodstock students.

Once upon a time the food situation was worse than we had ever experienced it. During the Partition, when the lorries could not bring food up to the school, Woodstock had to depend on local produce. Potatoes and squash provided the menu day after day. Some of the villagers shot a monkey and roasted it, but monkey meat was not an option for Woodstock.

"We did have bread and peanut butter," an alumnus wrote.

Paula's response was "Then what was the problem?"

Griping about the food was chronic. Even though food improved in a ten-year span from the terrible to the reasonably good, and sometimes very good, the students, while stuffing away vats of rice and curry, considered it appalling. Even on our last visit, the jokes most appreciated, next after bathroom humor, had to do with the terrible food. But what's new? Students have the same attitude toward college cafeteria food that I enjoy uncritically.

Many of the boarding school rules regulated dating, the hours and visitation and punishments for disregarding those rules. But there were other activities that could get one into trouble at Woodstock, among them, smoking, drinking, gambling, and using drugs. For students who came from high schools with no restrictions on these vices, Woodstock rules were a tremendous challenge. The students discovered ideal places for smoking (the tea stall at Cozy Corner and The Rock) only to have the administration declare them out of bounds. The problem of drinking and drugs was a concern for parents and administration, resulting in an occasional expulsion. These problems tapered off in the 1980s but are always present to some extent.

In the boarding situation where the school is responsible for students for twenty-four hours a day in a part of the world where there are no applicable community standards, a prodigious amount of time is spent in formulating rules, enforcing them, and talking about them. In earlier years a student gave her opinion of the then current rules:

> We have our student officers, who are supposed to keep us up to the mark, and we write down all our little sins in little books which are used as records against us. What gets me is that we must not have more than six faults a week against our names. I think that is trampling on our liber-

ties. There are seven whole days in a week, and I think a
girl ought to be allowed to make at least three a day. We
can't be, and it is not human to be, so *perfect*. We would
not need to have the same faults daily, we could skip
around. But only three a day is little enough to expect of
any healthy, normal girl, I think. That's my idea of self-
government.

The goal of discipline, as stated by one high school supervisor,
was to teach children to become self-disciplined. We did not have
total success.

One of the time-consuming responsibilities of the office during
Walt's tenure was the organization of Going Down Day at the end of
the semester in late November. Except for graduation, Going Down
Day was the most exciting time of the year.

The day had to be well planned by the Business Office. The date
was set in cooperation with the other schools of Mussoorie and the
railroad officials, for the railroad could not handle in one day all the
students leaving en masse from all the Mussoorie schools.

Tickets had been arranged for days ahead, with the parents send-
ing information and money needed for the migration. The students
from Woodstock were divided into parties according to destination.
Several days before Going Down Day, parent couples arrived to chaperone the parties going down. Students started leaving the Hillside at
5:30 in the morning and continued in groups until 2:00. The Madhya
Pradesh, the Ludhiana, the Calcutta, and other parties swept through
the bazaar in waves, exuberant and indefatigable. At Picture Palace
they boarded buses for Dehra Dun and the train station, where Mr.
Kapadia and his high-school helpers herded them into the proper
boogies (railroad cars) with their own luggage. (The high-school boys
formed a chorus line of singing and laughter that awed the coolies.)
A large party could reserve an entire boogie for themselves. The
escorts provided tiffin baskets and also made arrangements for food
from train stations. This routine has been simplified as more students
scatter to various countries and fly from New Delhi.

Usually the staff stays around for a few days. Woodstock School
without students is a particularly pleasant place during those early

winter days. Even for those whose duties extended through the three months, the pace was less demanding. The first joint celebration might be a staff sleep-out on Flag Hill or a wedding timed so that friends could celebrate with the bridal couple.

After ten weeks, we went through the reverse procedure, Coming Up Day. This was also exciting, but less arduous than Going Down Day. The parents on the plains made the arrangements for the parties to come up.

The most tragic experience of Coming Up Day occurred in 1970. The Raipur party was one day on the way when two adventuresome high school boys climbed up on the outside of the boogie to sit on the top and enjoy the moonlight. About ten o'clock one of the other boys heard a thud, woke the escorts who pulled the emergency chain to stop the train. They discovered that both boys had been killed, apparently hit by the overhead girders of a bridge at a river crossing. The tragedy was shocking for the entire Woodstock and missionary community. Climbing onto the boogies had been forbidden, but the students had not thought the lark to be dangerous. The lesson to the other students was hard, that rules are made for their safety, and each person must take responsibility for seeing that the community follows them.

On our first term in India, Walt was responsible for all the funds of the school and for managing the business office. He made budgets and negotiated contracts for the purchase of food and supplies; he scheduled and set priorities for the maintenance of buildings and grounds. An Indian supervisor worked in each of these four areas. About eighty persons were employed by the school in non-academic positions, most of them Indian.

Some of the decisions he found most challenging had to do with finding a way of allotting funds for housing and salaries that was fair to both overseas staff and to local staff. He struggled with a committee to provide nourishing and tasty food on a limited budget. Because of his cooperative and supportive supervisors, his first term was a positive experience.

Walt appreciated his staff. When he entered his office, he was usually greeted formally by the workers, most of them named Singh, who stood up when he first appeared. The clerk put flowers on his desk every morning. They gave him a formal farewell when they left at the end of the day. Walt found such respect somewhat overwhelming. (He was even more non-plussed when he was stopped on the road by a holy man who insisted on kissing his shoes.)

Although Walt was responsible to the principal of the school, his real taskmaster seemed to be the Finance Committee of the Board of Directors. They met twice a year, and budgets and financial statements had to be ready for those crucial dates. Walt's mandate from the Board when he began the job was to work within a balanced budget. He was not always successful. When all the teachers had submitted their requests, he always found that expenses were higher than income, and he would niggle at my request for typewriters and chalkboards. Auditors from Delhi kept Walt busy with such questions as "Why did the new library (or the Media Center) cost more than planned?"

Justin Singh, cashier, was a preacher in the local Methodist church, and on several occasions gave Walt moral support and reminded him to pray about a particular problem. Ron Kapadia, the building and grounds supervisor, asked Walt to go hunting with him. Ron shot a kakar. The next day he sent us a hindquarter of the venison.

When Walt thanked him and told him he had not expected a share of it, Ron said, "I know in America when a hunter shoots a deer it is his, but in India we divide it."

Chapter 8

Academe

W hen we were asked to go to Woodstock School, I saw the opportunity to excise my commitment to teaching the seventh-grade Sunday school class. This may seem like a radical kind of surgery, but I felt highly unsuccessful as a teacher of seventh graders. Upon our arrival in India, the principal asked me to teach seventh-grade English. I undertook the assignment without protest (I was there to serve, after all), but with a stone in my stomach. However, after I established my authority with the Woodstock seventh graders, I grew more confident.

These children came into class looking so young that I made the mistake of thinking they were innocent and naive. To me, they were polite and eager to please. With each other, they did not know how to cope with serious emotion and often responded with laughter. They aged noticeably during the year. After they had read all the good books in the library written for seventh graders, they turned to *Grapes of Wrath* and *Lord of the Flies*. Alistair MacLean and Louis L'amour were favorite authors.

I tried not to show how much I enjoyed their funny business, since seventh graders were adept at taking advantage of my lapses from the serious business of dangling participles. Some of it was not so funny. I could not understand how ink spots kept appearing on the backs of my wool skirts. Then Lynette told me that she had seen Peter give his fountain pen a flip with his wrist while I was helping the student at the desk ahead of him. When I confronted Peter, he pleaded with clear-eyed innocence that the ink spots had happened by accident. Three times? Yes. But they would never happen again.

Ink was one of my banes. At one time the whole country had

the idea that a document was not legal unless signed with pure Parker's Ink. But ink bottles were forever being pushed off those little desks, or students were forever running out of ink and having to borrow. When ballpoint pens became acceptable, I felt that they were the greatest invention since bakery bread and carried a handful with me back to India. Pencil boxes were also an affliction. They could be accidentally dropped on concrete floors with a satisfying crash.

Another of my irritations was the constant drumming of fingers on desks. Students of tabla drums are always practicing, consciously and unconsciously. It takes a strong nervous system to live with the constant thump of the fingers and the slap of the palm. Seventh graders received regular reminders that they were driving me crazy.

One incident almost undermined my disciplinary authority. I had just given a threat, reminding a group for the second time that they would stay after school if they did not *stop that noise*. At that climactic moment, a Sikh steel bangle fell to the concrete floor and bounced about with resounding clangs. Class action stopped as on a television freeze frame. They turned to me with apprehensive eyes. Was this a comedy or a tragedy? It was a comedy, and we all laughed. The frozen frame dissolved and the action flowed again.

My most recent experience in teaching English was with the eighth grade. I had read a book on teaching reading and writing in the middle school which I think should be read by every middle-school English teacher. My approval rating by students can be measured by two comments. The first was an unsigned note that said, "We want an ordinary teacher. Why don't you go home?" The other was a report to a colleague, "Mrs. Unrau is my favorite teacher. I love English!" The first kept me humble and the second restored my self-confidence.

Four years of my teaching at Woodstock included encounters with *The Tiger*, the monthly school paper. We were fortunate to have a good printer, meaning one who was willing to work with us and be sympathetic to our desire for an error-free paper. Once a month we set our publication date. Once a month we compromised either by postponing the appearance of the paper or letting it go to press needing at least one more proofreading.

We as a journalism class took a field trip to the "pressroom" at Art Press in Mussoorie. The owner, Mr. Sawnhey, was pleasant and cooperative. He took us back into the dark pressroom, which had, as I remember, a dirt floor. The typesetter, who could not read English, was setting type in English. That explained why words came through with interchangeable n's and u's, and c's that faced west rather than east. We understood why our corrections so often were corrected to unacceptable incorrections. Since then, the quality of typesetting has improved; computerization had come to Art Press, and we now receive printed material that is very well done.

We tried to connect with any literary movie being shown at the Rialto. High school students were encouraged to see *War and Peace*, so after tea, half of the Woodstock population trekked two and a half miles to the theater. The movie was old, but we soon became used to the flicker and poor sound. We found it difficult to follow the plot, however, and finally realized that the reels were being run out of sequence. We left the theater in an August rain and sloshed back to school through ankle-deep mud and water, wet and hungry. We felt a kinship with the French army in their retreat from Moscow. Never before had so many walked so far to see such a long, fractured production. A few students were inspired to read the book just to see what the movie was about. Now the school has the equipment to show movies rented from the bazaar or brought up from Delhi, and the Rialto no longer caters to Woodstock's taste for Western movies.

When the Indian boys discovered bookkeeping, they soon made up half the class. I realized that many of them came from families that ran businesses. I usually taught a typing class, and the ancient Remingtons and Underwoods were difficult to keep clicking. A man from Dehra Dun came up when called and always made a valiant attempt to keep their carriages moving. That department, too, has changed. Now everyone can learn to type on the computer keyboard.

Music and art have always had an important place in the curriculum. Mrs. Scott, one of the early principals, encouraged students in these areas, and when a friend remonstrated with her for placing so much emphasis on "mere accomplishments," she replied in the quaint rhetoric of her day: "In India, where young people in lonely stations were tempted to take part in many questionable amusements, it was well to have them supplied with sources of recreation that were pure and elevating."[23]

Woodstock gave our daughters the facilities to try their hands at a number of career-exploring activities. As a fifth grader, Paula was discouraged from art by a C on her drawings, but in high school Mr. Wesley persuaded her to try art again. She displayed her batik elephants at the Hobby Show and was commissioned to make one to order.

She became serious about Indian music, taking flute and sitar lessons; and then she got her father interested in taking lessons on the tabla with her. For a semester Paula and Walt sat cross-legged on our sun porch, aha-, dhiu-, dhin-, and dha-ing, learning the rhythm from Mr. Masih. The tablas are two separate drums. The left hand beats out the rhythm and the right adds embellishments. Although tablas were an interesting diversion, neither student became a professional drummer. Paula bought a sitar, itself a work of art. A teak neck with twenty strings is attached to a gourd. She learned to play the scale fairly well.

The music program was complete with choirs, a jazz band and an orchestra, music lessons on most instruments, and concerts that were often outstanding. Both Indian and Western students participated in programs of Indian and Western music. During our last visit, the Japanese and Korean girls were the impressive pianists.

Staging a major play at Woodstock was a dramatic and traumatic experience, and not all the drama and trauma took place on the stage. First to be dealt with was the problem of royalty. How can a shoestring budget afford, for example, to pay the royalty for *Fiddler on the Roof*? By negotiation. How do you develop the sophisticated lighting boards for which you have the know-how but not the facilities or the money? By creative improvisation. What do you do if the electricity goes off for some unexplained reason the night of the production? You arrange a back-up system. Surely drama was performed before footlights were invented. For Paula for a time, all the stage was the world as she became involved in the school drama courses.

Religion classes are required in the grades as well as in high school. A number of choices, including World Religions, are given. The current early morning assembly includes a short devotional period. There was a time when the devotional period was long with admonishment—"Morning worship to crush our spirits for the day,"

a former student wrote, but other students expressed appreciation for religious instruction.

> Though [Miss Jones] was extremely religious, she made every effort to teach the Bible purely as a subject, for in our class were many who were not Christians. One end-of-year found a Hindu girl with the highest marks in the subject—a tribute indeed to Miss Jones' inspired teaching.[24]

One of the Indian staff members told us that non-Christian Indian parents do not object to their children attending Christian services. In fact, they expect them to absorb high Christian moral values at Woodstock. Perhaps a statement by Bruce Nichols, a parent, expresses Woodstock thought on this subject.

> A Christian school will aim towards the personal conversion of the students to Christ but this must be primarily through individual witness and voluntary societies within the school. The classroom should not be used for proselytizing, and great care should be taken that dormitory activities do not bring undue pressure on children.

Woodstock offers all the courses any American high school offers to fulfill requirements for college entrance. It is accredited by the Middle States Association of Colleges and Secondary Schools. We watched our daughters find their way through chemistry, maths, French, Hindi, social studies, and art appreciation.

We were aware that American educational methods differed from those in other parts of the world. A memory system that eliminates logical analysis means that everything has to have a right answer. It makes teaching simple. We were given an example of teaching for tests when a colleague, Dwight Platt, taught for a year at a university in Orissa. His biology syllabus had omitted the respiratory system. He wanted to include it, thinking that a course on the human body should teach the fact that we breathe, therefore we live. But the students would have none of it. They were not interested in information that would not be on a test.

The criticism is made that such schools as Woodstock are little American ghettos where students learn nothing about the culture in which they live. Woodstock tries to overcome that problem with courses in Indian art and music, world religions, and Asian history, and with field trips. The teachers make special efforts to use the culture of India to enhance their courses. Ranjit Dass, as the Dan Rather of Woodstock, gave a weekly run-down of national and world news in Friday assembly, without notes and with the polish of a television anchorman.

It was after second and even third thoughts that we sent Susan with five other high-school girls and two women teachers on a tour of South India, giving her an Indian experience of her own. They survived a political riot the day Prime Minister Shastri died by hiding in the shop of a friendly tradesman. One day when they were at the beach and their bus didn't show up to return them to the town, they coped by hitchhiking.

During one week in spring, everyone in grades seven through twelve participate in some kind of off-campus experience. They have studied reptiles at Dodital, Himalayan tribal villages, plastic surgery at Ludhiana Christian Medical College, drama at Doon School. One senior spent a week selling peanuts with the Peanut Man; two went on a wilderness survival trek; one built a pipe organ with Indian flutes. One worked in the staff dining room as a kitchen bearer, much to the puzzlement of the kitchen staff. He wanted to know what it felt like to live the life of a servant.

One problem that we did not have at Woodstock was truancy. Day after day the report was posted, "all present." Only illness, dental appointments, and interschool games kept students out of class. Well, once a small boy decided to go home, but he was intercepted at the bus stand.

There we were, high on our hilltop, 10,000 miles from Columbia University or Wichita State. How could we be expected to keep up to date on teaching methods, new content for courses, or even the newest techniques of self-help, be it parenting or assertiveness training?

School buildings, clockwise from upper left: high school; Quad with elementary grades and middle school, dining hall, kitchen, and business offices; music building; and new library

Surprisingly, we had quite a few resources. Someone would find a book in Delhi, or bring a book from New York that we all wanted to read; and the school library ordered almost anything we suggested, if we knew what to suggest. Between the school library and the Community Center Library we could read through Jane Austen and Anthony Trollope, which I did over a span of several years. Traveling scholars were willing to come to our hill station, and they were probably more generous in sharing with us than they would have been at home. (A visiting researcher tested the grade school children for creativity, and we looked at Paula with new respect.) A man and wife performed Shakespeare; a classical guitarist gave a concert; the hat was passed for talent that would have commanded high fees at home. Furthermore, many of our problems and needs could be covered by resourceful persons from the larger missionary or business community.

I should not give the impression that we could rely only on Westerners to bring us professional and cultural enrichment. Many Indian nationals continue to share their skills and knowledge with the Woodstock staff. For example, Father Dominic George from South India led a staff retreat on the subject of teaching values.

At least we tried to keep up with the academic Joneses. "Behavioral objectives" was the key phrase for one professional workshop because that was what teachers were talking about in the U.S. In 1984 Kerm Gingerich as headmaster introduced the middle-school concept. We were years ahead of the Wichita school system on that. In 1986 Woodstock acquired a roomful of computers that, while not problem free, were preparing students for the world of electronic communication.

Worried about our accountability as teachers, we knew that something mattered in teaching, and we groped along with our Western colleagues to discover what it was. Perhaps as Kenneth Boulding once said to a group of teachers, "Our only function is to cheer students up."

A Woodstock brochure says,

> In a world where secular values and styles are blotting out the richness and variety of culture; where man begins to think that he created God and has power over his creation; and where intolerance is a prelude to destruction—our staff and students strive for sharing, for dialogue in ways that promote understanding, mutual respect, and even bonds of love.

Chapter 9

The Ladies' Staff Room

For a time I occupied a desk in the Ladies' Staff Room with ten or twelve other women. The walls were lined with desks, a table for coffee cups, and an old-fashioned fainting couch. Our view was to a garden below and a hillside beyond. I will take credit for one fixture in the staff room, the stove in the center. During our first term, that room and the classrooms were unheated. Through the cold months and even later, we sat there huddled in all our winter clothes, for though the weather could be pleasant outside, concrete walls continued to radiate the winter chill. I nagged the business manager and eventually a tin wood-burning stove was installed, but not soon enough for me to enjoy. Later it was replaced by an oil burner, a challenge to the patience of the high-school bearer.

The Ladies' Staff Room was our village well. In an Indian village, the women gather at a well or a pond about the same time each day to fill their large brass water pots or to wash their clothes. They talk woman talk: cooking, children, behavior of foreigners (those from another village). Gossip is an important part of their lives, helping them know who they are and who their neighbors are. They analyze and criticize their own world. American women use the telephone, the coffee break, the bridge club, the office lounge, or the sewing circle.

In the Ladies' Staff Room, we gossiped and questioned, reviewed and judged. During the thirteen-minute break at eleven, we all had a cup of coffee and some kind of snack. My cook provided peanut-butter cookies or coffee cake when I was on the rota for goodies. We were fond of cinnamon toast strips and Scottish pikelets (little pancakes), but bazaar biscuits (cookies) and *dal mot* (spicy, crunchy stuff) were welcomed.

There were times when we were bored with each other, and nobody said anything interesting or amusing. Then one of our characters would come swinging in with some outlandish observation and laughter restored us. Mrs. Cobble would relate some incident of her hundred years of missionary service in Africa; Miss Cowan would make a commonplace statement using Scottish metaphors; Miss Cressman would have a dumb student story to tell and we would be convulsed.

Our most frequent topic of conversation was the student body. The percentage of characters among the students was as high as among the teachers, and we would relate Stanley's latest smart/dumb remark or what Yashwant was wearing that day. The uninformed eavesdropper might have concluded that we hated students, that our lives would be ideal if we could teach—at Woodstock—without the trouble of student contact, lesson preparation, or paper grading.

Sometimes the subject of what had happened the night before was riveting. Landslides had narrowly missed a house; the rain had found a crack in the tin roof; the sunset on the Himalayan snows had been dazzling; or Ruth Hilliard, the courageous one of us, had tackled a burglar.

In my first few weeks at Woodstock, I wondered if I would ever be accepted by the group. At Woodstock, nobody knew how competent we had been at our jobs in Kansas, how much our friends had loved us, or how respected we had been as pillars of the church. (Well, maybe in retrospect we gave ourselves more prestige than we deserved.) In our new community, we had to establish rapport and build a reputation all over again. Furthermore, we were committed to this place for three years, even if nobody loved us.

The ladies in the staff room were for the most part ready to receive me, but I think they were a bit anxious, too. How could they relate to this middle-aged women who seemed rather reserved, no doubt snobbish because she had taught at the college level, no doubt uppity because her husband was a *burra sahib* who signed paychecks. Then, too, I had to overcome the stigma of my nationality. One of the Canadian women seemed to blame me for a story that *Time* magazine had printed about India.

Little by little they assigned personality to my hollow frame, and I began to ignore their church affiliations and nationalities. We soon learned to trust each other to act like the individuals we really were.

At one time we staff-room dwellers complained about the flimsy wall dividing us from the guidance counselor's office. We thought it was not appropriate for us to hear the conversations that took place next door. If we listened very carefully, we could hear quite a bit.

One noon hour, Saroj, Janette, and I were eating oranges and filling time until classes resumed, when Janette jumped up to tug at her clothes. "These wretched pantyhose! My mother sent them from bonny Scotland, and they are too long." (This was before most of us had adopted slacks.)

"What are pantyhose?" Saroj asked. "Always I hear 'pantyhose, pantyhose' and I have never seen any."

So we pulled up our skirts to show her the smooth practicality of our leggings. She laughed and laughed. Some ribald remarks were passed about our various bulges. As other women came in, they displayed their methods of holding up hose, and hilarity increased until we broke for classes.

Very soon after that, the carpenters came to make a pukka wall between the staff room and the office of the guidance counselor.

One cloudy day the high school supervisor, may his name be forgotten, decided that the day of women's liberation was at hand, and he was the one to cut our chains. He proclaimed that the staff rooms should be desegregated. Let the men and women share the same rooms, a man's desk next to a woman's desk.

I don't know how the men reacted, but among the women there was a loud hue and an outraged cry. We liked our staff room. Why would we want to mix with the men, hibited, inhibited, or uninhibited? We didn't mind meeting with them once a month. Their khansamas sent up some tasty cinnamon rolls. We had a better view than they did. They looked out to concrete steps. And some of them smoked.

The real reason for rejecting the idea was that we had our woman's world and we didn't want to be liberated from it. The Ladies' Staff Room remained as it was. A man might poke his head in, but no one invited him to stay. Something insidious happened during the next ten years. When we returned, we found that the staff rooms had been desegregated. The fainting couch was gone, and smoking was prohibited in the building. I wonder if the village well has also become unisexual.

An Englishman upon arriving in Bombay was told by an Indian acquaintance that he would probably feel comfortable in India. "You are a little eccentric and eccentric Englishmen in India—provided they don't get all walled up in the system within their first five years—tend to do very well."[25] Not all the eccentrics we met were Englishmen.

Walt and I quickly made the observation that many of the staff members at Woodstock School were characters, meaning that they were otherwise average people with strange streaks, stripes, and biases, even idiosyncrasies. Of course, coming as we did from all parts of the world, such individuality was understandable. Normal, average people stay home and find a job convenient to their relatives and television sets. Everyone who came to Woodstock was more or less a colorful personality, except for Walt and me and a few others of us who were ordinary, average, homeloving, colorless types. We were the ones who walked down Tehri Road not quite believing our good luck in being there.

In describing the types of teachers who are pulled in to stand behind the desks, one begins with the career missionary teachers, the old-timers, of whom there are few remaining in all of India. There was an era when young teachers went to India planning to work there until retirement. Francis (Frenchy) and Joan Browne taught for seventeen years, Ruth and Graham Hilliard about thirty, and Vera Frances Clark for thirty-three. Vera Marley came in 1918 and worked there for sixty years. The school has in the past depended on this group to give continuity and stability. A faculty meeting needs someone who can interrupt a discussion to say, "Ten years ago when this problem came up . . . ."

In Woodstock history, family names keep cropping up. Parents came to India as missionaries when the various denominations opened their fields, and their children attended Woodstock School. These children returned to India after college to join the missionary family or to teach at Woodstock. This group has almost disappeared. Now for most Western teachers the term of service is three years. The school depends on the Indian staff to give continuity and stability.

In our time there, many of the Western staff were like us: we wanted the experience of working in a foreign country and our mission was willing to send us. We became involved in the life of the school and believed in its goals. We all knew that we would soon return to the States or to a Commonwealth country and to our "real" lives. But even as we moan about the high turnover of the Wood-stock staff, we acknowledge that even the short-termers have made contributions to the school. (One of the least of my contributions was the introduction of the weekly staff news sheet. I wanted to call it Bean's Bulletin, for the headmaster, but he with his twisted New Zealand wit thought it should be called Ruth's Rubbish. It has since turned into the uninspired sheet of daily announcements.)

Loneliness was a problem for single women. Some women had come to India having heard the call to be a missionary, but few of them heard a call to matrimony. Miss Fanny Parsons, a dainty woman in a coal scuttle bonnet and a hooped skirt, is believed to have confessed in those early Woodstock years: "If some Colonel were to come along and ask me to wed him, I would go down on my marrow-bones and say, 'Thank you, Sir.'"[26]

I am convinced that it takes a special grace to be happy at Wood-stock as a single woman, although I think some have achieved that state of contentment. Perhaps happy people are happy wherever they are, but at Woodstock there is a high potential for unhappiness.

When I first joined the staff, most of the single women lived in a bedroom-with-bath arrangement in the Quad or in the dormitories. They were expected to eat either in the staff dining hall or with the students. Gradually the women collected equipment to cook in their bathrooms. The administration decided, *post facto*, that they be allowed to cook their own meals. Then the women started asking for apartments with proper living rooms, bedrooms, and kitchens. I tried to convince the business manager that they had just as much right to a nesting instinct as married women. By now all of them have apartments.

We came to expect a flow of anecdotes when a group of Wood-stock teachers met for a social evening. Over the coffee and cookies we usually started the game of "Remember Charlie?" Those of us who didn't remember Charlie or Fergy or Miss Frances were told how they had executed some preposterous venture, usually to the triumph and fame of Characters.

Sometimes Charlie was a student, sometimes a teacher. Diana Biswas could reach back into her pack of memories of students whom she had accompanied on hikes.

"I took him on a hike and he deliberately smashed all the eggs and threw away all the food that he was assigned to carry."

At one time, the ones with the most eccentricities were those who taught French, although colorful characters taught in every academic area. Either French teachers are inimitable or perhaps Woodstock School attracts only this kind to itself.

I knew Fergy. She was the French teacher with the heart of California gold. We all loved her and recounted the ways she had of sharing concern for everyone she met, often to her own economic disadvantage. But we all admitted that Fergy found it hard to say goodbye, and many were the stories of her tardiness because she could not shut down a conversation.

Another staff member we knew and loved was Fluff Flynn, her real name. She was on her solitary way around the world. What her parents were thinking of, letting this waif go on her own, I can't imagine. Probably they had not been consulted. She was so naive, so poorly equipped to take care of herself that she was often the victim of the avarice of taxi drivers who offered to change her hundred rupee note only to disappear with it, and postmen who demanded to be paid for delivering her mail. Presumably she made her way home safely after her interim of housemothering the little boys, who adored her. Fluff Flynn, where are you now?

"Miss Marley's memory puts an elephant to shame," was the common summing up of Vera Marley. She had served at Woodstock in almost every department during her sixty years there. Her name is set in brass in the Vera Marley Library, but in the 1970s her presence pervaded the Quad as she worked in her room on alumni records. Every visiting old student must see Miss Marley, and she, true to her legend, would remember the name of each and what famous or infamous record each had made at Woodstock, as well as who had been the plussie of whom from year to year. ("Plussie" comes from the John + Mary equation.)

Miss Marley was devoted to a number of expressions. One was "They will drive me to drink," whether she was talking about a student, the dhobi, or an administrator. One of the students she thought would drive her to drink was David Fiol (as I write this, the chairman of the Woodstock Board) when he substituted his own copy of a magazine for one in the library. As Miss Marley watched him, he chose that magazine from the rack, read through it, and then started tearing out pages. "Miss Marley pounced in holy wrath and my, the scene that followed." Later, she enjoyed the joke.

One student wrote: "Her most endearing quality to me was the ability to put the lesson across. It was always Miss Marley's final summing up that brought on the light."

While we knew we were living and working with teachers of outstanding personality, those who had gone before us seemed more outstanding as they were extoled in *Woodstock School, The First Century*. Some teachers were remembered for the way they conducted daily devotions. It was said of Mrs. Scott that if any particular girl seemed to be in need of prayer, Mrs. Scott would take care to mention her good qualities so that when the prayer was offered, the students had the feeling "that it was worth praying for one who gave so much promise." One grown-up student remembered that as a little boy he had been impressed with Miss Edith Jones' invitation from Isaiah: "Come for tea, come for tea, my people."

One housekeeper, Mrs. May Lincoln Mattison who survived a prolonged term of service, was distantly related to President Lincoln. She was eulogized as "one of those women whose mother heart enfolded the world about her . . . . For sheer nobility of character, there are few who could surpass her."[27]

Devotion and nobility were typical characteristics of our ancestral Woodstock staff members.

Chapter 10

The Great Rhododendron Hike and Other Sporting Events

"Skipping and strolling about" were the main recreations of the early years when Woodstock was a girls' school. A few played tennis, rounders (baseball), and badminton and arranged picnics on Camel's Back on the Library side. For the staff, all games were played in the long skirts and stiff collars of the era.

When Mr. Parker was principal, he delighted in recalling the first hike, in 1918, of the small boys, those few who had been admitted to this girls' school. The careful matron, not understanding the joys of hiking, bundled her charges off in dandies for their first hike. Every little boy became skillful with his catty, as he called the catapult, better known to American children as a slingshot.

Ophrysia, the little book published by the Woodstock Natural History Society, says, "Nali is a pleasant and easily accessible spot [eleven miles away] that is set in a pine forest."

Easily accessible by whom? By villagers, Woodstock intrepid trekkers, long distance runners, debt collectors, and other athletic types, I would guess. The statement is not true for some of us, but I am glad I made the hike because now I can say that I have been to Nali the way Sir Edmund Hillary can say he has scaled Mt. Everest. I take pleasure in the assurance that I don't have to do it again.

The event was called the Rhododendron Hike because we had heard that one needs a pillowcase full of rhododendron blossoms to make rhododendron jelly, and that the best place to collect the blossoms is near Nali.

One of the fringe benefits of living in the foothills of the Himalayas is the rhododendron. Unlike the bushes of western Oregon with their huge hybrid blossoms of various colors, these are red and grow on tall trees spotted on the hillsides. For a few paisa, little boys will climb the trees and bring down branches of the red clusters from which we arranged huge bouquets. Some of us made jelly. The Indian cooks used the blossoms in curry.

The making of rhododendron jelly was the excuse we needed to perform the first rite of spring, to take a hike. When we realized that we were in for a perfect weekend, there was nothing to do but reserve a dak bungalow, coolies, Diana Biswas, and sleeping bags. Ten of us, all women, started out Friday after tea, knowing that we had to make the eleven miles to Nali before dark to set up camp. Diana had reserved the dak bungalow by due process.

Here are the directions for reaching Nali. Walk east of Mussoorie on Tehri Road, a real motor road from which you cannot lose your way unless you fall off it. After about five miles you come to the small village of Suakholi where you stop for tea, which is highly regarded by Woodstock students. A twenty-minute stop is not too long for catching of breath and wondering how you, at your age, got involved in this foolhardy enterprise. The road to Suakholi is maliciously rolling, and you notice the inclines but not the declines.

A little beyond Suakholi, you find a path going down on the south side of the ridge. Don't take it, although it goes where you want to go. But at the next large curve, take an old washed-out motor road that goes down, beautifully, to meet the other path. It is a spiral road, and to save yourselves time and mileage, go straight down over the rocks from one zig to the next zag. This is more difficult than you expect and very hard on toenails.

Eventually you meet that other path you didn't take and go left, and after about two miles you come to another fork. Both tines go to Nali. The left is shorter but the other is prettier. (Since it was dark by that time, we took the shorter.) You are encouraged by your fearless leader telling you that Nali is probably about half an hour ahead. The path is described by *Ophrysia* as a drab path; all you will know in the dark is that it is slippery with pine needles. You will be dismayed by darkness, but your trusty torch (flashlight) keeps you from falling into the ravines. Walk along single file, but stop every so often to count torches.

I was usually on the end, my fellow trekkers said lagging but I said pushing. Everyone of the ten of us was a comedienne, and we enjoyed lots of camaraderie. Someone offered the information that bears were known to inhabit the area and asked what we would do if we met one. They thought I would be the first snatched off since I was at the end of the line, but I thought the bear would laugh himself to death when he saw Diana Biswas leading the group in her camouflage hat and hiking boots. Anyway, my toes were so painful by then that being eaten by a bear didn't seem such a terrible fate.

To return to the directions for reaching Nali: If you persevere, you will come to another fork, and this time you must take the right because the other goes down into the Doon Valley. After another few miles you find yourself at the dak bungalow, the time being about eight o'clock and the sun long gone.

Dak bungalows are one of the best ideas left over from British India. Some of them can be very comfortable for the traveler, even providing superior khansamas (cooks). But we were disappointed after all the pukka arrangements to find ourselves locked out. However, the coolies who had brought our sleeping bags had a fire going outside to welcome us. (How had they got there ahead of us?) We ate our packed lunches and drank hot bouillon. We looked at the moon coming up to silhouette the bottlebrush pines on a distant hill; we looked at the lights of Woodstock four or five miles across the valley. Following good British safari tradition, we practiced all civilized amenities and one of us put her hair on rollers for the benefit of her self-respect. We played Rook until eleven. I griped about having to play Rook when I was so tired, but after finally crawling into my sleeping bag, I was sorry we had not played longer. Even with my luxurious air mattress, I was uncomfortable and cold on that concrete verandah. The night was very long.

After a leisurely and bountiful breakfast, we packed a lunch and started back. This time we took the other path, the pretty one shaded by oak, rhododendron, and pine, and we were glad we had saved it for the daylight. We were disappointed that we could find so few flowers because the local villagers had picked all those within reach. On our climb out of the valley, we found that our toes were less painful going up than down.

We reached home in the early afternoon. A hot bath and a good night's sleep put me back to normal except for my black and blue toenails, a colorful reminder of the trek for a year after. The other visible result was the rhododendron jelly. I took the few blossoms I had gathered and added those that Paula found on a tree that grew in what you might call our front yard. I harvested two cups of juice.

The village of Suakholi deserves another paragraph. Though small, it is the center of an area of farming activities. Many paths come together here. Below Suakholi on the north side of the hill lies the village of Magra with a small apple orchard. Woodstock students come to this pleasant valley to camp overnight.

Suakholi can be explored in about five minutes. We stuck our heads in a stable, withdrew quickly, stood in the street to assess the food staples and cloth in a small shop, and visited the tea stall. It is hard to believe the poverty-stricken look of an Indian roadside tea stall. The table and benches are crude, the cups have been washed in filthy water, the floor is packed dirt, and everything is specked by the flies that live in the stable. We trust the boiling tea water to protect our health.

"There is no tea as good as Suakholi tea," the students of one generation told us. Their idea of a lark was to get up early in the morning, sneak out of the dorm and hike to Suakholi for tea. They woke the obliging owner, drank tea, and returned to the dorm in time for breakfast without being missed. A more legitimate time to make the hike is in the balmy moonlight of May or June after a class party.

Diana Biswas sent a note down one cold February Saturday morning to suggest that a group of us go to Cloud's End for the day. Even if I hadn't heard that it was an exhilarating hike, I would have wanted to go because of the name of the destination. Who can resist going to Cloud's End to discover what lies beyond?

Cloud's End is west of Mussoorie. We went all the way through the bazaar to Library, where we stopped at a tea shop to be fortified with tea and toast, the bread held on a fork over a charcoal burner. Reluctantly leaving the warmth of the tea shop, we took a road from the northwest corner of the Library square. We walked up past the Savoy Hotel, Waverley School, the Municipal Gardens, climbing amidst the greenery of oak and rhododendrons with alluring little jungle recesses and streams, past fairy-tale mansions built on cliff-sides. After the west toll gate, we came out into a less inhabited hillside area. We ate our sandwiches in a sunny spot, then continued on for tea at Cloud's End. After we reported to the *chowkidar* (caretaker), we felt free to explore the place.

The house at Cloud's End was built by Fanny Parks, that "distinguished Englishwoman" who came to Landour for the season of 1838.

> During her stay, Fanny Parks personally superintended the construction of the Cloud's End bungalow and would ride fifteen miles to and from her work on her pony each day. The walls were about two feet thick and at times she had as many as 500 men at work there . . . . At the top of Bhadraj [a nearby peak] she found a little shrine and a large rock with the inscription, "Lady Hood, 1814." Later she learned that Lady Hood never actually climbed the mountain but sent a man up there to chisel her name.[28]

Fanny Parks would not have sent a man to do a woman's job. She herself climbed the adjoining peaks of Benog and Bhadraj, and we wanted to do the same as we sat in the yard of the bungalow and looked across at the peaks with views to the east, north, and west. On our last visit to Mussoorie, Diana discouraged us from returning to Cloud's End. A mining crew with headquarters there had harassed the Woodstock students the last time they had gone there for an overnight hike. Cloud's End is another satisfying memory that cannot be relived.

Today, hiking is not as popular as it was in the 1960s and 1970s, although it is still an important part of the extra-curricular program. Earlier, Woodstock's schedule seemed to revolve around the sport of trekking. To paraphrase a quotation from tennis: "Trekking is not a matter of life and death. It is more important than that." "Long" weekends without homework were scheduled to accommodate hiking trips. The bazaar shoemaker learned to make good hiking boots, and top-of-the-art backpacks and sleeping bags were in demand, as were dehydrated foods. The students learned soon which new staff members were ready to chaperone.

In 1838 in her book *Up the Country*, Lady Emily Eden described the men coming back from a tiger hunt, delighted with having been very nearly eaten up and then stung to death. It was in such a mood that students came back from treks, happy to be exhausted and starved. Susan experienced her high on a trip to Nag Tiba, starting out with a full-blown cold, then enduring the misery of rain on slippery uphill paths and cold baths in streams. But she stumbled up to our third-floor apartment with a gratifying feeling of accomplishment.

Trekkers were given encouragement when the "high country" was reopened for hikers. Much of the area north of Mussoorie had been closed in the 1960s during trouble on the Chinese border. In 1974 the ban was lifted, and the famous pilgrim centers at the source of the Ganges became accessible. Hikers could even get to the top of Bandarpanch, the peak visible from the top of our hill.

My dream was to go back to India and join a party of trekkers, none of them walking faster than I. I would hire a man to carry my pack, and if I felt like it, I would run uphill, and with the wind behind me I would sail across flowered meadows and slide across fields of snow. That would be when I was seventy.

Actually, part of that dream came true, but it was not quite as easy as I had envisioned it. With a group of middle-school students, we took a bus to Gangotri, then hiked eleven miles on a path following the gorge of the Ganges to Gaumukh, where we camped in a moonscape of rocks and peaks. No flowered meadows there. Because of a temporary health problem, Walt rode a little horse, an unnerving experience, and he hopes to walk next time. I'm glad I made that Gangotri hike, but I'm also glad that our next trek, in the Colorado Rockies, was a bit less strenuous.

But there is more to the Woodstock sports program than trekking. India is a country that makes heroes of soccer and cricket players the way Americans make superstars of football, baseball, and basketball players. Cricket is the favorite national sport. Players are worshipped, games are followed on the front page of daily newspapers, scoring records are reeled off by fans. In a country where games are a national pastime, the schools must offer good athletic programs. Basketball, tennis, soccer, cricket, hockey, swimming, and field and track all have a place in the curriculum. (Note the absence of American football.) Classes were over at 3:40. After tea, a good number of both boys and girls went down to Hanson Field or up to the gym for whatever sport was in season. Basketball was perhaps the top sport for both participants and spectators. The court boasts a roof, three walls, and a concrete floor that becomes slippery in the monsoon season. There was a time when Woodstock boys' greatest competition came from Hillside fathers, but as enthusiasm for basketball grew in Indian schools, it became a Mussoorie sport.

Cricket became popular at Woodstock when Brij Lal joined the staff as Hindi teacher and cricket coach. One of his students, Tom Alter, writes about his love of cricket, that gentleman's game that requires a baseball field, a ball, and a bat but which has little else in common with baseball. The reader will realize by now that playing fields are rare on steep Mussoorie hillsides. Nevertheless, Tom lists eight in the area. Oak Grove, the railroad school, sits in a valley, so the players have the least trouble chasing cricket balls "rolling half the way to Dehra Dun," as would happen at St. George's, the Catholic school. But St. George's has such a view as to make playing cricket there "almost a mystical experience." The matches at Wynberg-Allen are memorable for the teas laid on by the school. (Unfortunately we missed the tea; not knowing about it and being bored, we left early.) The Woodstock ground, Hanson Field, "is so far from civilization that visiting teams are half-finished by the time they get there."

Tom Alter seems to speak for all Woodstock students who love the sport:

> The sun is out and a breeze is blowing and as you stroll through the bazaar, feeling cocky and confident in your whites, and with your arm around a friend's shoulder; shopkeepers wave out and wish you well and invite you in for tea, and girls stop and look at you; for a moment the world is yours.[29]

Sports Day, held about the second Saturday in October, is the Woodstock equivalent of an American high school's homecoming. All the parents who can possibly make it up the mountain come for the day. The competition takes place on Hanson Field, which is just large enough for the 110-meter track. The spectators sit on tiers of concrete built into the hillside or they sit on the slopes around the

Ron Flaming, principal, with his own and a few others' backpacks on the Gangotri path, high above the Ganges River

field. This is the Woodstock Bowl, with tree-covered hills rising around us.

Mussoorie Olympic games are held the following Saturday at Wynberg-Allen School which has a larger field and more bleachers. The place is crowded with Mussoorie spectators, for as many as fifteen schools participate in the Olympics. I love a parade, so I have a lump in my throat as we watch the March Past of the United Nations and school flags. Woodstock's colors are brown and gold. Our cheerleaders wear short pleated skirts handed down from generation to generation. The principal at Wynberg-Allen gives the invocation and welcome: "Jump higher, leap longer, and break no bones and all records."

The 100-meter hurdle was a delight to watch. The girls sailed over the hurdles in perfect rhythm, with long hair streaming, making us remember African gazelles leaping as they ran. Even the officials were entertaining. A stylish Indian woman in a flowing blue sari and matching umbrella (for the sun) walked onto the field to give last minute coaching to her students. A huge Sikh official in khaki strolled about, his beard neatly parted and tucked under his pink turban. He carried a musket appropriate to his size. When he fired the starting signal, the blast propelled the runners halfway around the first lap.

Not until 1938 did Woodstock have its own playing field. Mr. Parker, the principal, eyed a ravine between the Methodist's East-wood Estate and the school's Midlands Estate, five hundred feet below his office window.

Mr. Parker said, "Every engineer I have consulted tells me a playing field cannot be made there. I believe it can be done, so we are going ahead."

Even his wife did not encourage him. "To build that field one has to cut down a mountain, fill up a valley, and divert a stream."

He went ahead, but he should have listened to the engineers and to his wife. When the field was near completion, the hillside

Forming the W on Sports Day at Hanson Field

Hanson Athletic Field viewed from the tea garden at school

underneath the pushta settled, taking pushta, trees and all. The field was shortened by twenty feet, and it had to be used in that shape.[30] Later, about 1945, the Methodist Board of Foreign Missions contributed toward the improvement of the field and it was named Hanson Field in honor of Robert Hanson, a former student who had lost his life as a pilot in World War II.

But the monsoon season of 1950 brought a heavy rainfall, and the field was partially covered by rubble. Each year's monsoon added to the debris. When Walt arrived in 1965, one of the priorities of the Board was to restore the field. Energetic Tibetans filled two-wheeled carts and pulled them by man- and woman-power across the field, clearing the rubble from the north end and dumping it over the khud at the south end. The Tibetans uncovered bleachers on the north side that most people had forgotten existed. For several years the field was in good shape.

Then Eastwood Hill above the field began to shift. A fault in the mountain extended down to and across the field, and it became unusable. Eastwood with its eight apartments was also victim of the shift, and what could not be salvaged drifted down the hill. In later years, students manned the picks and shovels, trailers and carts, and moved rubble to fill the depressions and enlarge the field enough to hold Sports Day on the campus once again. But one cannot depend on the hillside staying put. It is important for Woodstock School to have a playing field, but providing one requires money and effort.

Chapter 11

The Flora and the Fauna

First the fauna. In Kansas we take for granted the surrounding wildlife until we happen upon baby skunks playing by moonlight in our backyard. In India, we had to stop to look at all new things and seek out names of birds and flowers, and even some of the animals. There was always animal life around us: choo-choos (shrews) in the bathroom, a monkey in the kitchen, a lizard on the dining-room table. And the ubiquitous goats and cattle and rats, mostly outside.

We had two kinds of monkeys to watch as we walked to school. The more common rhesus were brown and funny. They crossed our path or jumped from the Hostel roof to the live oaks without fear of us. Little ones watched wistfully through the kitchen window as I took muffins from the oven. They were as amusing as the squirrels in our Kansas elms.

The full-grown monkeys were not so endearing. I watched a troop of seven or eight on my way up the hill one morning as they crashed their way from tree to tree. When they got up to the Quad, they jumped from the tree tops to the roof of the office area, then galloped the length of the dining hall roof; they leaped easily into the trees and then on to the roof of Parker Hall. They crashed on up the Hillside and then, I suppose, down into the next valley. Later in the day during bookkeeping class I heard a freight train thundering over my head. I realized after one moment of panic that the monkeys were making a return trip.

One evening when I came home from school, I found the adult monkey population sitting on the fence snatching the flowers that bordered the yard. I assaulted them timidly with my umbrella, and they retreated briefly. The collective form is appropriate: "a shrewd-ness of apes."

The other type of monkey on the Hillside is the langur. They have black, old-man faces with white ruffs. Langurs are considered to be meaner than rhesus, but we never felt afraid of any monkey, especially when we were armed with an umbrella. Then one day Gloria, the secretary in the business office, was walking down the ramp from the high school when a half-grown rhesus jumped on her back, scaring her to the edge of insanity. Her screams and the yells of passersby sent him off, and Gloria was unharmed.

When Susan and her husband were traveling by train in Rajasthan during the hottest part of the summer, they were warned to keep the windows closed to avoid invasion by monkeys. But it was too hot to heed the advice. At one point Susan looked up from her book to find a monkey sitting on the shelf in the corner reading the label on her box of water-purifying pills. She was affronted to have this stranger invading her privacy and shooed him out the window. He took the bottle of pills with him as well as her train schedule. Then he stood calmly on the Jaipur platform, peeling the cardboard box off the bottle as if peeling a banana, and shook the pills into his mouth.

"He must have had the purest stomach in Jaipur," she said.

Later when they climbed to an upper balcony of the City Palace for a view of Jaipur, they found the train schedule on the balcony railing, just as they had marked it.

Monkeys are protected by law, but when a group becomes obnoxious, they are rounded up by government workers and shipped to another place where they are turned loose in the bush. Hindus revere monkeys as descendants of the great monkey god, Hanuman, who aided Rama in the Hindu epic *Ramayana*.

> The beautiful Sita, Queen wife of Ram, was kidnapped from their forest retreat by the cruel ruler of the Island Kingdom of Ravanna. En route to the home of the abduc-tor, Sita dropped pearls along the way and threw her choicest strand into a cluster of monkeys sitting on a hill-top. By this means she was traced to the stronghold of her captor and rescued by an army of their tribe.[31]

Another legend adds that the monkeys tied their tails together so that Ram could cross the distance between the tip of India and

Ceylon (now Sri Lanka) to rescue his wife from the demon-king of Lanka.

Villagers and hunters were sometimes badly mauled by bears. Leopards are the bane of little dogs on the campus, and even in our time leopards invaded the Quad. Pine martens, of the mink and weasel family, were common on Tehri Road. They are black with yellow throat markings and long tails. Their pelts are valuable. One sunny day on a hill path, we saw the pretty parade of a mother leading four young ones.

Some people (surely only women) are terrified of snakes, but snakes on the Woodstock campus seemed always to have slithered away before we arrived. A poisonous snake had wandered into the living room of our apartment the week before we moved in, but it had been dispatched by the sweeper. In the Woodstock history is the story of a python that invaded Midlands dormitory. The principal was called down from the school and he obligingly shot it.

When I tell my missionary friends that I did not see a single snake (besides the ones dancing in the bazaar for money), I immediately get a snake story. One snake inhabited the toilet bowl; another curled up on a favorite chair. Our missionary friend, Vernelle Waltner, tells of entertaining a visitor while a deadly krait hid behind a buffet, politely unmentioned by the khansama until the meal was over. One child kept a pet cobra until his mother discovered it in the clothes hamper. I gathered that one does well to learn the difference between the harmless and the deadly.

When we visited Paul and Nancy Conrad at Dhamtari, Nancy entertained us using her best white damask tablecloth and her crystal and silver wedding gifts. ("We plan to be in India for most of our lives so, not knowing what else to do with them, we brought them along.") During table grace, a six-inch lizard dropped from the ceiling onto the tablecloth in front of my plate and waited there repectfully until the prayer was over. Then one of the children removed him. Lizards don't bother me, and all of us took the episode as an interesting paradox of India, where one finds lizards enjoying the elegance of damask.

Our dining room ceiling at Palisades had no upstairs room over it, just attic crawl space. During the evenings when I sat quietly sewing in that room, I heard thumps and rattles above. I fantasized that two giant rats were bowling with stones and milk bottles. Whatever it was, the noise sent me out of the room in a nervous sweat to seek other company.

Then one warm January Sunday we were sunning ourselves in the yard when we noticed that other creatures had crawled out from their nests to enjoy the warmth. Two eighteen-inch lizards were flicking their tongues at insects on the walls of the house. When the children tossed pebbles at them, they skittered into a hole under the eaves. After that, those noises above the dining room sounded like lizards thumping their tails and clicking around on their toenails. We always had enormous spiders that carried pouches of eggs which hatched into dozens of tiny spiders that ran every which way. When Paula complained about them, Susan caught the spiders and carried them outside. But a place needs spiders to keep down the roach population. We had toads in the living room one day, a small army that came mysteriously out of the grass. We had a couple of scorpions, but never in our shoes where they are supposed to be shaken from. It is common knowledge that a scorpion will sting itself to death under trying conditions. Various curious Woodstock generations have proved this theory.

Snakes, lizards, and spiders I can take in stride, but rats make me uneasy. One of the questions I kept asking myself as we prepared to go to India was, Can I really cope with rats? For I had heard from missionary friends about their experiences with rats. Selma Unruh told a tale of a rat that had poked its head out from under a loose tile in the living-room floor; and she, rocking in her lovely rosewood rocker, had inadvertently executed it with a backward rock. I asked myself, Should I stay home from India because of this aversion to rats?

And there it was; on our first day at Woodstock, as we left the staff dining room we saw a dead rat lying in the middle of the Quad. I was appalled. It was indeed true that rats were so rampant that they were overrunning the place in broad daylight and dying wherever they chose. Mrs. Versluis, our hostess, explained that her cat was always bringing her rats to admire. I did not know then that this was the only rat I would see at Woodstock during that first year.

We bought a plastic lemon squeezer at Ram Chander's that had printed on its box: "Acid resistant, unbreakable, washable, and rat proof." I was more disconcerted than comforted by that promise.

Sometimes rats were a problem in the dormitories in fall. When we lived next door to the junior-high girls' dorm, we were always kept informed of adventures with rats. They jumped out of drawers, or they ran over the beds at night. Keeping a rat as a pet was forbidden. We had a visitor in our bathroom that year, but we could never discover how it made its way in and out, for we never saw it. Susan gave Walt a rat trap for his birthday. Using peanut butter for bait, he finally caught it, a large mouse, a small rat, or perhaps a shrew.

Choo-choos are not quite as bad as rats, but for them, too, I must collect my scraps of courage. Choo-choo is the pet name for *choochandra*, and the English name is shrew. It has a longer nose than a rat. We once attended a wedding *khanna* where the guests were seated on mats in two rows facing each other in an otherwise bare room. We women, modestly draped in our long saris, sat cross-legged with our plates of curry and rice in front of us on the floor. A shrew appeared soon after we had begun to eat, and he insisted on trying to eat from my plate. I shooed at him, but he was a very persistent rodent. I might have been willing to share my food with him (a statement of mock bravado), but I was afraid that he would run up the folds of my sari. I conducted myself with quite a bit of aplomb, I am told. I did not scream, I did not panic. I hope my children remember this incident as an example of how their mother behaved in the face of danger.

Some writers say that rats are the real inhabitants of India, and quote statistics that show that rats outnumber people eight to one. It is estimated that rats destroy half the grain and that they have increased because their natural enemy the snake is being exterminated. Snakes, like spiders, have their uses. Rats and roaches feed snakes and spiders, and so the environmental balance is preserved, but I don't know to what end.

Leeches can be described as one of the major annoyances of the monsoon season. A leech is a black worm about an inch long found in the fresh-water streams of the Himalayan hillsides and on the paths up and down from the school. They are not peculiar to India, but we had our first experience with them there. Leeches attach themselves to your feet and crawl up your legs. You do not usually feel the bite, but you look down to discover this animal has been drinking your blood. Bloated, the leech is now the size of an unshelled peanut. Your first reaction is horror. The simile, "sticks like a leech," is appropriate. A leech is difficult to brush off, and the easiest way to deal with it is to salt it; school children often carry little packets of salt for this purpose. Salting a leech is a simple but nauseous process, for the leech drops off and dies in a pool of your blood. Its bite contains an anticoagulant that keeps you bleeding for a time after his attack.

There is a good path that leads down from the dormitories, across the valley, and up to Wynberg-Allen School. A new member of the staff ventured that way for a Sunday afternoon walk and returned with thirty-two leeches. Back in the dark ages of medicine, leeching was a cure for almost anything, and we had a graphic lesson in how the treatment worked. "I'd rather die," is the common response to this information. But recently modern medicine has found the leech to be useful in controlling bleeding for skin grafts.

Having mentioned beetle collections earlier, I'll list here some of the common varieties that little boys collect in June at night under a lamp post: the reindeer stag with antlers three inches long; the clumsy cow beetles with two pinchers-like horns; the brown bamboo with antennae in sections, a great fighter; the fierce black Chinese stag; the rhino with one horn; the sweat beetle that grumbles when you stroke its back; the elephant beetle; the stone carrier; and others less often seen.

I know that I should say something about elephants in a book about India, but the fact is we saw very few in North India. We once picnicked in the Doon Valley where an elephant herd had tramped through, and though we said it would be fun to see some elephants, we were fortunate that they did not return our way. (We learned more respect for elephants during our two years in Africa.) One Woodstock graduate discovered as he sat at the top of a tree waiting for a herd of elephants to depart that the rumble of an elephant's stomach sounds exactly like an idling car engine.

Tiffany's advertised in the *Wall Street Journal* that you could buy an eighteen-carat gold camel with diamonds in the saddle, a cultured pearl in the topknot, and a pink ruby and lapis lazuli here and there for $2,850. You can buy a real one for quite a bit less.

Camels are used domestically as draft animals in Rajasthan and in the Punjab. They appeared infrequently enough that we stopped to laugh when we saw one in the countryside. They are mangy creatures, surely one of nature's jokes. Usually they were pulling something. I'm told that a camel is not as easy to ride as an elephant.

My last glimpse of a camel came as we were traveling by fast taxi on the multi-lane Ring Road around Delhi, comparable to I-70 through Kansas City. Traffic was stopped by a camel drawing a hayrack across the road at his own leisurely gait, viewing with contempt the trucks, taxis, motor scooters, bicycles, and rickshaws that were forced to swerve around him. You could have bought him for $300.

There are, according to folk wisdom, ninety-nine names known for Allah. Only the camel knows the hundredth one, and that is why he is so arrogant.

The first color in spring comes in March when the rhododendron explode. Then we notice that the hillsides are being blanketed with tiny white daisies. Then come mayflowers, purple iris, peacock iris, yellow and white Bankshire roses. Blue periwinkles spread over the shady slopes, and pink daisies decorate the stone steps and hang from the pushtas. With the first raindrops of the monsoon, we become aware of flowers and ferns and all manner of vegetation that has lain dormant under dry grass. Trees light up with color.

"What is the name of the flowering bush just below the fence?" I asked the mali. (What I really did was point to what I supposed was an ornamental cherry and say, "Nam kya hai?" hoping he would understand my kindergarten Hindi.)

"Just jungly bush," he replied in English, giving it no name. Anything from bushes to people with an untamed look are called jungly.

Ferns were rampant. Red-bearded Christmas, polypods, walnut, four-eared membrane, nail, all grew along the paths and on the forest floor. The maidenhair and Crete were common along the stream below Midlands. The common male, comb lady, and mouse ear were also gathered by biology students.

The most interesting to us were the light green Bible ferns that grew from moss-covered walls and tree trunks. The stone parapet of the bridge over the stream on our path was prettily decorated with velvet moss and lace ferns. In the bazaar, little ferns decorated the mane of the enormous lion carved out of the rock below the Roselynn Hotel. There were 120 kinds of ferns in our area. We used a three-foot frond to make a Christmas tree on the whitewashed wall of our dining room, and decorated it with tinseled strings from the

Fifth grade class party during fair weather; Paula is by the tree

bazaar. We used fern foliage to enhance bouquets, but I can't remember that anyone put them in a hanging basket or set them on a flower stand in the living room.

We saw cosmos at the desolate Haunted House, where the cultivated plants had washed down the hill. Walking over to the edge of the neglected yard and looking over the khud, we were surprised by this cosmosic sea below us. I understood how William Wordsworth must have felt about his host of daffodils. Cosmos, I know, are common everywhere, but when you come upon an acre of them growing wild, that is a memory to take with you into your old age.

Along with cosmos, dahlias have become wild, progeny of once planted hybrids. Their brilliant deep red combined well with purple plumes of Mexican salvia, probably called Himalayan salvia in that area, if anyone gave it a name. By October the tree dahlias are out. They have spindly branches about ten feet tall with lots of pale lavender flowers. They are not so beautiful as their cultivated cousins, but they are a part of the perfect October Indian summer.

We accepted an invitation to hike down to the orchid beds, a Saturday's excursion in April. We didn't know what to expect, but what we found were small, white irises among the green foliage on the walls of a deep, dripping ravine. Nothing spectacular, just a charming setting of stream, miniature waterfalls, greenery, small caves, and white orchids. On the two-hour climb back, we stopped at a cinnamon tree to collect a little of the bark. We carried with us starts for an orchid garden that never materialized and cinnamon bark that we never used.

We were never much as bird watchers in Kansas, but when we settled into an unfamiliar part of the world, we needed to know the names of flying things. A number of people were glad to help us, particularly biology teachers Robert Fleming and Robert Waltner, both former students.

In the hills we learned new names: kalij pheasant (which I thought was an educated bird until I saw the spelling), great Himalayan barbet, rosy minivet, black-headed yellow bulbul, and leaf warblers. We went bird-watching with missionary doctor Arthur Thiessen on the plains and were introduced to another avian caste: Indian roller, Indian poppet, black drongo, cattle egret, gray wagtail, coppersmith, and green bee eater.

Leaf warblers are small yellow birds that decorate the trees and bushes along the road. One gray day, walking along Tehri Road, we were delighted by a flock that suddenly appeared out of the wall of mist. Small, soundless, they added only motion and color. We were attracted by the bright green parrots that perched in jungly trees near the children's playground in the Quad. The yellow-cheeked tit and the magpie were morning visitors on the balcony of our upstairs apartment. Of course sparrows, doves, mynah birds, and crows were common. But crows in India do not say "caw." They say "quark ark" or "arrag." By my unscientific research, crows outnumber other birds one hundred to one, and they would certainly win an election if noise and numbers counted.

I have a message for you who have been gone from the Mussoorie hillside: the Indian cuckoo still calls as one strolls on Tehri Road on a spring evening. He arrives in early April and for weeks we heard his four-note call, "kaiphal pakkyo," (the kaiphal berries are ripe). This mating call has been put to good use by at least one student: "When six years after I left Woodstock and I was courting a girl in the university, I used to summon her to her dormitory window by whistling its distinctive four-note call."

My favorite bird was the laughing thrush. We could have used him for an alarm clock, when his musical laugh would be prolonged for almost a minute. He lived somewhere along the stream below our Palisades house. We didn't know whether he was a variegated, striated, white-throated, streaked, lesser necklaced, large necklaced, white crested, white spotted, rufus chinned, or red-headed laughing thrush.

Chapter 12

Weather Report

> In America it is the spring which blows the breath of life into woods full of skeletons; in India the rains perform the magic of life giving.[32]

My favorite poem in my sixth-grade reader was by Robert Loveman, declaring that it was not raining rain, it was raining violets, daffodils, and roses.

In India, the clouds of gray rain wild orchids, peacock orchids, ferns that grow like gentle swords out of moss on tree trunks, and emerald rice stalks that fill the Doon below the Himalayan foothills. But even a poet is aware that the Indian clouds are raining water, so much water that after a few weeks it sloshes around in your mind and you forget the poetic possibilities. Your metaphor is more likely that of the old-fashioned water closet that sends its gallons down with a roar from the overhead tank. Or you understand better the bedroom images of blankets of fog, pillowcases of cloud, sheets of rain, curtains of mist. Our splendid storms come up with rumbles of thunder and slashes of lightning and pounding rain that pass over and then go raging off into the next valley.

A monsoon is a wind. We usually spoke of it as though it were a rain. There are dry monsoons and wet monsoons. Ours was wet, and the good ones lasted three months. Monsoon winds are caused by changes in temperature as air moves over ocean and land. Weather scientists know the cause, but the riddle is when and where exactly the formation of the monsoon begins. What is the exact air-sea interaction which helps the monsoon develop? Why do some fail?

In the deserts of Rajasthan there is not enough water to support life, and it is said that three-year-olds in certain villages are frightened by their first sight of rain. On the other hand, the village of Cherripungi in Assam is one of the wettest spots on earth, flushed annually by 426 inches. Raindrops as large as marbles pound on this village, and the wind sometimes drives them with such velocity that the inhabitants of the town dress in wicker armor and carry small shields to protect themselves.

"Is this true?" I asked a student from Cherripungi.

She ran to her room and brought me a miniature wicker raincoat and showed me how it was fastened to the shoulders.

Everyone looks forward to the coming of the monsoon as a release from heat and dust. The economy and agriculture of India, as well as that of a third of the land area of the world, depend on the monsoon to bring rain to the crops. Famine follows a monsoon that does not begin on time; famine follows the monsoon that ends too soon.

Mussoorie is drenched by a rainfall of seventy-five to one hundred inches during the three months of July, August, and September. In May and June our Hillside is dry, grass fires are a real danger, dust rolls up from Rajasthan and cuts visibility, water is rationed. We scan the news to learn how the monsoon is progressing as it blows its way up the country, skipping around here and there, loitering in Madhya Pradesh. When we read that it has reached Delhi, we know it is in our neighborhood. A graph in the *Statesman* showed that the "normal" date is June 29. Only once in twenty years has it begun on its normal date. The local Delhi wallah could only conclude that the astrologer could give him better advice than the statistician. The monsoon receives as much attention in Indian newspapers as do harvest conditions for wheat in the Wichita *Eagle*.

One year the monsoon began while we were in church in Parker Hall, the high ceilinged, iron-roofed auditorium in the high school building. A crack of thunder, a wind, a fistful of rain against the window, and then a downpour nearly silenced the speaker. He raised his voice, but the attention of the students and other worshippers was diverted by the rain. We looked out the windows to watch the dusty foliage of the hillside turn green. The morale of the congregation rose with the tide.

The rain stopped toward evening, but this was the pitcherful that primed the pump, and it started again in the early morning. Students wearing *chuppels* (plastic thongs) sloshed through water six inches deep pouring down the ramps. Nevertheless, goodwill prevailed. The rain had washed away tension, and students and staff became easier to live with.

The Hillside exploded with color. The brown of the blue Tehri Hills began to green. Grass sprang up in places that had appeared to be barren. The mali's garden by the tearoom bloomed luxuriantly. On the rock faces along Tehri Road, flowerets popped out: tiny daisies, pink rock begonia, also called saxifrage, meaning "to break rocks." And indeed these fragile plants fracture boulders. In their earth-shaking alliance with wind and water, all these pretty little flowers are changing the face of the Himalayas, aging and shaping them with the same process that has subdued older mountains.

Very often we enjoyed a sunbreak during the day, or the sky cleared toward evening. Sometimes the Doon filled with mist, and St. George's School across the valley, red and white on green, floated in a pool of clouds spotlighted by the sun. When the clouds cleared, we saw the town of Dehra Dun in the valley. The greens of the groves and fields, the blues of the Jumna and the Song Rivers, and the white stones in the dry rivers flashed like rain-washed jewels. The low-lying Siwalik range formed a boundary to the Doon, and then the India plain stretched forever. The rain had cleared the haze from the air and surprised us with a fresh world. If our eyes had been just a little sharper or our glasses a little stronger, we would have been able to see to Delhi. It was the most beautiful view in the world. That was in the early seventies. What with the pollution from the cement factories, the view has never been quite as breath-taking since.

The feeling of euphoria and gratitude to the weatherman lasts about two weeks. The monsoon becomes a routine presence; cloud, mist, rain, sheets of swinging water. A curtain of scrim drops between us and the valley. We know from having lived for half a century that into each life *some* rain must fall, but it falls with such a dreary, nagging dailiness. We settle in for three months of mildew, putting a weak bulb in the closet to keep it off the shoes and the camera. The air chills, and we begin to add layers of sweaters and build trash fires in our ineffective fireplace to take the damp off the house. But India is a country with little trash.

We all buy umbrellas, big black cotton ones. These we have to replace from time to time, for umbrellas at the school are considered common property, and if you need one, you take one. If you are honest, you return it to the same place. Our daughters disdain umbrellas. They would rather get wet than carry one, and they go into the bazaar expecting a baptism. They arrive home having been immersed rather than sprinkled on.

One July evening I left Walt at home with a bad cold and accompanied my home-room students on a class party to the bazaar. The object was to eat moo-moos at the Tibetan restaurant and then watch Music TV. The weather was balmy, perfect for such an excursion. We all ate moo-moos, but only *they* watched MTV. We were to start back by eight o'clock, but by then the rain had started; no taxis in sight, and few umbrellas among us. During all our times in India, I had never before been in the bazaar during a real immersion. The rain increased in a crescendo that continued during the time it took to walk from the Clock Tower to Northern Stores. We each took our own pace, and I found myself alone splashing up Mullingar Hill. The water poured from the sky, from rooftops onto the narrow street, down stairways and ramps from buildings above the street. The street itself was a virtual storm sewer. The streetlights and the lightning brightened the rain. The experience was exhilarating, and I related a bit to Gene Kelly in the movie *Singing in the Rain*, except that I don't dance as well as he does. At Northern Stores I stopped under the overhang to wait for someone, anyone with a torch, to walk back with me on Tehri Road. Several teachers soon appeared and we sloshed back together during the diminuendo of the storm.

Monsoon snapshots: two little girls under an umbrella sing as they whirl on the playground merry-go-round; three coolies squat, each under his own big black umbrella as they share one cigarette; two serious trekkers set off for Dhanaulti with plastic capes over their backpacks.

Housekeeping becomes more of a chore. Our newly whitewashed dining room walls grow black patches of mold. Towels smell sour; the bannister feels as if it had just been wiped with a wet rag. Dampness makes the broom push hard. The sheets are cold and damp unless we have the luxury of an electric blanket. The dhobi, too, has his problems and doesn't call for the laundry on the scheduled day. I learn not to strip the beds until I see the whites of his laundry bundle. Our academic world shrinks. Fog limits our space. Rain on the roof makes teaching in an upstairs classroom a disquieting experience

Landslide, the two-man shovel in use

as student hum rises to compete with roof rumble. Soggy boots and umbrellas inhabit the halls, and the floors are slippery. At the high school as I come down the stairs into the large hall below, I see the mist rolling in through the front door. It swirls up the stairs to meet me, and I feel that I am moving through a dream sequence of *Wuthering Heights*. The cloud moves on up and out the doors at the back of the building, joining a company of clouds to move on up the mountains to muffle the dudh wallah who is coming down the path.

We were sitting in the Ladies Staff Room after school when Miss Marley burst in.

"I have to tell somebody," she announced breathlessly. "I just escaped death by inches."

She had been walking along Tehri Road toward Cozy Corner when she heard a rumbling that stopped her short. Ahead of her the rocks of the pushta just above the road came tumbling down. Shaken, she turned to come back to tell us about it. We all went to assess the disaster.

The Kirkwoods, Poores, and Floras, residents of Woodstock Villa, were leaning on the fence above us, looking aghast at the debris below their yard. On a steep hillside, pushtas are built in tiers. While we watched, a crack deepened in the top pushta and rocks and chunks of cement rolled down, leaving a sagging fence and a narrower yard for the Villa.

No one was hurt but the damage was formidable. The families living there wondered if they should move out, but Ron Kapadia, the supervisor of buildings and grounds, assured them that the Villa was built on solid rock and that they were safe. So new pushtas were built and the fence strung around the new perimeter.

The view from Woodstock across the valley to the Landour bazaar gives the illusion that the town is slipping off its mountain; the houses appear to have spilled from the ridge and are lying scattered on the slope. The fact is that buildings do occasionally fall off their pedestals during the rains.

In August, Dwight and LaVonne Platt, colleagues from Bethel College, came to visit us on their way back to the States. The rain persisted through every minute of their short stay until the last half hour, which LaVonne and I spent walking leisurely through the bazaar looking for a few mementos. We entered the Art Emporium, a tiny shop across from the Clock Tower, to look at ivory and wood carvings. As we were poring over the walnut elephants, we heard a rumble. The proprietor came from around the counter, took each of us by an elbow, said "Leave, please," and guided us out to the street. We discovered that the back of the shop had dropped down the hill. The situation was not so dangerous as it sounds. The slide had been expected but was not considered so imminent.

Landslides introduced us to the two-man shovel. One man shovels from the handle end and another pulls on a rope fastened to the shovel so that the load is lightened. This method makes the work more sociable and it also employs twice as many people.

Many incidents of landslides are recalled in this community, some with tragic results when people are caught while walking along the road. Everyone who has ever stayed in the Lee Memorial Home in Calcutta is reminded that it was built in memory of the six Lee children who perished in a landslide near the hill town of Darjeeling.

Old-timers in Mussoorie speak of the earthquake of April 1905. The shock came just before the rising bell, and all the girls moved out into the Quad for safety. Landour residents thought they were at the center, but learned that the epicenter was at Kangra, about 150 miles northwest in the Punjab, where many lives were lost. The earthquake totally destroyed a new church in Mussoorie that was nearing completion, killing a number of workmen. The superstitious said that the earthquake was an expression of the gods' anger at the community for allowing a white sahibs' church to be built.

A devastating earthquake occurred on October 20, 1991, in the Uttarkashi area about 35 miles due north of Mussoorie. It measured 6.1 on the Richter scale and lasted for about forty-five seconds. Although it rocked the campus, only minor damage occurred at Woodstock School; but the loss of life and property in the Uttarkashi area was stunning. A group of Woodstock students and staff members spent the week of their October break distributing relief supplies and helping dig through the debris. Two years later in 1993, we could tell where the damage had occurred as we drove past villages with new bright tin roofs, evidence of rebuilt homes and shops.

By August the monsoon becomes depressing. How could any event so anticipated become so dolorous? Happy people can survive a monsoon by looking ahead, remembering Noah's rainbow after the flood. Unhappy people can brood about leeches and lost umbrellas. During the latter days of the monsoon when plodding to the bazaar on the running river of a road, we thought, "What are we doing on this dreary mountain?"

The monsoon is nearly over when the ferns on the tree trunks curl up and turn brown. And then the October sun appears, not only once in a while, and the staff can again take teacups out into the garden. We housewives spread our flour and spices in the sun to be debugged. Trekking starts in earnest. October in our area has all the loveliness of a Kansas Indian summer, warm days and crisp evenings. The rain is suddenly over, and we cannot believe our good fortune to be living in such a perfect environment.

We know there is the cold dampness of February and March ahead, but for now we are happy. Did I say the monsoon lasts for about three months? The space I have given to it is out of proportion to the time it took in our lives, or of the time during which we found it oppressive. But the monsoon seems to dominate the year, as it certainly dominates the economy of the country.

Even as cold weather approached, we tried to live without fires in our house. There was something about admitting the need of a fire that diminished one's manhood or womanhood.

"You have a fire in the daytime?" a visitor catching us out asks incredulously.

Besides the importance of avoiding a smirch on one's hardihood, there is the matter of frugality. Wood is scarce and expensive, as is kerosene. Trudy Nelson never started her winter fire until after Christmas, but she was a hardy Canadian and we were thin-blooded Kansans.

Hillside homes were built to withstand the hot sun and winds of the Indian plains, but they were poor habitations for winter dwellers. That was why the school was dismissed for a long winter break: there was no economical way to heat those tall, dark buildings. The classrooms became colder as the end of the semester approached, but the prospect of Going Down Day kept student morale high.

After Going Down Day, the staff who were left settled into their winter pattern, still taking outside as many tasks as possible. One year we spread both our Thanksgiving and our Christmas dinners on the picnic table in the sunny front yard. After Christmas, families left for various tours, the beaches of Goa or South India, many with invitations to visit homes of students. But some of them wanted to be on the Hillside when the yearly snowfall of white lace and velvet drifted in. Snow came seldom enough that it was an event, and we wished we could save the scene for the children when they came back to school.

Walt lived with chilblains, for his office depended on heat from a stove in the outer room. The chill from the floor seeped through his hiking boots and two pairs of socks. We envied the Farleys next door in our duplex; they had a fake fur toilet seat. We tried as much as possible to live in the one room we heated. But the views from our yard were almost enough to compensate for the discomfort. Every morning during winter break as Walt left for the office, we walked out to our railing to see what the world was like, and it was usually beautiful. The sky above the mountains was such an intense blue that I can find no name for the color. The winter line grew deeper each evening.

Then in late February the students returned, back to a dreary part of the year. Before warm weather crept up from the plains, a few weeks could be dank, cold, and fraught with equinox storms, dramatic with thunder and wind. One head cold followed another, and students were stacked in the infirmary with various respiratory ailments. Students were sometimes able to prevail on the principal for a reprieve from the weather. "By wearing bathrobes to school one day that spring, we persuaded the faculty that it was too cold for classes and promptly dashed outdoors for the rest of the day."

What of the Indian families who lived without stoves and hot water heaters? They, too, lived in one room and cooked and slept there. They, too, sought the sunshine, and when it was not shining they huddled under shawls and shivered. After the October rush, the bazaar shops that catered to tourists had closed and moved their wares to Delhi, so the town, too, seemed to close in.

Before long, winter melted into spring, and by mid-March we were absorbing the warmth of the sun on stone benches while we made tentative plans for a hike. We took our students from their refrigerated rooms to outdoor classrooms on the library steps and gymnasium bleachers, although I never had the courage to take thirty seventh graders into the wide open spaces for a lesson on the adverbial prepositional phrase.

Then there was the long spring, never getting too hot, making us smug when we heard of the soaring April and May temperatures on the plains. We watched new pink leaves push off old green leaves on the live oaks. A few warm weeks, and then the welcome monsoon.

During 1986, the year of Halley's Comet, the press published stories about its last appearance in 1910. Some people had expected the world to end.

The community of Woodstock School took note of the comet of 1910. The girls at Midlands rose at 4:30 to see it from the balcony. The forecast was for the earth to pass through the comet's tail on May 18, and marvelous disasters were predicted by the papers. The students looked forward to that day as to Judgment Day. The Reverend Andrews was principal that year, renowned for his long prayers, and when the great day came, he prayed them through Halley's Comet.

The winter line

But the day dawned, and nothing out of the ordinary happened . . . .

[Small breakfast], study hour, prayers, classes, breakfast, classes, study hour, play hour, supper, prayers: the day was moving on just as they always had done and always should do, and the tension of Judgment Day which had shown itself in marked politeness, hushed voices, and unnatural obedience all the day, was visibly lightened . . . . Well, the prayer-bell rang. The girls lined up outside and filed in decorously to take their seats. The teachers filed in and took their seats on the platform. Daddy Andrews arrived—the hymn, the Bible reading, the prayer. All heads were bowed, the younger ones in thankfulness Judgment Day had come and all but gone. They could look forward with confidence now to the ending—study hour, beds, and sleep. And then one of those sudden gusts sprang up which are so well known to old Mussoorie residents. Without so much as a breath of warning it sailed across Mussoorie, ripping off roofs as it went. In a trice it struck Woodstock and with one mighty blow it tore off that three-year roof immediately above the assembly hall, depositing it in the housekeeper's garden at the back. This nearly killed Mrs. Keogh, the housekeeper, who, Judgment Day notwithstanding, had decided not to go to prayers that evening but was walking in her garden instead. The wind rushed in through the open windows blowing out every light [lamp] and filling the whole place with flying sticks and leaves and what not. Immediately there was bedlam. One little girl danced up and down screaming, "The comet's tail's come! The comet's tail's come!" over and over. Girls clung to each other in tears— loud sobbing, screaming, wild running around the place. But when nothing more happened, quiet once more settled down so that they could hear something else beside their own noise and confusion, and this was Daddy Andrews' voice, steady and clear in its supplication to the Almighty. He had not paused in his praying.[33]

King Edward VII died in 1910, and his death was attributed by a few astronomers to Halley's Comet.

My own assessment of India's weather, countrywide, is that it goes to extremes. The rainy season is too wet, the hot season too searing. What I missed were the filigree of new leaves in spring and the lushness of early summer, the gold coins of cottonwoods in fall and the brightness of winter. I like rain followed immediately by an equal amount of sun. Jane Austen said that no country is completely perfect that doesn't have four seasons.

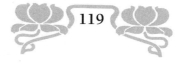

Chapter 13

Coping

As children of the Depression of the 1930s, Walt and I enjoy the challenge to tighten our belts, husband our resources, cut expenses to the bone. Our children did not understand this attitude and used to tell us often that they would rather not hear about how we walked to school and wore hand-me-downs.

In India we learned other lessons about living economically with what was available. All paper goods were expensive. We learned to like cloth napkins (serviettes). We vowed to use cloth when we returned home, and we did briefly, but abandoned them because of the washing and ironing. I thought the use of napkin rings a nice touch, rather aristocratic, but I have learned since that no aristocrat approves of napkin rings. Napkins should be laundered after each meal, certainly not carried over to be reused.

I never threw away a good zipper when discarding a dress; I salvaged the zipper and looked for material to match it. We lengthened the life of typewriter ribbons by adding vegetable oil, never mind the spattered look of our correspondence. (I should have given the ribbon more time to marinate.)

Packaging in the bazaar was simple. If we did not remember to take a shoulder bag to carry home our carrots and mangoes, the *subzi wallah* produced a bag made from notebook paper, the math or English lesson still readable. Paradoxically, simple aspirin was packaged in little foil sheets, each pill in its separate pocket. By now, however, the plastic industry has given India many of the little conveniences we take for granted. Plastic bags now bloom from shrubs all over the Hillside.

The bequeathing of appliances to the person who takes your place is part of the outfitting system. American-made refrigerators can be repaired and sold over and over, as can small appliances, cameras, and typewriters. There was a time when missionaries thought they had to bring barrels of the amenities with them to India to make life bearable. By now most essentials, even by Western standards, are available. And those products not available, such as pantyhose and cheese spreads, are not necessities.

In a chapter on coping, mention must be made of water, electricity, and fuel problems. But since our last visit, I must admit that many of the problems we experienced in those first terms are fewer or no longer exist. Still, India is a country short of energy.

Electricity was an on-and-off affair. Whether or not we had *bijli* depended on the weather, the state of the wiring, and the mood of the man at the power plant who giveth and taketh away. His power was limited, for he controlled only our section of the Hillside. Across the valley we could see Mussoorie in full glow, and down on the plains the lights of Dehra Dun twinkled spitefully.

In 1993 a new system was installed that was to eliminate those problems. The school was just waiting for someone to cut the red tape before being able to realize all its promise. The word today is that the system is working well.

While the unpredictability of electricity was an inconvenience, the scarcity of water was a real trial. There seemed always to be a water shortage, and the reasons were many: it was the dry season and so no water; it was the wet season, and so the pumps had been washed out; it was the time to irrigate the rice in the valley, so the farmers had priority, understandably; it was the cold season, so the exposed pipe along the path had frozen; it was a religious holiday, so the man who turned on the water had forgotten his wrench. (This became an example of a non sequitur for English classes.)

Mussoorie advertises the virtues of its climate without advertising the problems, which are compounded by all the new hotels being built and all those visitors who expect to have water for drinking and bathing. Woodstock has in the last few years installed plastic storage tanks and tapped a stream on its property, so the problem of water for the school is no longer so acute.

The shortage of wood is still a problem. India had not begun its forest conservation program early enough, but now the government is very strict about cutting of trees. Kerosene is sometimes in short supply for stoves and oil heaters, but charcoal is usually available for cooking. Burshane (propane) was the more convenient fuel, but we were not allowed to have an extra tank standing by for our hot plate, and Burshane has a perverse way of exhausting itself on the weekend when one is having guests for dinner.

The telephone was an exasperating instrument with a consistent personality, surly. During those two years when we were unfortunate enough to have a telephone in our house, we wondered at the credit given to A. G. Bell. Often it rang when no one was trying to call us; other times we irritated the caller by being the wrong number. The operators could not understand our English and demanded that we speak Hindi. A telephone conversation from any place was often a shouting match, but when we tried long distance, communication seemed impossible. This conversation took place in our living room between Walt and the Delhi operator.

Walt: I can't hear you.

Delhi: Why can't you hear me? I hear you.

Walt: But I can't hear you.

Delhi: You should listen more loudly.

Walt: I am listening as loudly as I can.

Even here, India is coming into the high-tech age. Now Mussoorie callers can direct dial to the States, and sometimes even receive calls and faxes. The real improvement has come with the new internal system that links all offices and staff homes into the system.

Mail time was the high point of the day. We expected letters from our families once a week. In this age of instant communication, we wrote letters knowing that we could not have a reply in less than fifteen days. A ten-day reply was a conversation piece.

The school library subscribed to the overseas editions of *Time* and *Newsweek*, which were delivered to our mountain within a week of publication, although they were easily "lost in the mail" because of their considerable value. Radio reception in our area was poor, but we listened to the Voice of America for early morning news. I hope the Voice has improved over the last twenty years. When we listened the announcer always ended with a little homily such as "Let's work together. You tell me what to do, and I'll tell you where to go." Or, "If you see someone without a smile, give him one of yours." After we had heard those clever remarks for a year, we became cynical about the philosophical IQs of program directors. The British Broad-

casting Company announcers seemed more intelligent, or at least
more dignified. The announcer on Radio Moscow read the news with
a good American accent. You had to listen carefully to learn that this
was Moscow rather than Washington. In the 1980s it did not have
the invective against "imperialist Americans" that we had heard in
earlier years. By the 1990s, middle-income Indians had televisions
and VCRs. "Dallas" was one of the popular American exports, but
the India movie industry was developing its own programs.

We met Doma on our second day in India. She spread out her
wares on the upstairs Quad verandah, and we Unraus joined the circle. Doma flung a sheet over the concrete and with graceful ceremony brought out one piece at a time from her pack. There among the
heavy balustrades and Persian arches we watched her lay out an
array of baubles that could have come from Aladdin's cave. Filigreed
brass and silver plates; Tibetan necklaces with jade, topaz, and car-
nelian settings; bracelets, unset stones, chunky rings, brass candle-
sticks, jingling silver belts with turquoise sets. All at a price we middle-class consumers could afford.

An ambitious and scrupulously honest Tibetan wallah, Doma
soon prospered enough to set up a shop in the bazaar where she was
always busy during the tourist season. Then she expanded to a shop
in New Delhi. Unable to read or write, she kept accounts in her head,
even as she urged us to "take home now and pay later."

One of many peddlers (in respect for their dignity, a better word
is merchant) a gray-bearded, white-turbaned old man came to our door
followed by a coolie carrying an enormous and obviously heavy pack.
The peddler had cloth which surely the memsahib (I) and the missahib
(Paula) would like to see. Of course we would like to see it, but we were
not in the market. He implored us persistently to only please look, no
need to buy, and sat down on the verandah floor to untie his bundle.
Soon the floor and the couch were spread with one hundred pieces, fifty
of which we wanted to buy, and three of which we bought.

In spite of the many immunity shots that were required for living in India, some families came out for three years and spent six

months of the first year convalescing from hepatitis. Other epidemics were predictable: rampages of measles, mumps, and pink eye. During the monsoon when summer turned wet and cold, respiratory ailments and flu were common. Students returned from field trips with stomach flu or dysentery. Spring brought hepatitis. The bazaar was too close, too seductive, for students to stay free of unsanitary food and water. The matron of the little boys discovered to her astonishment that they thought that only at mealtime were they required to drink boiled water.

After three tries, Paula reacted largely to her smallpox vaccination, but still while on a retreat she went swimming in the Ganges. The holy water did not restore her pox to health, but we were surprised that it was not further infected. Our family was blessed with good health for most of the time. We were also fortunate that we survived all the physical rigors of the place. Walt had the most dramatic encounter with near disaster. When coming home one afternoon on Tehri Road, he heard horses galloping from behind. He moved over to the open khud side, and a horse and rider came around the corner and passed him. It was the second galloping horse that hit him, tossing him perilously close to the edge of a deep ravine. Walt was bruised but not broken, much to the relief of the frightened rider who helped him to his feet.

The list of things I did not miss when we were in India includes sirens. No sirens screamed down Tehri Road. News of accident and tragedy was announced to us by the survivors. We were all expected to be part of the rescue squad.

During the years we knew him at Woodstock, Frenchy Browne owned a jeep which served as ambulance, fire truck, and wrecker. He called Walt out from supper one evening to help with a fire above the Eyebrow, a narrow path that runs above Tehri Road. Paula and I, curious thrill seekers, went along with Walt in the fading daylight. We found one small seventh grader carrying pails of water up from his house in a desperate effort to put out a grass fire. Neighbors soon joined him, and the fire was extinguished. We gave the boy considerable credit for battling the blaze until we suspected that he had been responsible for causing it.

A number of more tragic fires occurred during our times at Woodstock. They were on the north side of the hill and away from the school. During the dry season, grass fires threatened homes on the Hillside and villages beyond Mussoorie. High school boys and sometimes girls were always ready to take off to fight fires. Sometimes they were helpful, but we often wondered how they kept out of each other's way. Soldiers came from Dehra Dun for fires that defied the resources of the local military personnel.

Fire was always a danger to the villagers and school employees in their cramped quarters. In winter people hovered over little charcoal burners in a crowded family circle; at night they kept the burners under their beds. The end of a sari floating over the coals could envelop the woman in flames before she was aware of her carelessness.

My first operation in India was at the Landour Community Hospital, an institution I can recommend. The doctors, both Indian and Western, were kind and competent and the nurses friendly. Residents of Landour had collected the capital to build the hospital, and it has been serving the community from this location above Tehri Road since 1939.

The doctor had invited me to come in for an overnight stay and a breast biopsy. I was shown to the women's ward, a large room with six steel cots. My first embarrassment came when I was told that, besides toothbrush and pajamas, I should have brought sheets and towels. But never mind, the nurse could lend what I needed. I had the feeling that this was the concession made for the very poorest of their Indian patients. Eventually we received the report from Ludhiana Christian Hospital that the tumor was benign, as we had expected.

Walt and I were on the list of emergency blood donors. There was no formality to giving blood. Once you were typed, no one asked if you had forty-eleven different diseases or had had a cold in the last week. No orange juice, no sponge to squeeze.

My other medical experience was at Ludhiana Christian Hospital when I stayed for a week of observation after minor surgery. Walt was a relative in the Indian fashion, sleeping right in the room with me and eating hospital meals like mine. He could have brought food in and fixed it for me in a kitchen down the hall. The Ludhiana Christian Hospital is an awe-inspiring institution. Patients, nurses, doctors, bearers, chaprassis swarmed all over the ground floor corridors. Doctors from all over India come to train in the medical school connected with it. An extensive building program was underway, and the new wing was to have the most modern equipment and design. However, LCH was not equipped at that time for the procedure I needed, so we returned briefly to Kansas City Medical Center for that.

Walt came home from the office one evening in August 1965 to report that by orders of the city officials, Mussoorie was to be under a modified blackout. Because of the impending war with Pakistan, we were not to turn on our lights until we had covered the windows. While Walt cut up cardboard boxes, the girls and I determined how many thicknesses of newspapers we needed to make the windows opaque.

The hostilities were caused by the debate over Kashmir. Pakistani troops were encroaching on the border and refused to give up that territory unless India called for a long-promised plebiscite for the Kashmiris to vote on which country they wanted to join. India sent her troops toward Lahore and refused to hold the plebiscite unless Pakistan removed its troops. (Our Kashmiri houseboat owner told us later when we visited there that Kashmir did not want to join either country; it preferred to be independent.)

Then war was declared and we had to take the blackout more seriously. Enemy pilots flying overhead must not be able to distinguish Mussoorie from the mountain shadows. The border town of Ambala, eighty miles away, had been bombed, and who knew where the Pakistani air force would strike next.

Our Indian friends predicted that the conflict would not last long, since neither country had the resources to wage a long war. The greatest concern of the parents on the plains was for the safety of Woodstock students. Our concern was for the parents of our students who lived in Pakistan and in the border towns. The American Embassy sent complete plans for our evacuation. The Indian army commandeered all the trucks, so the school had difficulty getting food. Staples were rationed, and the chaprassi stood in line for us to get our allotment of sugar, flour, and rice. In spite of these concerns, school continued as usual with an added level of excitement.

And then in three weeks it was over. Not quite over. The cease-fire was declared, but border skirmishes and accusations on both sides continued, and then indignation when India found that the tanks used by the Pakistanis to kill Indian soldiers had been made in the U.S. We Americans were advised to stay out of the bazaar for a time to avoid embarrassing incidents. The outcome of the short war that affected us most was the decrease in American prestige in India. Only the good name of John Kennedy remained untarnished.

Our second term was half over when the third India-Pakistan war broke out, this time over the plight of the Bengalis in East Pakistan. The Bangalis had long been treated as second-class citizens by the Pakistani government; and when the election of their popular leader, Sheikh Mujibur Rahman, was set aside, East Pakistan declared its independence in March 1971. West Pakistan sent its army into East Pakistan and the brutality was widely reported. Ten million refugees moved from East Pakistan into India. On December 3, 1971, India declared war on West Pakistan.

In spite of the terrible bloodshed in the east, the war was only a small inconvenience for us in the north. We felt that we were in the safest place in India. Dehra Dun was mentioned in news reports abroad because it is the location of the military academy at which the leaders from both sides had studied war. Expecting the war to be short, we had blacked out only the back bedroom with its one window, and there we spent our evenings.

On December 16, after a thirteen-day war, the Pakistani army surrendered. The one casualty from the Mussoorie community was the only son of one of the bankers. The boy was killed on the last day of the war.

Before school closed, the Social Action Committee, of which both Paula and Walt were members, put on a campaign to help the refugees. They collected money and clothing from the school community and solicited help in the bazaar from the merchants. The money was used to buy 700 light-weight blankets which the Indian railway shipped free of charge. A blanket can be used to sit on, to give a degree of privacy in crowded quarters, to provide a suitcase to bundle up one's belongings, or to serve as clothing if a man loses his dhoti or a woman her sari.

Often we felt like the central characters in a soap opera that leaves the viewer at the end of every episode with questions: Will Walt have the servants' strike settled before the Board meeting? Will Paula learn to eat curry? Will Susan pass chemistry? Will any of my students learn to type?

But those were only the questions of day-to-day existence. We also had worrying ties to home. The health of our elderly parents was a concern. It is hard to be away from the family during times of grief—or celebration. My sister had a baby. Walt's father died, and we received the cable the day of his funeral. Absence from the family circle was one of our few sacrifices.

Some of us don't really know ourselves until we face life in another culture. We hadn't known that our stomach turns over at the sight of a dead rat or the smell of urine. Or that we really are not comfortable working with strange people, or that we get tense if our plans don't work out. Or, a common problem with visiting mission board members, that we can't wait patiently while the taxi is fixed or a swollen river subsides. We find out what it is that we really need to be happy. That we can't live without beef in a pork-eating area. Or that hairspray is one of the necessities of life, no matter what it costs. Some of us found that we can't live without Bach and Mozart.

At least one reader, having endured with me through the tribulations of this Indian bed of thistles, may ask why we didn't just stay home, where the electricity is dependable, the telephone has touch dialing, and the wars aren't quite so close. The truth is that these tribulations, along with the satisfaction from the work we did, energized and challenged us. True, I may have had less culture shock than some women because I have never been a fussy housekeeper. And I relied periodically on the solace of a Cadbury chocolate bar.

Chapter 14

Food

Happiness in India or any foreign country may depend on one's attitude toward food. I first realized the importance of food when I worked at a voluntary service project in Germany with a group of college students. We were being well fed on substantial, simple food. As we reveled in the castles and culture around Stuttgart, what was our main topic of conversation? Food. What they were eating at home. How our mothers prepared goulash. How to make the best hamburgers. We lusted after hamburgers. I had considered this preoccupation with food as an American obsession until I read *Waiting for the Mahatma*:

> The prisoner said, "If I ever leave this place, I am going to spend a hundred rupees on Badam Halwa at the corner shop. You know, Krisha Vilas's. The shop is small but it is a wonderful place, he serves on clean banana leaves and not on plates. You know his idlies are almost as if made of the lightest . . . ."[34]

In India we soon came to realize that food was important to the morale of students and staff. We Unraus, too, were sometimes undone by our love of food, even though we had made a solemn pact among ourselves before we left for India that we would not complain about the food, not ask for food parcels from our relatives, and not talk about food all the time. We broke all three resolutions.

First, we complained about the food. Paula, aged ten, would not eat most Indian food; at a curry and rice meal she would eat only plain rice, adding sugar and cinnamon when possible. Since she would not eat the noon meal at the dining hall, she was reduced to fixing her own peanut butter sandwich every day. None of us could drink the buffalo milk unless we added cocoa or Bournvita. Children who have been raised in India like, in fact demand, the taste of buffalo. We liked the cracked wheat cereal; but suji, like cream of wheat, was my personal trial, as was rice cereal that came in the shape of noodles.

Second, we asked for food parcels. At the time of our first sojourn, we were none of us gourmets. Paula had always been on a two-track program: first pears and pablum and then hamburgers and honey (not together). Susan ate everything except broccoli and margarine. Walt had a more cultivated taste, preferring foods that gave him either nostalgia or hives. I want food to be inexpensive and easy to fix. Surely there would be no problem with a family who approached food so casually.

Two weeks after our arrival in India, we wrote home asking for Koolaid, chocolate cake mixes, chili powder, pumpkin pie spice, and Velveeta cheese, all to be compactly stuffed into a box with Kleenex in the crevices. The food was to entertain our friends. Why ask for chili powder in a land redolent of spices? Well, because we didn't know how to combine the spices in the bazaar to make chili taste like it did at home. And home cooking was what we yearned for. There we were, in the land of rice and curry, homesick for the cheese and chili of our homeland.

By the end of our stay, we found fewer reasons to order special foods from home. Soups, both dry and tinned became available; Prakash at the top of the hill began to make cheese, and we learned to like bazaar fruitcakes.

We broke our third resolution. We talked about food all the time. So did everyone else. It ranks at the top of the list as a subject for table talk, at least as important as dysentery and travel. *The Landour Cookbook* is given by the hospitality committee to the newcomer, and we treasured it as a sensible guide for cooking in high altitudes.

So much for good resolutions. But they were good resolutions and we recommend them to anyone who goes abroad.

We had a variety of kitchen experiences during our time in India. I tried making soda crackers with such limited success that I didn't try again. Living without a refrigerator one year made me appreciate the facts of Indian life, but I never got good at it. The proper mother provides abundance for her family, I had been taught, which leads to leftovers and the need for a refrigerator to store them until they collect enough mold to cure infections.

I bake reasonable sweet rolls, an accomplishment that served me well with students. Our standby menu for entertaining was chicken and dumplings, when chicken was available. For a number of years, the Skinners had a dairy and chicken farm, and they brought their products to the Quad every Wednesday afternoon. We became very possessive about our orders of chicken. If you invite company and plan to serve chicken, and then someone takes your chicken, you are apt to lose your Christian perspective.

Most of our problems with cooking came because we tried to be Western in a non-Western culture. An Indian woman does not depend on electricity to put a meal on the table. But when I made a pie for a company meal, tucked it into the crib of the borrowed electric oven, and then discovered that the electricity had gone off, I developed the Western mentality toward all the inconveniences of living in a foreign country: I thought the meal was ruined because I had to serve cookies and fruit from the bazaar, while my beautiful pie sat gray and greasy in a useless oven.

However, most of our get-togethers were not elaborate affairs. The usual menu was Nescafe and a snack from the bazaar, and we could always add peanuts if we wanted to be festive. I try to remember: What food did we really miss? We never saw a strawberry, and only a few ripe peaches. No frozen orange juice but lots of oranges. We missed salad food, celery and lettuce. What is a BLT without bacon and lettuce? Of course, we all missed hamburger. You can pretend that ground pork is hamburger and make it into sloppy joes or pizza, but a Western student on leaving India heads for the first hamburger heaven or Pizza Hut.

Much of the produce was brought up from the valley, but some was grown out east in the Tehri Hills, especially potatoes, beans, and cabbage. As I look back, it seems that something was always in season and that was the only thing we could buy. We welcomed cauliflower when it came on the market, despised it in two weeks. French-fried eggplant was greeted with good appetite the first week, but after that we snubbed Sadiq's embalmed circles.

The local fruit season started with the dudh wallah's raspberries, but we were really waiting for the mangoes. A good mango, once you get used to the slight odor of turpentine, is a wonderful and satisfying fruit. Some people think Eve's forbidden fruit was the mango and not the apple. Mangoes, oval and about the size of a large pear, have a texture like peaches, but a distinctive flavor.

Guavas are another popular fruit. They have such a distinctive flavor and odor that perhaps a taste for them is inherited only through the mother's milk. They can be made into guava bread, pudding, and cheese. They are a rich source of vitamin C. But beware. Any mixture that includes guava becomes guava. It is the onion and garlic of the fruit world. Papaya looks like cantaloupe, but needs lemon juice added for flavor. Very versatile, it can be made into pumpkin pie, applesauce, or sauerkraut. Meat can be tenderized by being wrapped in papaya leaves. Pomelo is like our grapefruit, but twice as large.

We learned to like litchees, which appear just before the monsoon. They are a beautiful fruit on the tree, growing in clusters, greenish brown with red cheeks. The cook served them on a plate, branches, leaves and all, an unusual but pretty arrangement. About the size of a golf ball, the litchee has a brittle shell with goosebumps, and you peel it like a hardboiled egg to find a slick, juicy, white grape. However, the pit is large, and you eat only a thin layer of wet, perfumed fruit.

We saw a thorny, giant, cucumber-shaped fruit in the bazaar, *kattal*, or jackfruit. Indians use the unripe fruit in curry.

"Sadiq, why do we never have jackfruit?" I asked.

"You not like," he replied. "Only Indian people like."

I learned that the fruit has a very short season and cannot be preserved, but that Indians consider it a delicacy. However, it is tedious to prepare, for the flesh is surrounded by a sticky pulp that glues the cook's fingers together. I suppose that is why Sadiq thought we would not like it.

Oranges were our most appreciated fruit and were available for a long season. They tasted like California sweet oranges and had a loose skin like a tangerine. Bananas were usually available. Cherries, peaches, and pears came from Kashmir or the Kulu Valley for a short season. Local peaches from the hills were small and green and had to be allowed to ripen.

Our favorite Landour subzi wallah in the bazaar arranged stair-step shelves of fruits and vegetables. The carrots were rosy red and

The subzi walla. Photo by Vic Reimer

sweet, the radishes foot-long icicles. But the place to see the glory of
subzi is in Mussoorie bazaars. The subzi wallahs compete with artistic arrangements of their produce in mounds, flares, and spirals,
using variation in color, shape, and line.

Fruits and vegetables were not our only bazaar foods. Students
are fond of jalabies, a corrosively sweet pretzel. The children stand
before the sweet shop watching the cook's boy make them. He
squeezes the batter through a paper funnel into the hot oil, zigzagging
a lacework. These fried tangles are then soaked in hot, sweet syrup,
and the students buy them still warm from the kettle. Nothing is more
tempting than a hot jalabi nor more repulsive (to me) than a cold one.
Burfi is the Indian's candy, made from sugar and milk. Some people
are addicted and prefer it to Fannie Mae's chocolate turtles. Pyramids
of *laddus* were featured in sweetshops. I think they must be related to
a sweet named for Lady Canning who was fond of a sweet known as
ledikeni, a ball of flour, sugar and curd.[35]

Woodstock students had their favorite tea stalls where they
exalt the Hindustani tea. I kept hearing about Cindy's sweetshop,
and I wondered how a nice English girl named Cynthia could be running an Indian tea stall. When I went there with Paula, I learned that

a middle-aged, stubble-chinned Sindhi was the proprietor.

Since much of bazaar food is prepared in the open, we agreed that a good slogan for Indian food stalls would be a perversion of a United Airlines' TV ad: "We fry the friendly flies."

Tinned food was expensive, for much of it came from abroad, although India developed a food-processing industry over the years. Gelatin, called jellies, had the virtue of jelling overnight on a cool floor. We had friends who subscribed to a service that provided yeast from Canada, something like "yeast-of-the-month club," but yeast was also available in the bazaar. We bought our bread from the *roti wallah* who came to the door carrying his trunk of bread on his head. A pound loaf was firm and substantial, good for toast. Cakes were available from the bakery, as were tart-sized mincemeat pies. At Christmas Walt received from school venders two or three fruit-cakes, mortared with icing in wild colors, which he shared with his staff for their tea breaks.

Paula heard this tale from a Woodstock classmate. I did not give it credit, until back home in Kansas a colleague told me the same story and asked if it were true. The rumor was that a well-meaning person in the States sent a package of used tea bags to a poor missionary in India. I asked Vernelle Waltner, former missionary, if she had ever received used tea bags. She had never received tea bags, she said, but she had sometimes wondered, during the war, if the yeast she received had not been used once before she baked with it.

We bought meat from the pork wallah who came to the door. When Sadiq took vacation leave for a month, I was besieged by wallahs who said they were delivering meat the cook had ordered. I protested weakly and uselessly.

The most entertaining place to buy fish was at a fish market on a side street in Dehra Dun. We chose a shop with a good screen door and found ourselves in a narrow little place smelling pleasantly of fish and dampness. The fish wallah was seated on a low platform. His fish, mostly *elatchi*, white bellied and handsome and about two feet long, were lying in a bed of green leaves. We chose our specimen and the fish wallah whacked off the head and the tail with his machete. What fascinated us then was the way he held his long curved knife between his toes, rapidly deboning and cutting the meat into frying-sized pieces. Then he wrapped it in fresh leaves and put it into our plastic bag.

Occasionally we had to buy mutton in Mussoorie. By mutton I

mean goat. The carcasses hung on hooks in the dark little shop, and this wallah, too, sat on his platform and sliced the meat with the knife between his toes. He was very skillful, and more generous than we could appreciate. He weighed out everything including the hooves, which we returned to him. Most of our Indian friends preferred mutton curry to pork.

Pork was our main meat dish, but I did not visit the pork wallah's place of business. A number of our friends had been there, and they had immediately taken pork from their menus. But the pork was very good, not at all fatty. Beef, even buffalo, was the least expensive meat, but it was not available in Mussoorie, a predominately Hindu town. Some of our friends brought it up from Dehra Dun. We received welcome gifts of wild pig and venison. A chowkidar gave us a pheasant he had killed on our path, but it was such an athletic old bird that I could not make it edible.

When we were hungry for something that was not available, we tried making it. Marshmallows were popular, but they were never quite up to expectation; they melted too fast in cocoa, they were not toastable, but they could make a children's party memorable. At Easter I heard one of the missahibs say that she had once made chocolate Easter eggs by using mashed potatoes and powdered sugar. The idea challenged me, and I made up a recipe. I dipped the fondant into melted chocolate chips (already melted into a chunk en route to India) to which I added a bit of candle wax. The neighbor girls and Paula thought my Easter eggs were special; to me they tasted like mashed potatoes. We made grapenuts from a recipe in the Landour Cookbook. Our substitute for cranberries was roselle, a red flower that grows wild in mission gardens. The petals are crushed and added to red gelatin to make a cranberry-red dessert.

Over time we learned to enjoy curries and, in fact, preferred Indian food to Western food.

Our wonderful cook was wonderful because he could speak English and because he had several recipes that he prepared for guests. Very often my guests asked for his recipes.

When I relayed the request, he would say, "Memsahibji, when you leave, I give."

I asked for his recipe for a much-admired meat dish which he called glahssy steak. I had wondered what exotic spices he added to this dish to make it so delicious. It turned out to be nothing but slivers of pork fried in onions and tomatoes.

Indian cooks have at least one thing in common with our pioneer German-Russian cooks. They used what was inexpensively available to make food that was tasty, or maybe it was just that we got used to the taste of it. Then years later nostalgia takes over, and we yearn for chappatis and zwieback the way our khansamas or our mothers used to make them.

Chapter 15

Clothing

Krishnalal Shridharani, studying in America, wrote nostalgically of the sari:

> I look forward only occasionally and by way of contrast to the day when I have returned to India, and can feast my eyes on a woman dressed in elusive rose and blue and violet saris, the color reflected in the satiny wings of her hair, with gold at her hem and throat, with invisible legs and covered brow.[36]

To write about clothing in India, we start with the sari. This six-yard length of material is the Indian woman's national costume, and although the city woman is becoming more liberated from it, women in the rest of India rarely exchange it for any other garb. I predict that the sari will never be completely replaced. It is too convenient, too traditional, too becoming to young figures to have any real competition. "The sari is perfectly simple and simply perfect," a writer in *Times of India* proclaims, aghast at a fashion designer's plans to add padding, lace, scallops, and frills.

To don a sari, start at the right hip and wrap to the left; pull it around once, make six or seven pleats down the front, go around with the cloth once more, bring it against the right hip, tuck it all firmly into your *saiya* (long half-slip). Bring the leftover cloth up over your breasts and toss the yard or so that remains (the *pallu*) over your left shoulder in a graceful gather. If you are dressing in South India, reverse the directions by starting at the left hip. (I can tell that these directions will be hard to follow unless you can watch someone doing it.)

You may have decided that a sari makes playing tennis or scrubbing floors difficult, and you are right. You can bring your pallu around and tuck it in at the waist so that it won't catch fire as you cook over a charcoal bucket; or you can bring the pallu between your legs and tuck it in at the waist and hitch up your skirt to make pantaloons so that you can plant rice. For many village women the sari is a more or less modest covering by itself, but the women in our area always wore a *choli* (blouse) with a sari.

A sari can be handed down from mother to daughter to granddaughter, and an inherited sari may be highly prized. The bride asks for saris from her prospective husband, and these are her wealth; they belong only to her. Her bridal gown is flaming red, the symbol of joy, ironically for the unhappy girl who may be leaving her family to marry a stranger.

The sari is versatile. The pallu can be a shawl, a headcovering, a handkerchief. The ayah can make a small pouch in the waist to hold little things, such as an egg or a packet of tea and sugar. Western women do not adapt well to the shape of a sari. Most of us do not have the bearing that makes the Indian woman look dignified and elegant. Most of the early missionary women who worked in the villages did not adopt the sari, but later some of them defied British custom and did, earning approval from the Indian women they worked with.

Also prevalent in North India is the Punjabi costume. The *salwar* (trousers) are wide-bottomed, tapering down to a neat ankle. The *kameez* is a tunic falling above or below the knee, depending on the fashion. Across the throat, a long *duppatta* (scarf) is worn, the ends free to float over each shoulder. The duppatta is always in the way and takes endless adjustment, but one would feel immodest without it. Although it is the North India costume, one sees it in Delhi and other parts of India more and more. The style compliments the girl with a slender figure who looks willowy; but pillowy matrons from the Punjab wear these exclusively, often in satin and brocade.

I could never get the hang of a sari, but the Punjabi salwar and kameez were comfortable. Slacks were appropriate in our bazaars where people were used to Westerners, but in the village we wore saris or long skirts. Shorts should be forbidden to Western women visiting Indian towns and villages, although they may pass in Delhi where people expect anything from unrefined Americans.

Indian men wear the loose fitting pyjama trousers with the *kurta*, a loose shirt that is not tucked in; or Nehru jodphurs with the

long, tight-fitting coat; or increasingly seen, the Western business
suit. The strangest-looking costume to Western eyes is the *dhoti*,
yards of thin white cotton wound around and around the waist with
the end brought up between the legs to be fastened—somewhere—
leaving the unlovely calves exposed.

We could have gone berserk buying saris, for there were many
to choose from in Mussoorie, where the merchants catered to the
holiday crowd. We made saris into tablecloths, curtains, and dresses.
Susan bought a white silk sari with a heavy gold border to make into
a gown for her junior-senior banquet, and Paula chose burgundy silk
from Champa for her dress-up occasions.

Bedcovers came woven, printed, embroidered, tie-dyed, and
batiked. Bedcovers could be made into skirts and caftans. One of the
traditional kinds of bedcover is called *phulkari*, flower work, used as
temple hangings in some areas. The cotton material is literally covered with embroidery in a geometric pattern. From his village Sadiq
brought us two in the traditional shades of gold, red, and orange.

Mr. Abhinandan, the cloth merchant

While the men work in the fields, the women sit in the winter sun to embroider them, taking many months to finish one cover. Our phulkaris each have a row of bright blue stitches that show up as imperfections, and here and there a variation in the pattern. We were told that such "mistakes" were made to deceive the gods, jealous of human perfection, or who desire anything so beautiful for themselves. I have heard of this little ruse being used also by Amish quilters, but the explanation was a bit different.

We used Indian shawls for bedcovers, jackets, skirts—and shawls. They came in a variety of patterns depending on the area in which they were made. Almora produced heavy woolen shawls. The Tibetans sold shawls of coarse wool in jewel colors—sometimes I thought that burrs and thorns had been woven in. Sheer Kashmiri shawls of soft wool were embroidered in traditional floral patterns. The shopkeeper boasted that the finest could be drawn through a finger ring.

Woodstock School once promoted a uniform for students and staff which included a brown blazer with a gold emblem, but such institutionalism went out when individualism came in. Woodstock at one time had a dress code. Back in the dark ages of fashion in the middle 1960s, girls had to wear skirts to school. Then the code was relaxed so that they could wear warm slacks on cold days. But the code inevitably became impossible to enforce and finally was stated in such general terms that almost anything could be worn to school. Almost anything is. The issue during our last visit was about the permissible shortness of a miniskirt.

Yashwant, the grandson of a Rajmata (mother of the king) of Jodphur, liked to flaunt his royalty with a very princely, bright blue velvet cape, a purple velvet pantsuit and a satin shirt. He would enter the typing classroom with a flourish, swirling his magician's cape as he sat down to plunk out mistakes at the old Remington. Most of the students, however, dress from wardrobes of paupers rather than princes, and every student owns uniforms of tee shirts and jeans.

I have a theory that divides all people who wear clothes into four classes. We are familiar with the class of conspicuous consumers, those who spend money on expensive clothes hoping to be admired or at least noticed. Or to shock.

The non-conspicuous consumers are those with real class. They dress conservatively but expensively, with understated, exquisite taste. The point is to have something new often enough not to be conspicuous among people who often have new clothes.

In India, Paula was a conspicuous non-consumer. She converted her worn-out jeans into long skirts with patches and wore wrinkled 1940s shirts and coats from the Goodwill store, the uniform of her friends. In India where so many would have liked to dress more decently, patchwork poverty puzzled, even affronted, the Indians.

I, now in my mature years, try to be an example of the non-conspicuous non-consumer. I like bright colors and interesting textures (I expect to have a red or yellow shroud). But I don't want to stand out from the crowd in something too striking. I put together a somewhat dowdy wardrobe from sales, cast-offs from my daughters, and thrift shops. India was a good place to flaunt my style.

There was a time when a Western man in India had no trouble deciding what to wear to church. He donned his dark suit, white shirt, and other pair of shoes. He might ask his wife's advice about which of two ties to wear. A revolution in men's apparel exploded while we were in India. Staff members returned from furloughs with plaid trousers and floral printed shirts. Soon only preachers and missionaries who had not been home recently were wearing dark suits and white shirts.

Even at Woodstock a man stood by his closet door and asked, "What shall I wear to church?"

She said, "Your blue sport coat with the plaid pants."

"I wore that last Sunday."

"Well, how about the red and white check with the maroon bell bottoms?"

"That shirt is at the dhobi's. Could I wear the bright blue shirt?"

"No. You don't want to display the American flag in this community. Too many Canadians. The church bell is ringing."

"And I still have to pick out a tie."

Even when Walt had to decide on what to wear to social events, he was in trouble.

"Should I wear my fancy kurta with the chikan embroidery to the wedding?"

"No. The Indian businessmen will feel insulted. You should

wear your dark suit and white shirt, just as they will."

"Should I wear my fancy kurta to the Christmas program at the Hindustani Church?"

"No. If you had a pyjama outfit or a Nehru jacket, they would be delighted."

We were fortunate that Mussoorie had a number of good derzis. We could boast that we had tailors who could look at a picture in *Ladies Home Journal* and make a dress without a pattern. Or if you gave them a dress to copy, they might even duplicate the mends and patches. Only a few of them were that good, but these you could trust with expensive cloth and complicated patterns. They sat in little cubby holes, their work spread on clean cloths over gritty floors. Most of them sat cross-legged at their machines, spinning the wheel with one hand and guiding the cloth with the other. A few had treadle machines and could sit on a chair to sew.

But the good ones were very busy during certain seasons. Paula, along with five other girls, had the derzi make a Swedish costume for a folk dance for a PTA tea. On the day of the performance he had still not delivered it, and Paula was furious with anxiety. Just minutes before she was to perform, he brought it, basted together, *kutcha* style. I sympathized with Paula, but I knew that he had been frantically trying to get the costumes done on time. "He should not have said he would do it when he knew he couldn't," she said. But he knew that he had to take on all the work he could get during the school year to carry him through the winter break.

Some tailors specialized in men's suits. You selected your material and they made it up. The tailor made a very nice suit for the headmaster, but the pants were made with the material wrong side out. So who's perfect.

The shoemaker in the bazaar was a wizard. I bought a second-hand pair of fur-lined boots, cowboy style with pointed toes and run-under heels from a friend. I didn't feel like wearing them in public and the family laughed when I wore them at home. Budha Ram restyled them by rounding the toes and attaching new soles and straight heels. He also made sandals for us from a picture in Sears catalog, but his chief claim to fame was his desert boots. There were Western men who declared that they returned to India whenever they needed a new pair of desert boots.

Students brought back from abroad new fashions in dress and hair styles. Finally after years of waist-length hair, a head returned from the States with a shag cut, and then another appeared after winter break with a curly permanent. Soon there was no stopping the scissors. Where once I had surveyed a class of shining curtains dropping from center parts and tangling the keys of the typewriters (one of the girls got her long hair caught in the electric beaters while making a cake), now there was some variety.

My daughters and I had a recurrent ear-piercing argument. I kept remonstrating with Paula until she really was the only girl in her class with unpierced ears, and then what can a mother do. Some of Paula's classmates were also getting their noses pierced to wear diamond or gold nose studs. I think ear-piercing is harmless, but an Indian friend told me she was sorry she had had that permanent hole made in her nose.

In a country where jewelry is a conventional part of the apparel, where earrings, finger rings, toe rings, and nose rings are investments; where pendants are worn in the hair and on the forehead; where bracelets are worn at the wrists and sometimes from elbow to armpit, we Westerners could not help being fascinated with jewelry. We also wanted to avoid looking conspicuously unornamented. We waited to buy gold bangles until we could no longer afford them, but inexpensive, attractive, and unique handmade jewelry was affordable.

When we first went to India in the 1960s, I took along hat, gloves, and high heels, and a shoe bag so that I could climb the hills in walking shoes and change to heels before going into church. Sensibly, we quit all that in the next decade. In the early 1970s we in the Staff Room were discussing the miniskirt. In the 1980s we were discussing the return of the miniskirt. In the 1990s we conceded that we were all too old to give it a thought.

Mention is made in the Woodstock history of Miss Cameron, she of the waspy disposition, who had a unique claim to fame.

> This was in the days of wasp waists, and of all the wonderful wasp waists that circle around Woodstock, Cammy's was the waspiest. It was whispered among us girls that it could be spanned by two fair-sized hands when she was all toodle-faddled up, ready to go to some affair.[37]

Another teacher of a few years earlier, a Miss Condit whose favorite expression was "Hark," was of a different opinion. She would as soon try to squeeze her feet into a pair of Chinese shoes as her body into a fashionable pair of corsets, she maintained. Corset stays were not the only freak of fashion of the time. Pictures of the early years show bustles, flounces, tucks, and celluloid collars. How those long, heavy skirts must have swept up the dust of the road. And then came the austere, unbecoming, straight dresses of the twenties worn with long necklaces and short straight hair.

When Edward VII, king of England, died in 1910, Woodstock cancelled the June concert, to the disappointment of the performers who had gone to the trouble of ordering new frocks. Someone observed, "I trust the fashions of June will not be quite out of date [for the concert in] September." The derzis of each generation must have delighted in all the sewing to be done.

Nor were the men exempt from the foibles of fashion. Until the 1930s, the proper attire for office wear, even in hot and steamy India, was a suit with jacket and waistcoat. If you became very warm, it was permissible, unless you were to call on the burra sahib, to remove the jacket but not the waistcoat, thus eliciting the expression of "working in his shirtsleeves." The topi, the white pith helmet worn by both men and women, disappeared during World War II when it proved to be a nuisance for military wear. Civilians, who had trusted it to keep them safe from the dangerous Indian sun, discarded it also.

Down through the years, all the funny fashions of the Western world were exported across the sea and up the mountain by buffalo cart to Mussoorie to amaze and delight and impress, and, especially, to puzzle the Indians.

Chapter 16

Shelter

We did not know what to expect of Mussoorie housing. Dirt floors and thatched roofs? During our various terms in India, we lived in six different locations. The accommodations were comfortable and some of them even had charm. Since we are natural nesters, we enjoyed making a home in each of them.

As you look down from the Chukker with a view over the Woodstock Hillside, you realize that there must be an acreage of red corrugated iron roofs enough to cover the state of Kansas. The thatch of earlier days would have been more attractive but not as practical.

The British built houses on the plains that were intended to compensate for the inhumane climate and outrageous distance from civilized England. They imported as much of England and Europe as was needed to make themselves feel at home. Houses on the plains were built to cope with the heat, houses with thick walls to insulate the interiors, high ceilings to let the heat rise and escape through high little windows called *havadans*, wide verandahs all around to shade the inner rooms and provide a place for sleeping during the stifling nights. Every room had access to a verandah. The doorways were curtained so that air could circulate from room to room and still allow for privacy.

Before electric fans, public buildings as well as the bungalows had been equipped with *punkahs*. The punkah was a wide flounce of cotton or jute matting attached to a rod suspended from the ceiling. A rope was attached to the top of the punkah that went over a pulley and out a hole near the ceiling. The rope dropped down on the verandah where a servant, usually a young boy or an old man pulled at it to create a breeze as the punkah was pulled leisurely back and forth.

All these heat-reducing ideas were imported to the foothills and incorporated into buildings that were intended to be used only during the hot months. And then demands for housing changed, and residents stayed year around and endured the discomfort of the cold for six months of the year.

The early furniture was dark, heavy mahogany, suggestive of the permanence of the Empire. It perspired during the monsoon. Every house needed a number of almirahs, those huge cupboards in which personal property could be locked up. The more transient residents, military and missionary personnel particularly, sold their furniture to the next occupant and bought another set just like it in the new location. "The furniture had a twenty-second-hand look," one woman wrote home. Some of us were still furnishing our houses this way when we lived in Mussoorie.

At the top of the hill was the cantonment where British troops were once quartered. Many old homes on the Hillside were built by the British military who were more or less permanently stationed in Landour with their families. After Independence in 1947, the homes were sold by the departing British to the school or to various missions as vacation homes. When many of the missionaries left the country, the homes were given to the school or sold to Indian nationals.

My friend Beth Taylor lived in Landour Villa, built in 1832. The Taylors' living quarters had been the military mess hall, evidenced by the *chulha* in the kitchen with its holes for ten cooking pots. The ceilings in the living room are so high that Beth could raise her clothesline to the ceiling and still have room for entertaining below. The ghosts of proper English gentlemen must occasionally give the sheets an insolent twitch.

Tafton, just above the high school, was leased from Colonel Reilly in 1856. Originally it had had a thatched roof, but now it has a proper corrugated roof that leaks around the bolts. It is a charming house with the aforementioned features of the British Raj. During Walt's tenure the Woodstock maintenance crew was unable to stop up all the holes caused by rats chewing through the concrete. When he inspected the house, Walt thought it should be pushed over the khud, an unfeeling statement to make about an attractive old house. Since then it has been renovated and I believe the rat problem has been solved.

Oakville is another of the old houses. Once owned by a Colonel Peacock, the estate lies east of the school and above Tehri Road. Oakville must have been in its time as romantic a place as any Southern plantation. It was self-sustaining with a herd of dairy cattle and a spring, horses and bridle paths. People came to parties from as far away as Cloud's End. Five malis were employed in the greenhouse.

Originally owned by the British army, Ellangowan had once provided officers' quarters on the upper floors and stables below. During our years in India, it was owned by our Mennonite mission and housed parents who came to the Hillside for vacations. Scenic though the location, Ellangowan living was not perfect. It was easy to remember that those dark, dank lower apartments had once been stables.

Our various living quarters had much in common. The furniture was typical of that found on mission stations and other housing on the Hillside. Some of it was antique, some more modern teakwood, all with a natural "distressed look." Our divans were sometimes upholstered, but some were teakwood with caned seats that could be made comfortable with pillows. Most of us added touches of Indian art and souvenirs. Cranes made from buffalo horn, brass dishes, colorful batiks, mirrorwork pillow covers lifted our spirits on dull days. Little tables made from feet and tusks of elephants we resisted as not being our style.

The living situation was like a deluxe camp-out. We had the scenery to make up for the inconvenience of the kerosene stove. We had the wonderful weather to make up for the lack of hot water. Every apartment had a Western flush toilet rather than a cubicle with a hole in the floor and a faucet to fill a plastic bucket for flushing. What we whimsically called our "roughing it" style represented poverty to wealthy Indian families, but enviable affluence to many of the Indian workers we knew at Woodstock. Coming to terms with the visible paradoxes of life styles, trying to determine how we should live and act among the multitudes, was a continuing education for our conscience.

I doubt that anyone on the Hillside hesitated to move from one place to another just because of the difficulty of transporting household goods over the terrain. When the householder sent out the word, coolies made themselves available immediately. Indian Van Lines was a procession of coolies carrying our desk, barrels, refrigerator, and stove (a two-burner hotplate) on their backs. If we had had a grand piano, they would have moved that. These were not the regular bazaar coolies who followed us with our accumulated parcels. These specialized in moving heavy loads. Often they were the small, Oriental-looking Nepalese, sadly with short lifespans.

The staple type of floor covering in India was coir (coconut husk or jute) matting. It comes in strips three or four feet wide, and carpets are made up to fit the room. The common color, like the one in our living room, was brownish tan, following the maxim that if you can't beat the dirt, join it. We decided that concrete was preferable to road-colored coir and bought small cotton rugs in the bazaar to replace it. The matting is inexpensive but wears through quickly, comes apart at the seams the day it is sewn, then looks obviously mended. This type of carpeting improved when it was manufactured in prettier colors and patterns. It has the advantage of being easy to take up and clean. When we bought a camel-hair carpet for the living room, I learned that I was allergic to camel hair.

During much of the Mussoorie year we thought nothing about cooling or heating. And then the dampness began to tell on us and we needed a little fire to dry things out. Later in October the nights were cool and we asked for something in the evening that radiates a little warmth, and finally in January and February, we kept a fire going in at least one room.

Our first apartment had a small open fireplace, as all the old houses do, although many of them are now cemented over. It ate mounds of wood and warmed only the chimney. Later we enjoyed a tin stove, cleverly designed with baffles which kept some of the heat in the room. But once we started a fire, we had to give it constant attention, opening the damper and closing the damper, adding a stick and encouraging the bigger logs. Once we bought a little iron stove, Queen No. 5, from the kabardi wallah. It was about eighteen inches high, a very pretty thing with curlicues, sliding doors, and two small lids on top. It could be compared to an oversized ashtray. We enjoyed owning it, but it was so small that we had to have the wood cut especially to fit it. It took the chill off a room and was a great conversation piece. We had no trouble selling it when we left, for it had a warm and outgoing personality.

When we noticed our guests shivering or when we could not read comfortably even when embracing our little stove, we lifted it off its metal tray and installed the Duo Therm, an oil burner. The directions for starting it were to turn on the oil, wait one minute, and throw in a match. Nobody in our family had one minute to waste, so we would go off to read the paper or talk to Sadiq. When we remembered the Duo Therm, the burner would be flooded and we could not start it for another hour. We drained and cleaned it periodically, flooded it by mistake twice a week, cherished it, and coaxed it. It did its part by keeping the room at sixty-five degrees. I like to think that working on that stove improved my character.

Could it be that central heating is responsible for the lack of family togetherness? When we had but one source of heat, we spent our evenings around that fire. We arranged ourselves under the main ceiling light, Walt with his budget or Board report on the table at one end; I with my papers to grade on the other; Susan with her chemistry on the sofa; and Paula with her arithmetic on the end table.

The rooms that we glimpsed from the bazaar street looked barely adequate for survival. Even some well-to-do Indians live in circumstances that suggest poverty. In the 1970s, we observed that the wife of the wealthy shopkeeper might live in clean rooms, but with chipped plaster, broken shutters, and moldy paint, just as her neighbors did. She might breathe the same vapors from the open sewers. Neither the outside nor the inside of her house proclaimed her husband's wealth. Benares saris and gold jewelry did that. This disregard of surroundings has changed for the middle class, and we were later guests in well-appointed homes.

I have referred to Mr. Abhinandan, the Indian cloth merchant. He liked to entertain Westerners, and we enjoyed his hospitality. He helped us to understand the life of the middle-income people who lived in the bazaar. He may not have been typical of his group (who is?), but we would like to think he is, for our respect for him grew as we learned to know him. The Abhinandans were one of six or seven Jain families in the town during the 1970s. Mr. Abhinandan lived with his wife above his shop, three stories up from the bazaar street on the front, seven stories up from the street that runs behind the building. He invited us several times for a Sunday noon vegetarian meal, which his wife began cooking on our arrival. She worked in a corner of the verandah while squatting on the floor in her pink silk sari, preparing the various vegetable curries and *puris* (fried bread) over buckets of glowing charcoal. Our host served us but did not eat with us. He joined us for coffee, and his wife came in briefly to receive our compliments. She spoke no English. After the meal we settled down to the conversation for which we had really been invited. After his wife died, his daughter prepared the meal; and since she knew English, she joined in the conversation.

The room in which we had been served was furnished with a small table, a single bed, a few straight chairs, and a sewing machine. The room was functional, with no thought for aesthetics beyond a few Jain religious prints and an embroidered table cover. The kitchen and toilet rooms were off the back verandah. The Abhinandans also used a bedroom on another floor of the building, but he rented out all the other rooms.

The owner of Art Press invited us for a meal. This family lived in the bazaar on the hill overlooking Picture Palace in a spacious and comfortable home furnished in Western style. Our superb Indian meal was served on a table with a complete set of cutlery while the beautiful white refrigerator hummed an accompaniment to our conversation.

Most of our Indian hosts offered us chairs for dining or visiting. But I suspect that they would have been more comfortable sitting on a mat or against a bolster. Krishnalal Shridharani sees the chair as the symbol of the difference between the cultures of the East and West. He attributes our fallen arches to the use of the chair. He believes that Indians are philosophers because they are floor sitters and Westerners are doers because they are chair sitters.

The chair has dictated our style of clothing. The floor calls for loose clothing and the chair for tailored and fitted. Loose garments hamper one's pace in walking and interfere with vigorous work, and they affect one's state of mind, calling for leisure and contemplation. Chair sitting, he says, is half standing, making one ready to spring up ready for any occasion, work, or sport. But getting off the floor is almost like getting out of bed, "and everybody knows how difficult that is." Because the Westerner cannot squat comfortably on the ground for a considerable length of time, he cannot become oblivious to time and he can never become really chummy in an Indian group. And so the Indian "has become a philosopher and has distinguished himself in cosmic and spiritual reflections, while [the Westerner] has become a businessman, swift and capable of plucking advantage, as far removed from the world of Hindu philosophy as any man could be."[38]

We are what we are because of our chairs?

Chapter 17

The Support System

"Cheap labor was another jewel in the crown of the Raj."[39]

"I wish I could take that one home with me," Margaret Toews said as she watched her ayah spooning rice and dal into one-year-old Andrew. The one Margaret wanted to take back to the States was Indira, along with Andrew.

Somewhere in the records of the Woodstock Executive Committee is a resolution that the servants will be referred to as "maintenance staff." The directive would give those who serve and maintain the school their proper status. The Woodstock maintenance staff came from different villages according to the type of work they did. Sweepers came from near Moradabad, the only group from the plains. The kitchen staff, electricians, and chaprassis came from the villages to the east in the Garhwal districts. They arrived as untrained hillmen. The school trained them and offered education to their children, a number of whom then joined the Woodstock staff. Now employees come from the third generation of Woodstock caretakers, some of them having had longer tenure than anyone on the academic or administrative staff. Most of them are either Christians or Hindus. During our time, the head carpenter was the only Sikh and the audiovisual technician was the only Muslim.

Boarding school children will speak with affection about their beloved khansamas or ayahs. Their khansama was really one of the family, and they played with his children as with their brothers and sisters. It is true that many servants are remembered as jewels; many stay for years with one family until retirement.

On the other hand, some people become unexpectedly psychotic about their helpers. Otherwise even-tempered adults can be irritated to adolescent rages. Intelligent women can be made to feel like fools. An American housewife coming from a carefully controlled, sanitized, pasteurized kitchen, from a routine of shopping that pays attention to cents per ounce, can be thrown into an economic depression for which the only cure is lunch at the Oberoi in New Delhi.

There are families who frequently change servants. The ayah tucks eggs into the folds of her sari, the khansama will cook but not dust; the mali steals the mangoes before they are ripe; or the sweeper isn't allowed by his caste to clean the bathrooms.

"I hope I did not deserve some of the servants I had in India," a missionary said.

Workers keep little packets of references from their former employers; they guard them carefully and show them proudly even when the recommendation is not favorable. "Samuel was a good cook but he had tantrums when we had guests." "Ranjit can make a good shepherd's pie, but nothing more."

Upon our arrival in India, we were besieged by Indian men who came to our door offering to cook for us. I sent them away, for I knew we could manage well without a cook. After all, we were three almost grown women, cooking for one man. Furthermore, I could remember the puzzlement of friends over the fact that missionaries in India seemed to need helpers. Life progressed smoothly for us that first semester. The dhobi took away our dirty clothes and brought back clean, ironed ones; a sweeper came in each day to sweep and raise the dust. Our older daughter did the cooking for the privilege of spending a semester in India. For two dollars a month a young man from the school kitchen came in to wash the day's dirty dishes.

But all was not perfect in our Indian Eden. We did not find the time to do all those leisurely things that we had planned. Walt's job kept him more than busy and my teaching was full time. We discovered that we could not trust half the laundry to the vigorous ministrations of the dhobi. The sweeper made dusting necessary every day. We looked forward to the three-month winter break when the routines of life would be less demanding.

But with the winter break, our dishwasher left for his village, and our cook left the nest to fly back to college. Paula and I were on our own for three months of simple living. But there was the milk to boil and the rice to clean; drinking water to sterilize and raisins to stem. We picked the stones out of the beans, browned the wheat cereal, cracked the nuts, and made the buffalo butter. We washed all those dishes, and the dishes always lasted longer than the hot water. Two or three times a week we walked to the bazaar for produce.

We also spent time answering the cough at the door. The dudh wallah brought the milk, the roti wallah dropped off a loaf of bread, the pork wallah weighed out two kilos of meat once a week, the luckri wallah brought the *maunds* of wood every few days; the kabardi wallah solicited our paper, bottles, tin cans, and old shoes. The dry cleaner stopped weekly, as did the dhobi and the derzi to solicit business.. The sweeper came daily and the paperman left the *Times of India* on the kitchen table. We were never lonely during those winter mornings.

Relief came when we went to the mission field for the Christmas break. In each of the mission homes we observed the efficiency with which those households were managed. The missionary wife spent the morning at the hospital or school going about mission business, then came home to a meal already prepared for family and guests. The washing and ironing were done on schedule by the ayah, and the garden produce was brought to the kitchen by the mali. The khansama, the ayah, and the mali made it possible for the doctor, the nurse, the teacher, the engineer, and the evangelist to do what they had come to India to do.

I explained to one of the teachers that we had no khansama, alluding to the expense and involvement that accompanied the presence of an employee.

She protested gently, "But they need the work. That can be one of your contributions to India."

She had a point. We could raise the standard of living of a number of people by employing one helper. But was that our responsibility? Certainly we could not employ all the unemployed cooks on the Hillside. In some respects, life was much simpler without servants. We valued our independence and privacy. The employer must become involved with the lives of his employees. They receive low salaries by our standards, so the employer must see that the workers and their families have what they need in clothing, education, and medical care. Furthermore, the helpers are often inefficient. The common knowledge is that the khansama uses twice as much Burshane as the memsahib. Once he lights the burner, he leaves it on all morning, to save matches, I suppose.

But then thinking again, cooking is not my favorite sport. I have a long-standing reputation for burning the potatoes and letting the milk boil over.

"If we had a cook," Paula reminded me, "he could make the cinnamon rolls while you are teaching school."

"Then what would be my claim to fame?"

"Liniment fudge." She was referring to the time when I had mistaken the liniment bottle for the vanilla bottle, long years ago.

When we moved to Palisades, we acquired the Brownes' cook. We were privileged to have two years with Sadiq Masih. He was a neat, stocky, grizzled Punjabi from Moga, a long day's journey from Mussoorie. His six children had all been educated. We first met him when we were invited to the Browne's for Sunday dinner. Sadiq appeared very impressive in his white coat and starched *pugree*, a many-layered turban that ends in a stiff fan and adds a good nine inches to the height of the wearer. (That was the last we saw of the pugree. He must have decided that none of our occasions merited such formality.) Sadiq, Muslim by name, was a Christian and a faithful member of the Hindustani Church. He lived in the servants' quarters back of the house with his son who was attending the Mussoorie business college. His wife came to visit him once a year and he returned to his village for a month during winter break.

Sadiq's domain was the kitchen and back verandah. Luckily, guests did not invade that part of the house. Casual housewife that I am, even so I despaired of keeping the kitchen sanitary. At least we never caught our cook straining the soup through the master's sock. ("It's all right, Memsahibji. It's not one of his clean ones.") Jokes about servants were serious laughing matters.

"Sadiq, what shall we do about a sweeper?" we asked after we had moved into this new arrangement.

"Surat, hospital sweeper, came to door yesterday. He say he sweep."

"Will he dust?"

"No, Memsahibji, sweeper not dust."

Inquiry revealed that Surat wanted Rs. 20 a month for coming in each day to sweep. His references were not enthusiastic; he had not acquired the Protestant work ethic.

While we were pondering, Sadiq came to ask if we would help his son with his college expenses. He needed books for his business administration courses. Our decision was to do our own sweeping and use the money to help his son with his books. Sadiq accepted the arrangement, but we were aware that it bothered him. He, as a cook, would lose face by sweeping, but he was pained to see me doing it, at least in his territory. Whenever I took up the broom to sweep the dining room, he took it from my hand. To save Sadiq's pride, Walt wiped up the kitchen and dining room floors in the evening after he had gone home.

Sadiq had been a good student of cooking during his many years with the Brownes. Here I pay tribute to all those women who taught Indian men how to cook so that we who came later could reap the benefit. One of Sadiq's endearing qualities was his ability to plan the menus. But I gave him a little more guidance after one Sunday dinner included rice and curry with potatoes and a dessert of cinnamon rolls. Once he amazed us and our guests with gingerbread covered with lemon sauce of an astonished green, his attempt at elegance. He set it before me impassively, but he was gratified by our surprise.

He baked two kinds of cookies, peanut butter and oatmeal. Then when I told him I needed fancy cookies for the Community Center tea, he made iced sugar cookies in star shapes. He had recipes he didn't waste on our family. Paula dictated a recipe for her favorite snickerdoodles, which he took down in Urdu, but she didn't warn him to add flour to compensate for the high altitude. They turned out flat.

He apologized for them. "Missahibji, they taste good, but they don't see good."

Sadiq could also boil milk. Milk should boil for twenty minutes, and Sadiq never to my knowledge let it boil over. On Sunday when I boiled it, I sometimes had to scour up the burned pan before he came back.

Having a khansama changes one's lifestyle. No more clearing off a corner of the dining table to set two or three places for a meal. All our papers and sewing must be cleared so that Sadiq could set the table properly. No more cleaning out the refrigerator and setting the odds and ends on the table for a scavenger meal. Sadiq must plan a meal with a main dish, vegetable, and dessert. No more curling up with a book and a sandwich if Walt was traveling. Sadiq must serve us in the style to which he was accustomed.

The job description for "cook" does not quite cover the duties of the khansama. He is also the marketer. We considered him the most honest of cooks. When he made his weekly report of what he had spent and told me he had bought one dozen oranges for Rs. 3, I believed him, for that was exactly what they would have cost me. Still, he was never happy with me when I picked up fruit in the bazaar, and I am fairly sure that he got things a trifle cheaper and kept the difference. But that was probably the customary perk, taken by a person who worked for pennies from an employer who worked for dollars.

Most servants were run-of-the-mill humanity with some flaws. Our only complaint about Sadiq was that he filled the house with the smell of his *bidis* when he sat on the back verandah smoking with his friends. All in all, we considered him a person of integrity, a real Christian gentleman.

Again, an inordinate amount of space has been given to the subject of food and those engaged in its preparation. There were other workers who made up our support system.

The sweeper is one of the almost invisible people of India. Although he (or often she) is at the bottom of the social ladder, he is one of the necessary Indian workers for both Indians and Westerners. Outside sweepers clean the roads and paths. Others come into the buildings to sweep and mop floors. At the school, with their *jharus*, short-handled, long-strawed brooms, they start duck-walking through the classrooms as soon as the students leave in the afternoon.

Every family with a working mother has an ayah for baby sitting, washing, ironing, bedmaking, and sewing. I did not regularly hire an ayah because we did not have enough work for one; nevertheless, I tended to collect ayahs.

I became involved with Shanti for a brief period, just to give her a little work. Although she had terminal cancer, the doctor said she should work as long as she felt well enough, and for a few months she ironed and mended for me.

Rosie's was a different story. She told me how much she needed the work, that she had three children, no husband, no job. I was already aware that I could not hire every ayah that needed work, but I told her to come home with me and I would find something for her to do that day. Shanti was already doing things I didn't need doing. I gave Rosie a little ironing and a lunch that she took home for her family in our tiffin carrier. After that she came half a day a week.

There was a certain coolness in Sadiq's attitude toward the Rosie project. Here he was, a tried and true servant deserving of favors, and there Rosie was, undeserving. The problem resolved itself when we left for a quick trip to the States. Rosie found a job in Dehra Dun, but she quit after a few weeks because she did not like the family. Too many children. When I met her in the bazaar, she asked for work, but I didn't feel that I should help her. The help I had given her had not solved her problem, and to my family's annoyance I had lost the tiffin carrier.

My third and last attempt was with Jayti. The second time she came I put her to washing windows. Evidently Jayti didn't do windows. She never came back.

"Everything you do to help people hurts them," a development worker said. Translated, I suppose this means that economic development problems do not have simple solutions. Another aphorism is "People should get what they need and people should get what they deserve." These two ideas are not always compatible, and such an approach leaves little room for grace. We discovered that "helping" is a tricky business. Some people, both at home and abroad, seem to look frantically for people to help, and others seem just to be at the right place at the right time to extend a hand.

When the British established the cantonment in the 1840s, they brought in the dhobis from Lucknow to do the laundry. The Dhobi Ghat is a small village down the hill from the Woodstock Estate. Originally the dhobis bashed the clothes clean and thin on the rocks of a small stream. (All the clothes, not just jeans, were stone-washed in our time there.) Now they have the water piped to cement tanks, and they beat the clothes on the sides of the tanks.

When we moved to Palisades, we were assigned to a dhobi whose deaf-mute son collected and delivered the clothes. He was a friendly fellow who communicated with grunts and gestures. He once brought me the first rhododendrons of the season and tried unsuccessfully to tell me where he had found them. I could have wept for him. After our thirty years of coming and going, he is one of the few constants on the Hillside, always greeting us excitedly with a salaam.

The dhobi. Photo by Vic Reimer

Every morning during the winter holiday, our daughters went jogging on Tehri Road to the east tollgate. They met what they called the Dudh Wallah Relay Team coming from villages ten or fifteen kilometers away, walking in groups of four or five carrying cans of milk of twenty or thirty liters. At some point they poured milk from the large cans into smaller cans for distributing to Hillside homes.

When I didn't have a cook, I had to remember to leave a pan out for the dudh wallah to fill with a seer of milk, two cups. He looked unkempt in his patched and torn jodphurs, a shirt that hung below his black vest, all of him the color of Tehri Road. To our kitchen smells, the dudh wallah added the aroma of buffalo and sweat, an earthy and, I suppose, healthy smell. Our dudh wallah was always cheerful, polite, and stubble-chinned. He obligingly came into the kitchen and filled the pan I left out. If I forgot, he would rummage around in the cupboard, find a *degchi*, take the sieve off the hook, and strain the milk. Once when he couldn't find a clean pan, he washed one. So he did, after all, have his own standards of cleanliness. He carried his milk in small cans on his back, slung together in a macrame net of rope. The cans were stoppered with a wad of leaves, some of which flaked off into the milk.

Our dudh wallah was once boycotted for drunkenness and neglect of his customers. When he was allowed to solicit business again, he became very faithful and never missed a day. Sometimes he asked for five or ten rupees on his account and indicated that we were to write it in our book. He seemed to trust us to keep accounts for him, but I am sure that he always knew exactly where he stood.

The standard of living of the dudh wallahs has risen with India's economy. They dress better, more of them own horses for delivering milk, and some of them own jeeps.

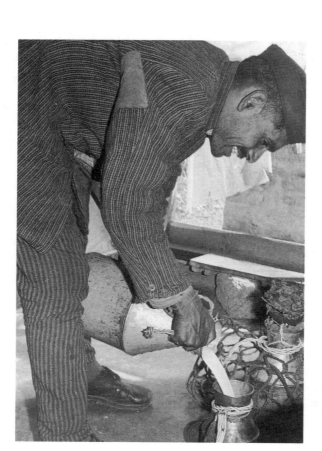

The dudh wallah.
Photo by Vic Reimer

Every building needs a *chowkidar* to guard it, and ours was provided by the school. We never lost anything, but there was widespread thievery from locked property on the Hillside, once from the other side of the duplex where we were living.

The advice we received was that a householder cannot possibly do without a chowkidar. Yet, the common complaint was that when real thieves come, he is useless. He must be employed because that is his profession, but he will have the habits and courage of a rabbit. I quote from Francis Yeats-Brown:

> The only recorded instance of aggression on the part of a chowkidar is that which used to be found (it has now been erased) upon the tombstone of the Reverend Isidore Lowenthal, a Protestant missionary of Peshwar: "Accidentally Shot by His Chowkidar. Well done, thou good and faithful servant."[40]

Probably the tale is apocryphal, for it appears with changes of the name of the victim in other biographies. The whole profession of security guards should not be discredited by all the stories of chowkidars who sleep through grand theft. Because a chowkidar is one of the many workers needed for an orderly life in India.

Chapter 18

The Society Page

Call this section "A Day in the Life of a Woodstock Teacher Which Happened to be her Fifty-first Birthday."

As usual, we are awakened by the racing of crows on our tin roof. The new snow we see on our hillside is picturesque, but we don't have much time to admire it as we shiver into several layers of clothing. In the frigid dining room we wrap our hands around hot cups of coffee and comfort our inner core with the hot wheat cereal that Sadiq offers.

Walt leaves for his office, and half an hour later Paula and I climb up to school. We estimate that my classroom is ten stories above our front door. Paula disappears into the senior homeroom and I stop in the Ladies' Staff Room to huddle around the oil burner with Saroj, the Hindi teacher, the first to remember that this is my birthday.

After a morning of English classes and a departmental meeting (having the longest tenure—this is my third year—I am head of the English Department), I go home for lunch. Over rice and dal, Walt tells us his troubles with the pork wallah. Walt has spent the morning trying to convince this man that he should keep to his contract for the school meat. The pork wallah had bid for the contract, but now prices have risen. Should Walt be sympathetic and compromise?

In the afternoon I have two typing classes and a bookkeeping class, and then it is time for tea. I gather my papers together and go down to the Quad, where the presence of Skinner's jeep reminds me that I have forgotten my egg basket again. So I put my weekly dozen in my purse along with a handful of rain.

Usually we have tea and read the mail at school, but today Paula and I gather up a family of four to take down to our house for tea. Walt had said yesterday that he had seen the Ditmanson children standing together in the rain before going down to their various dorms. He thought they would welcome the opportunity to get together as a family. We take them home with us, quickly build a fire, and set up the tea tray in the living room. We learn that their parents had met during World War II in the Shantung concentration camp where one of our friends had been interned. So we have a starting point for our conversation. After tea they leave, animated and warmed.

We are invited out for dinner. Those who had gone to Kashmir for the October break are getting together to show their color slides. Mrs. Vonk, wife of the headmaster, presents an angel-food cake and a candle in honor of my birthday, and even more special, a beef roast.

The slides are good, bad, repetitive, and lots of fun. Walt and I had not gone to Kashmir, having been there earlier, but we had entrusted our daughter to the good characters of the headmaster, the chaplain, and the French teacher. And then we see on the slides in living color each one of the party trying the hubble-bubble pipe, also known as the hookah. (None of them in later life has adopted the habit, but I wonder if the experience might keep one of them from becoming president.)

As we come home, a star-studded sky and the clear twinkles of the lights from Dehra Dun promise a change in the weather.

Before going to bed, I look over my birthday cards. I have one from a church group that did not write in it, suggesting on a separate note that I could use it again. I write Saroj's name on it for two weeks from today. Paula's card is a one-of-a-kind batik. Susan's includes the design of her kitchen curtains in Zaire where she is teaching English.

"What happened about the pork wallah," I ask as we prepare for bed.

"He wept. And finally we compromised on the price of the pork."

On a windy, rainy March night, Walt and I climbed up from our house to Cozy Corner where the path met Tehri Road. We waited there for two other couples, shivering under the eerie road light.

"This is silly," I complained. "We would never do anything like this at home."

"Kansas doesn't have wind and rain? Only blue skies and sun?"

Two couples approached from different directions. One froggy voice suggested that we toss Dick Allison's umbrella over the khud for arranging this questionable affair for a rainy night. We puddled on together toward Landour. At Mullingar Hill we started climbing the cemented jeep road to the right, twisting up and up, challenging Dick's sense of direction. Finally we found the house we were looking for and joined others already waiting.

"Surprise," we shouted as we trooped into the Marks' living room.

For good administrative reasons, our Indian friends had been moved from a convenient apartment on the campus to one in Landour. The family felt displaced. To help them start off with our best wishes, we Westerners planned a surprise housewarming.

Housewarming was a new idea for the Indian staff, but we blithely planned for an evening with gifts and refreshments; the Indian staff joined us, for they were ready for a party.

The occasion turned out well as far as we could tell. If there were feelings of resentment, we didn't try to uncover them. We hoped that as foreigners we could get by with a few cultural gaffes. From housewarmings we went on to baby showers, which later became large affairs.

Most Woodstock weddings made good use of the setting. Frances Hilliard had grown up in India, with her parents on the Woodstock staff. She returned to Woodstock for her wedding, held in St. Paul's church. Each window was decorated with a nosegay of freshly gathered jungle plantain, fern, and dahlias. The bride's dress had been made from a white silk sari.

I will draw one striking contrast. At formal weddings in our home church, the service begins with the ceremony of candle lighting. Two charming children with brass candle lighters come down the aisle and solemnly light the seven tapers in the candelabra on each side of the altar, performing a simple ballet as they eye each other to light the corresponding candle in unison.

Witness this part of the ceremony as it happened at St. Paul's. The candles were in the brass candelabra silhouetted against the impressive background of stained glass windows and embroidered tapestry. In came the caretaker-janitor of St. Paul's wearing his uniform, a drab shirt outside his drab trousers. He shaves regularly once a week, but this was not his day. We watched expectantly as he lit the candles, using matches from a Tikka matchbox, and typically one out of three flared. He was not embarrassed by our attention, knowing that he had a job to do, which he did properly, and also knowing that he was not part of the wedding party, only the facilitator. The Western bride could now come down the aisle on the arm of her father.

Indian Christian weddings often borrow from Western culture. The niece of one of the Indian staff members was married in Parker Hall, with rather casual plans. The match had been arranged, and the couple had met each other once, a month earlier. On the morning of the wedding day, the bridegroom arrived from Calcutta.

Diana Biswas gathered armloads of hydrangeas and arranged them artfully across the front of the stage in Parker Hall. Friends swept out the place and laid the orange aisle carpet that changed the space from an auditorium to a church.

We presented ourselves at three o'clock, the announced time. At three-thirty the groom and his best man entered and sat down in the front row. Slowly the seats began to fill. About four o'clock the bride appeared at the back door with her party and the pianist began the traditional Mendelssohn wedding march. Three pretty little girls in peacock-blue ruffled dresses appeared and were gently pushed down the aisle and reminded to scatter their flower petals. Then the bride and her father crept in so slowly that the pianist had to play on and on. The bride wore a white satin sari, the Western wedding color. Two bridesmaids followed the bride, holding the corners of her long bridal veil. The little bride was downcast and unsmiling, but the photographer was completely unabashed, moving everywhere to get his unique shots, directed by members from each family. This while the vows were being spoken. I think the picture-taking performance had been learned at Western weddings.

After the ceremony, the bridesmaids passed out little bags of confetti. When the half-happy couple came up the aisle, we showered them with confetti, which is certainly more appropriate in India than rice, a precious food as well as a fertility symbol.

The couple then went for a taxi ride, to become better acquainted, I assume. When they returned, the school bearers served an abundant tea, and later the bride's family provided a curry meal. The wedding probably cost a good deal more than the family could afford, but wedding extravagance is not uniquely an Indian weakness.

We did not see a Hindu wedding, but we were invited to a number of wedding dinners. Invitations were bright, tasseled cards, printed in English and Hindi. The auspicious time for weddings in Mussoorie is in winter. On a cold March night we attended a Hindu

wedding dinner at one of the Mussoorie social clubs. We were ush-
ered to folding chairs in the shamiana (a colorful tent) and shivered,
realizing too late that we should have dressed warmly rather than
smartly. Our hosts brought pots of charcoal for us to toast our feet
over, but how many feet can you crowd over a small pot of charcoal?
Finally we were asked to gather at the wedding feast in the long hall.
The curries were fiery, causing tears to flow and voices to disappear.
Indian food gourmets said this meal was superlative.

Walt, but not I, received invitations to village weddings in the
families of dhobies, sweepers, and other school employees. A small
wage earner goes into debt for life for his daughters' weddings, even
borrowing on his retirement fund. There must be food, saris, jewelry, music, and flowers. A bride's dowry of clothes and jewelry is her
economic security. Supposedly, her husband cannot sell them, for
they are to be passed on to her daughters.

"When you go out to eat, you will go to Kwality's," our
returned-missionary friends told us as they prepared us for our trip
to India. "But you won't go often."

Every time we went out to eat was memorable. We always
invented some reason for celebration to justify the expenditure of
time, energy, and rupees. We once celebrated at Kwality's with a
teacher who had just one hundred days left in India. She had hated
every minute of her two-year stay, but she survived the last hundred
days and then returned for another term.

There were other places to eat in Mussoorie, and more sprang
up with the coming of more hotels, more tourists. The Tavern was
popular for its tandoori chicken and Chinese food. We liked Green's
vegetarian. Eating at the Savoy Hotel, noted for its somewhat dowdy
grandeur, was an experience in elegant loneliness. We ate there once
and happened to be the only diners of that hour, overwhelmed by the
number of bearers at our service. Library Bazaar boasted a revolving
restaurant on a pedestal that operated during the season. We heard
that the food was brought up from the street vendors.

We entertained every acquaintance who was passing through,
even though they were only friends of friends. How do visitors
amuse themselves at our hill station? Some of them walk to the
bazaar every day to take pictures and to have tea. Other come for

trekking and amuse themselves by spending whole days walking off in all directions.

We had planned a trip to Nepal during winter break, but the December war intervened and we cancelled our plans. However, a small group did go trekking there, their goal the base camp at Annapurna. Part of the challenge of their trip was "living off the land"; that is, they depended on the villagers to sell them food and furnish them with supplies.

When school began in February, we asked the trekkers to share their mountain-top experience with us, so they invited the staff to a Nepalese banquet and an evening of slides, all for Rs. 2.50 (35 cents) per person. When we arrived at the dining hall, we were asked to be seated on the floor. We were curious about what kind of delicacy was bubbling in the barrels that had been split in half and were now suspended over charcoal fires. We could smell only boiled potatoes. Then for half an hour while we became hungry enough to eat anything, our hosts regaled us with anecdotes of their cooking skills.

Finally came the banquet. As the comedian says, the jokes were depressing but the food was hilarious. Cooking in the barrels were small potatoes about the size of walnuts. These were scooped into large bowls and set before us along with side dishes of salt and pepper. We were taught the trick of slipping the skins with our thumbs and popping the potatoes into our mouths in one smooth motion, a trick at which the trekkers were already adept. Tea was also served. That was the menu. Our hosts explained that this had been their diet during several weeks of trekking. As a peace offering, they brought out apple pie. In vain we demanded our money back. We were given left-over potato marbles to carry home in whatever doggy bags we could improvise.

The *piece de resistance* of the Nepalese banquet was the after-dinner program. The slides were worth the price of admission: pictures of brilliant sky, ice-covered mountains, veils of blowing snow, emerald green valleys, the trekkers who looked like Lilliputians set in a Brobdingnagian background, the Nepalese people who inhabit those defiant mountains, coolies who ran uphill, suspicious hoteliers who had to be persuaded to trust the Westerners who wanted to bunk with everybody else in the one sleeping room.

Like pictures of India, those of Nepal showed us the slick, glamorous aspect of the country. Nepal is indeed beautiful; it is indeed impoverished, exploited by rulers as well as by conquerors. Deforestation has caused much of it to wash away into its rivers; the same diseases that ravage India are present there. Nepal needs simple technology, basic community health programs, a more complete highway system, and an economic structure that makes better use of its resources.

Dick Wechter, the math teacher, asked if I wanted to visit the Mushroom Lady who had quite a business of growing and selling mushrooms. Dick wanted to buy fresh ones, but all she had at the time were the tinned ones which she sold wholesale. I was surprised to find that the Mushroom Lady was a red-haired Hungarian, married to an Indian from a royal family, now associated, if I remember correctly, with the army. Their house was a museum. Royal families often hoarded beautiful heirlooms as a hedge against devaluation of the rupee. Mr. Lal said that the family treasures, though priceless, had lost much of their value when the government passed a law that all antiques had to be registered and could be sold only to the government. The Lals would not be able to get the price for them that they could have received on the open market. We left, with Dick promising to deliver tulip bulbs and pick up mushrooms when Mrs. Lal had a new crop.

I did not know many Indian women apart from the Woodstock staff. When I attended Rotary as Walt's guest, I had difficulty making conversation with the women. I tried to joke with my dentist's wife, saying I had not really enjoyed my visit to his office, but she seemed to take me seriously. Mrs. Singh, who ran a Montessori school, was easy to talk to and I would have been interested in her experiences, but she was a busy woman and we lived at opposite ends of the town. When Sadiq's wife visited, a friendly, motherly woman, Sadiq presented her with good-mannered formality, but we did not have a common language. I don't think Mr. Abinandan's wife would have accepted an invitation to our house.

I look back on my efforts at entertaining in India with regret that I didn't try harder. I heard an international development authority say that one of the principles of development is "If it is worth doing, it is worth doing badly." Badly in this case means doing it as well as you can, even if your effort is inadequate by your own standards.

At Woodstock School, Christmas was celebrated just before Going Down Day. The maintenance crew installed a tree in the corner of the balcony of the Quad, and then concerts, banquets, and farewells followed. The real Christmas for school children happened in their homes. Although we usually went to our mission field in Madhaya Pradesh sometime during the break, we spent a number of Christmases at the school.

We asked the luckri wallah who supplied wood for our stove if he could find a nice pine branch that we could decorate. We knew that cutting a tree was illegal. Well, anything for the burra sahib. Delivered to us was a ten-foot pine, overwhelming and embarrassing us. Walt's birthday was coming up, so we had the tree moved to the study hall and invited everyone left on the Hillside to a tree-trimming party. We provided the popcorn for stringing and can lids and bits of foil from candy bars and the tinseled strings that girls tie around their brothers' wrists on Rakhi holidays.

That was the year that Janet Starr decorated the Brocade Room with ivy and ferns from the Hillside and added gold and silver snowflakes made from someone's precious foil wrap. In this setting, Bill Starr led us in a formal Christmas Eve communion service. Surprisingly, the formality seemed to affirm the physical and emotional closeness we felt. The British, Texas, Southern, and Midwestern accents were no barrier. We were touched by Dixie Roelof's thanksgiving prayer for her first-born, and we felt a kinship with Mary and Joseph as they rejoiced in the birth of their son, knowing that tribulation comes to all born into this world, but not really believing that it will come to this perfect child.

The gifts we gave each other were not hard to find. Doma, the Tibetan wallah, always had brassware and jewelry that we coveted; and there were enough different kinds of shawls for every gift-giving occasion.

India is the country of shepherd boys, camels, poinsettias, jewels, and little villages that look the same as they must have looked in Bible times. It is a country where giving and receiving are important to both the giver and receiver. We wish we could say it is a country of peace, but it was not when we were there, although the people we knew were just as interested in peace on earth as those anywhere else we have lived.

In a land that loves fireworks, Americans observed the Fourth of July with ear-shattering gusto. It is not a school holiday because Woodstock is an international school. Nevertheless, every child of every nation got to know that American Independence Day was for shooting Roman candles and sprays of colored stars into the rain.

At Ridgewood, the young boys' dormitory, we watched from the road above as the fountains of rockets sizzled up into the black sky. Then the huge bonfire was lit and sparklers were handed out to the children. Someone, either dorm parents or pranksters, had planted firecrackers in the bonfire so that it blazed and exploded at intervals, a fine American celebration to delight the international gathering. An alumni wrote:

> We were asked to use some discretion in our celebration of the Fourth since some of the descendants of those early British oppressors were our peers at the school. In the early years of Woodstock, a certain amount of tension existed between English and American children. But on one point they were agreed: they would have liked a school holiday declared for the Fourth of July, and the English girls goaded the Americans into going to the principal to ask for it. And our request was always refused, always with the same patient explanation: "The Fourth of July is an *American* holiday. We could not possibly keep it in India. What would the British think? It would be a slap in the face to them."
>
> "They want it too!" the girls would murmur parenthetically.[41]

India observes its own Independence Day on August 15. Indians, like Americans, were celebrating their freedom from British rule. A flag raising ceremony was attended by the entire student body as well as by staff and employees. At noon the employees prepared a meal for themselves to which we were invited. The evening meal was a large Indian banquet for all the school, followed by a program of Indian music, dancing, and drama.

Indian Christians joined us in our celebration of Easter and Christmas, but the Hindus and Muslims had their own holidays. More than once we went to the bazaar to do business, only to find the shops closed down for a religious holiday. The hill villagers observed still other holidays.

Republic Day on January 26, another national holiday, marks the anniversary of the adoption of India's constitution in 1950. The colorful four days of festivities in New Delhi draw people from all over the country for the parades and pageants. We were never brave enough to become part of the mob, but in 1972 we participated by way of Vic Reimer's slides of the twenty-fifth anniversary celebration of India's independence.

The Republic Day parade must be the model by which other parades are measured. All that was missing was a platoon of seventy-six trombones. After the fly-by of the air force, the army display on the ground included an array of conventional equipment and uniforms, a band of Scottish bagpipers, and a company of drummers in tiger skins. The cavalry sent in its horses, a cavalcade of camels, and a line of elephants decorated with bright colorwash. Floats from every region showed off the people; many troupes danced by in costume. What other country has such variety of people? Certainly, not all the participants in the parade spoke the Hindi language of their national anthem.

The parade wound down Rajpath (Path of the Kings) and past the grandstand to be reviewed by the nation's leaders. Taps sounded at sunset and the Christian hymn "Abide with Me," taught by the British generations ago, was part of the Beating of Retreat, when the flag was lowered in the presence of the President. Even when viewed on slides, it was an emotionally moving ceremony. It included traditions going back to Akbar as well as those of the British Raj, a blending of the ancient with the old to honor the new India.

Chapter 19

Wordwise

The lecturer for the travel series knew his color photography but not his Hindi pronunciation. Rajpath Road rhymed with badge pat, Agra with Niagara. Say these words: Rahjput, Ahgrah, Mahatma Gahndhi, Punjahb, Rahjustahn.

Not only were the sounds of Hindi of interest to us while we were in India, but also the picturesque metaphors of other English-speaking nationalities. We Unraus speak a broad American mixture of mid-Kansas and northern Indiana with just a touch of Oklahoma drawl. In the Ladies' Staff Room the Scottish, Australian, New Zealand, and Texas accents took some getting used to.

Missionary Harold Ratzlaff tells of attending language school for missionaries with an Australian woman. She greeted him on his first appearance after a week of illness with "Howja fail to die?"

Taken aback to be asked why he hadn't passed over, he quickly sorted through the vowels and realized that she had asked, "How do you feel today?" Another Australian missionary preached dramatically of the "wild wives" washing over the ship when the apostle Paul experienced a storm at sea. The interpreter, puzzled but dutiful, translated, "Those jungly women took over the boat."

Students from abroad brought the current slang to add to the babel. Indian students and teachers spoke with a British accent, having learned English from teachers whose ancestors had learned it from pukka Englishmen. Susan and Paula picked up babu English, the accent of the Indian clerk and merchant that is a combination of Hindi and English. Both Western and Indian students mimic each other hilariously.

Understandably, the language of India has been influenced by the different conquerors for whom the subcontinent became a military and linguistic cul-de-sac. Fifteen national languages had developed before the English added the sixteenth. The Aryan invasion from 2000 to 1500 B.C. brought languages that when synthesized with original dialects created the Sanskrit language, a remote relative to most of the languages of Europe. It is the classical language of India, the Latin of the school child, and very complex. The Muslim invasion which began about 1000 A.D. brought in the Persian influence. The vernacular in North India is Hindustani. Two literary languages have emerged from it: Hindi, considered the language of the educated Hindus, and Urdu, the language of educated Muslims, derived from Hindi but incorporating Arabic and Persian influences. The two are dissimilar in written form. Hindi is a Devangari script that hangs its letters on a straight line, but Urdu uses the Persian alphabet with flowing curves that move from right to left. Sadiq, our cook, wrote his recipes and marketing lists in Urdu. Although the Urdu language is looked down on as a language of the military camp, its correct use is considered an accomplishment. The village people spoke one of the Pahari dialects, related to other dialects used by Himalayan villagers.

The country was named by the Persians who called it Hind. Then the French came in who had no sound for the h and wrote it as Inde. The British changed that to India, but the Indian name for the country is Bharat, from the Sanskrit.

Because the British needed English-speaking clerks, they saw to it that English was taught in the schools. Now English and Hindi are the official national languages; but there are 225 distinct languages and 600 dialects in India, or 845 or 872, depending on your authority. A box of powdered drink gave instructions for its preparation in eleven languages.

English was to have lost its official status and been replaced by Hindi in 1965, according to the 1950 Constitution. That objective proved to be impractical. Hindi is a North Indian language and foreign to the southern states that did not accept it. Today English continues to be required in the upper grades of public schools and is usually the language of instruction in universities. It is a requirement for many top-level government posts, especially for interstate communication. English has in effect become the *lingua franca* for the country.

English has borrowed some 900 words from Hindi and other Indian sources. Examples are bungalow, verandah, path, dungaree, chintz, khaki, calico, gingham, cummerbund, shampoo, and punch (from panch, meaning five, the number of ingredients in the drink). The word posh was contributed by the well-to-do who could choose their cabins on the voyage to and from India: they avoided the heat by booking cabins on the port side going out and on the starboard when returning to England. Thus, port-out, starboard-home, and you were posh.

We early became aware of the Landour Language School, even though we were not a part of it. Most missionaries were required to learn Hindi before they were assigned to mission stations. Now the school offers intensive courses for college students who are pursuing research in India.

A doctor will chafe at sitting in a classroom learning the language when she thinks she should be out there saving bodies, and the evangelist will chafe because he thinks he should be out there saving souls. The firm rule that missionaries must learn the language before attempting a vocation is important to the success of the work and the morale of the worker. The shining model for all Hindi language students is Dr. William Carey, missionary in Bengal from 1793 to 1834. He wrote dictionaries, translations, and grammars in Hindi and translated the Bible into Bengali, Oriya, Marathi, Hindi, Assamese, and Sanskrit. He was broadminded enough to translate the Hindu epic, the *Ramayana*, into English. Literally, he had the gift of tongues.

A learned scholar can be humbled to find how ineffective he is with the language during his first attempts. Missionary J.A. Ressler told of a colleague who had delivered what he supposed was an understandable sermon in the dialect of the area. A kindly Indian church leader in his closing prayer thanked the Father for having sent so wise and good a missionary to them; but, he added, "Teach him quickly to speak our language, for you know we do not understand English."

There are comic examples of the Westerner using the wrong word of his newly-learned vocabulary. Others have to do with the lack of communication between employer and servant. Vernelle Waltner tells of her tea cozy, that necessary little bonnet with which the hostess smothers the teapot to keep it hot. Vernelle had received a pretty embroidered cozy for her birthday. Soon after when Dr. Gass visited, she asked the khansama in Hindi to use her best china teapot and put the cozy on. Which he did. He brought in the teapot at the proper time, wearing the cozy on his head. The Waltners and Dr. Gass restrained themselves until the khansama had retired to the kitchen. Dr. Gass used the story often, and it became known all over that part of India.

What about us Unraus? Did we return to the States speaking Hindi? I taught classes in English to English-speaking students. All the men in Walt's office spoke English, as did the merchants. Our problems in communication were due to culture rather than language.

Of course we picked up words that are necessary for survival in India. Some of them were such good words that it took us a long time to eliminate them from our vocabulary. I throw a few Hindi words into this manuscript now and then because there may not be a good synonym in English, or I like the sound of the word, or using Hindi makes me feel internationally ept.

We liked the word *aachchaa*, spoken with the accent on the last syllable, as in a strong sneeze. Like a sneeze, it has an infinite variety of intonations. It can be a short, excited, "Yes, I agree," or a rising and falling crescendo of sympathy or understanding. It can mean anything from "I'm listening," to "Isn't that perfectly wonderful!" The superlative of aachchaa is *shabash*, "You have my unbounded admiration."

Then there is the word *buss*, Hindi for enough. The girls used it to indicate that I had filled their teacup full enough, and I used it to stop an argument. "*Koi bat nahi*" is accompanied by a shrug and means. "Never mind, it doesn't matter." The word for "thank you" is *dhanyavad*, but Indians think Americans overuse it. You don't thank people for what they should do as a matter of courtesy. I have used the word *khud*, meaning the face of a cliff, and *pukka* (or pucka or pucca), meaning ripe, solid, but is expanded to mean good, genuine. The opposite is *kutcha*, used to describe something raw or crude, poorly made or half finished. A pukka building is made with bricks, meant to last. A kutcha road is temporary or so poorly built that it will wash away in the next monsoon. A *godown* is a storage room, and *chits* are sent around in the absence of the telephone.

One of the words that I wish were in the English vocabulary is *tamasha*. The sound expresses what it means: a spectacle, an excitement, a pageant. The colloquial use means a fuss or commotion. You listen to a violent argument, or you are part of an event that doesn't go as planned, and you say, "What a tamasha!" I also like the sounds of *ulta pulta* (upside down), *ranga panga* (naked), *nutcut* (little rascal), and *badmash* (big rascal). You may find these words spelled differently by other authors. We are all spelling phonetically when we go from Hindi to English.

When Paula was in fifth grade, I learned to count with her, ache, doe, teen, char, panch, but I used memory devices: back ache, bread dough, teen age. When a man on the road asked the time, I had to debate whether it was back or ache o'clock. I suppose the man wondered at his bad luck in asking someone who could not tell time.

When we returned to India for a three-year term, we were determined to learn the language. We signed up with Brij Lal to take three weeks of language study during the winter break, meeting two hours a day. I looked forward to the experience. I had done well with high school Latin some thirty years before. I probably had a natural affinity for languages, I told myself. I wanted to learn the language so well that I could have fun with puns and jokes.

I was doomed to linguistic oblivion in Hindi. We learned the alphabet and a vocabulary of about three hundred words and all about the preposition and the postposition. I found the study very difficult, some of it sheer drudgery, some of it humiliation. I could have five problems with a three-word sentence. If the girls had not kept correcting my pronunciation, I would have practiced more at home. How, they asked, had I ever learned English?

We don't use much Hindi at home these days. Oh, we throw in a tamasha here and there, and it is hard to find a good English word for pukka. But we have stopped saying aachchaa and shabash.

A Japanese student once said to me, "The number of languages a person speaks is the number of times she is a person." I am, alas, only one person.

At our first Woodstock School retreat, the suggestion was made, not by me, that to improve morale, interested staff members should form a poetry club.

I do not consider myself a poet, but I have a fondness for rhythm and metaphor. Whenever I am singing Happy Birthday, I become anxious about how to get the honoree's name into the music with the correct meter. I had little interest in hobnobbing with poets who take poetry seriously. When the poetry club was organized, I was expected to be a member; and because I do those things that people assume I will do, I went to the first meeting, intending to tell them that poetry was not my forte. Only five or six of us had responded to the call, and I decided that those enthusiastic few needed my body in a chair in the circle, so I continued going.

The poetry writers of Woodstock were a demanding group. We met weekly, and we always gave ourselves an assignment. Sometimes we took on a verse form; sometimes we wrote according to subject, such as animals or sunsets or the sea. The assignments may sound uncreative, but the poetry was not. We had models to emulate, poets whose work had been published, particularly Myra Scoval and Mary Esther Burgoyne.

Poetry Club met at four on Thursday, and I would be reminded of it during my last typing class of the day. While the students pounded away on the quick brown fox, I frantically called forth my Muse to tackle sunsets and sonnets. I took many an unfinished symphony of words to those meetings. In Mrs. Burgoyne's living room, with her khansama serving tea and cookies, we read each other's unsigned poems and wrote criticism. Some of the criticism was helpful; all of it was kind. It is hard to tell a poet that her idea has been expressed before, immeasurably better. On the other hand, if it is a new idea to the poet and she (all of us were she) receives satisfaction in expressing it, well, shabash!

Eileen Ferguson, the French teacher, sometimes took unfair advantage of us by writing poems in French. They sounded beautiful, but for all we knew, she could have been reading from the French Congressional Record.

The club lasted for one semester. I have not since written a poem a week. I'm glad, though, that I was compelled to write a poem about the sea. A college student set my Emily Dickinsonian piece to John Denverish music (even the Bible says there is nothing new under the sun), and I felt temporarily immortalized when my sea-of-wheat poem was sung at a college festival.

In India we became aware of books and writers that we would not have heard of at home. R.K. Narayan is a South Indian who set his novels in the town of Malgudi. His people are ordinary: the financial expert, the English teacher, the bachelor of arts, the sweet vendor. He wrote uncomplicated fiction about real people. My introduction to the bloodbath of the Partition was *A Bend in the Ganges* by Manohar Malgonkar. The independence of India was achieved through non-violence, but the Partition was not. Kushwant Singh's *Train to Pakistan* is also about the Partition and my choice of the two novels. Nirad C. Chaudhuri is considered by some other writers as the best Indian writer in English. The Indian Renaissance Man, he has an astonishing breadth of subject matter. *Continent of Circe* was new when we were in India in 1965. "An essay on the people of India" is fascinating, enlightening, encyclopedic, controversial, humorous, and infuriating to many Indians. Ruth Prawer Jhabvala is a current writer of novels and screen plays, not an Indian but married to one. She perceptively portrays foreigners in India as alien and estranged and dependent on each other. These were current authors during our time in India, and I have since read with pleasure Anita Desai and Rohinton Mistry.

Occasionally I see short pieces by Ruskin Bond in the *Christian Science Monitor*. We met Mr. Bond at a dinner and I immediately started thinking in terms of a Ruskin Bond Day for all English classes with a special luncheon at noon. He agreed to come, but Ruskin Bond Day never materialized. We asked our lion to roar, but he would not. He sent a chit shortly before the event to say he would not be in Mussoorie on that day. A friend who knew him better said that Mr. Bond, a shy man, is not a speaking writer. He must be one of the few literary figures who has never been on a talk show.

Along with their devotional literature, the Muslims have preserved proverbs and humor of the Sufis, the seers of their religion. The history of these wise men goes back for centuries, but some of the classic stories seem contemporary. People have always laughed at the same situations.

The Sufis probably did not have the word for it, but they did know what committee work was like: "Tie two birds together. They will not be able to fly, even though they now have four wings."

We say, "To do nothing is to make a decision." The Sufi said, "We wrote a hundred letters, and you did not write an answer. This, too, is a reply."[42]

Sometimes we subscribed to the *Times of India* and sometimes to the *Statesman* or *Hindustani Times*, depending on which one the newspaper wallah wanted us to have. We had to admire the vocabulary of these newspapers, the platitudinous acknowledgment, the expired mother who left for her heavenly abode, the dilatory Uttar Pradesh government. Wrongdoers were always miscreants. Diplomats acted with elan. A bank clerk was accused of defalcation. Cricket players were known for their eclat. Congress made a retrograde move. Some words sent us running to the unabridged dictionary. Pakistan had resiled from its threat to quit the Commonwealth. The scrammel voices of the unemployed were heard. The crowd was maficking on Republic Day. People and committees were often flayed for bad judgment.

Commodities seemed to be physically active. The markets didn't just go up and down. Groundnut (peanut) oil spurted or hardened or firmed up. Coconut oil flared up or drifted lower. Wheat sagged, jute traded dull. Some commodities were mentally ill at times: hedge castor was better, mustard oil was subdued, pulses were depressed but moong was easy.

The English newspapers did not ordinarily run comic strips. The Laxman political cartoon in *Times of India* was popular, and the Sunday edition ran a page of color funnies. Dennis the Menace and Beetle Bailey were popular; little kids and army privates can make people laugh anywhere in the world. In a Hindi language newspaper with a Bumstead's comic, I could easily follow the story line, but I was startled to see Hindi characters ballooning from the mouths of Blondie and Dagwood.

Even the advertising was educational. Mundane articles like thermos bottles, shampoo, garlic pearls, and soap were well covered. New in the last ten years were ads for fitness and weight control centers and advertisements against smoking. Eicher Tractors of India, Ltd., ran a public service ad entitled, "Keep Delhi Clean": "It has been determined that a speck of dirt, however small, can be the precursor of a grave disease for yourself and those around you."

A grave disease sounds very determinating.

Chapter 20

The Villages

Mahatma Gandhi said, "I have believed and repeated times without number that India is to be found not in its few cities but in its 700,000 villages." The number by now may be closer to 900,000.

Armies from the North have invaded India, and traders from the West have exploited it. Kings, emperors, and maharajahs have built states and cities. All the while, villagers have observed and endured. Even today, the village is the social unit of India.

Writers about India give equal time to village beauty and village poverty. The sight of women winnowing is one of the most pleasing in the Indian countryside. They stand tall, holding their *soupas* above their heads.

> Like the opening movement of a dance, when from stationary feet movement would shiver upward and end in the finger-tips, these women would gently tilt the trays with quivering movement into the wind and shake them like bells. The wind would sweep the chaff while the grain fell into a heap below.[43]

Another attractive picture is that of the graceful Indian woman carrying water. "As every Italian artist of the Renaissance painted the Madonna and Child, so all Indian artists . . . have painted the Indian woman with brass pitchers on her head returning from the river."[44] And perhaps everyone with a camera takes the same picture. On my bulletin board at Woodstock I tacked a picture of women returning from the well, their colorful saris blowing, their brass vessels balanced on their heads. The picture was the winning photograph in a contest of an American magazine. We saw this same picture from our train window whenever we traveled to the plains, women walking along the narrow banks of rice fields, talking and laughing, stopping to look at our train, one lifting a foot to remove a thorn, all without spilling a drop.

The simple life of the village is extoled, and the cow dust haze of evening is much admired. The *Vedas* describe an age when everyone, the poor and the rich, had plenty to eat, and the peasant returned from his fields each day with a song in his heart.

We tried to imagine that long-ago time when we visited a village. Each path that branches off from Tehri Road ends in a village somewhere behind a hill. One might look out over the Tehri hills with their terraces of corn, barley, mustard, potatoes, onions, and a few fruit trees and think only of the beauty of the scene; but life for the villager is not simple; it is a long struggle, especially if he lives in a remote crease of the hills with no dispensary to treat accidents to man and animal. Even so, the mountain villagers come closer to the good life than do many of the plains dwellers.

I cannot believe in the benign effects of poverty. I concluded that the picture of the simple peasant, the happy villager, is a myth. I have heard an environmentalist hold up the Indian society as a model that makes do with what surrounds it, using buffalo chips for fuel, linoleum, and salve; being self-sufficient with sun power for warmth and wind power for blowing chaff from grain. But Indian farmers work from sunrise to sunset and longer, with a plodding, unresting pace that our forefathers might have endured but few Westerners today would tolerate. Non-materialism as a way of life should be a choice and not a predestination.

The rhododendron hike took us near a village with the fictitious name of Sirkanda. Gerald Berreman, a sociologist,[45] chose this village to study because it was typical of villages in the area. The people are Paharis, kin to the five million mountain people of the lower Himalayas from Kashmir through Nepal.

Fewer than five hundred people live in Sirkanda, which is accessible only by foot or horse. It is about six miles from the nearest road and bus service. Some adults in Sirkanda have never been to Dehra Dun, about ten air miles from their village. Their contacts with outsiders, police and tax collectors, had made them wary of strangers.

The villagers rotate their crops, grown in small terraced plots, some of which they leave to fallow for a year or two. There is little hunger among hill dwellers. For the most part they eat what they grow, but the milk is sold as raw milk, butter, or ghee, much of it in Mussoorie, especially during the summer season. Every housewife in Mussoorie knows (assumes) that once the milk reaches the edge of town, it is fortified with water from the tap to make an adequate supply. Buffalo milk is preferred in the bazaar, but the villagers prefer cow's milk. They reason that if you drink too much buffalo milk you get buffalo wisdom: you become stupid.

We saw the village women and children on the school campus in their never-ending task of gathering wild grasses and leaves for their animals. They gather wood for fuel rather than burning manure, which they use for fertilizer. Plains farmers, on the other hand, use manure for fuel since there is so little wood available.

Suakholi is the trading center for the village where farmers bring their produce to be trucked to Mussoorie and Dehra Dun. A shop in Sirkanda sells cigarettes, matches, kerosene, cooking oil, sugar, salt, spices, and tea. It is within this area that one can find all castes and occupational specialists necessary to the economy. Everything is within half a day's journey. The postman comes occasionally, but letters can be mailed whenever someone goes to the valley. In the 1970s, the maximum village education for the men was five years.

The houses are substantial. Many are two-storied with the family occupying the second floor, the animals the first. Furnishings are sparse. A hearth for cooking in brass and iron pots, a wooden churn, wooden vessels for storage, and baskets that we admired and bought when hillmen came around with them. They used small lamps for lighting and string cots for beds. Since there are not enough beds for everyone, blankets are spread on the floor.

Water is a quarter of a mile off by way of a rough, steep trail over a ridge. Berreman quoted an Indian woman as saying as she lifted a heavy water pot to her head, "I'd like to set fire to the beard of the man that founded this village here."

Hill villages are apt to be scatterings of small clusters of six to ten families under one panchayat, the governmental unit. They are often isolated from government aid programs, or if it is a block program, it will be plains oriented and considered irrelevant by the Paharis.

Some aspects of hill villages have changed since Berreman did his research there. The farmers have added other crops and their produce goes as far as Delhi. More men wear Western clothes, and most of them now wear shoes, albeit plastic. Most of the dudh wallahs have horses or ponies to haul their milk over the mountain paths. Everyone still works hard and few of the children attend school, but the transistor radio has come to the hill village, and with it mass communication. Now it is movie music that one hears more than flute playing or mule bells. With the better road, small trucks have taken the place of mules. People can now depend on a daily bus within six miles of a village. School employees who live beyond Tehri City can now reach home in less than a day rather than two days.

Village development is becoming more effective as villagers themselves become involved in listing their problems and working on the solutions. Robert Alter, Presbyterian missionary and former Woodstock principal, was associate director of village development activities in Chamasari, a collection of fourteen settlements scattered over twenty-five square miles below Tehri Road. In 1983 it had no schools, no water supply system, no irrigation schemes, no roads below Tehri, no health-care facilities, no electricity, and no veterinary service. On our last visit in 1993, the community was inaugurating the new water system that was to pipe water to some of the settlements. The occasion was one of ceremony and deserved self-congratulation: this was a project for which they had supplied the labor, with financial help for the pipe. After Alter's retirement, a young Indian woman, educated in the U.S., took over the position.

The Paharis have a reputation for honesty, Robert Alter told us. However, at the time of the Partition when the Mussoorie town authorities suddenly decided to round up all Muslims to take them to the safety of Rampur House in Dehra Dun, an ugly incident occurred. The Muslims had no time to make arrangements for their businesses, and all they could do was leave them locked but unprotected. The word quickly spread that the Muslims had departed. That night the Paharis streamed in from the hills, looted the shops, and in the morning hurried back to their villages carrying piles of merchandise.

An old villager watched them, tears coursing down his face. He said, "We Paharis don't do this kind of thing." He was right. The Paharis do, in fact, pride themselves on their honesty. They don't lock their houses, and they are the last suspected in case of burglaries.

Many of the sweepers, bearers, and cooks at Woodstock School come from the Tehri Hills, leaving their wives and children home to farm with the joint family until the employee is in a position to establish a home in school housing. Separation of families is a common custom, but the school is building more and more housing to alleviate this situation. One of the Indian supervisors at the school described the background of these employees. They come from responsible families and own land. Most of them are semi-educated; that is, they can read and write. They are improving their homes and educating their children.

The villages we visited on the plains had a different look from those we saw in the hills. Appearances change according to the season: after the monsoon, the mud walls are pitted and crumbling, the courtyards smelling of mud and manure. With the coming of the mild winter, the walls are repaired and even decorated with drawings. In some villages, neat, narrow sand lanes run between the homes, and the children crowding around us are clothed and combed. In other villages the lanes and the children look uncared-for. Our missionary friends suggested that the well-kept appearance is characteristic of Christian villages, and even non-Christians agree that this is more than just a self-serving assessment.

In a village near Dehra Dun we watched the winnowing of rice. The threshing floor was from Bible times. The women tossed the grain in a soupa, a willow basket scoop, to let the chaff blow out. But the wind was modern. An electric fan stood on a stool and was hooked by a long wire to an outlet somewhere. The stiff breeze was consistent and effective.

Victor Zorza, a political columnist, came to Mussoorie to write about the Indian village. "I wasted a lot of time looking for the 'typical village.' Yet no such thing exists. Conditions vary too widely. But the villages I stayed in had much in common—poverty, dirt, ignorance, exploitation."[47]

We saw a few model villages that demonstrated Mahatma Gandhi's vision of the happy community: where the children play in the warm sun while their mothers wash clothes at the village well and pound grain in stone mortars; where the smells of dung and spices and wood smoke mingle pleasantly; where the yards are tidy and the mud huts with thatched or tile roofs look inviting; where the floors are leeped to a fine glaze with a solution of cow dung and water.

From the 1920 Quadrangle we have this report of students on a walking tour to Chakrata, a village west of Mussoorie:

> Lakhwar village, which we passed a mile beyond the bungalow, was most picturesque. Houses very like Swiss chalets, with carved wooden balconies and gables, were embowered in a grove of walnut trees.
>
> The Lakhwar women are famous for their beauty, and we certainly noticed some charmingly pretty girls. They wore brilliant handkerchiefs on their heads, and full skirts, and little velvet jackets. We photographed a group of them clustering round a spring with their big brass jars.

I keep thinking of the home of the school dhobi where we were invited to help celebrate his young son's auspicious birthday. The small room was dark and grim. On the rough, uncovered table was an aqua plastic tumbler with one red plastic rose, the only "pretty" spot in the room. Do the marvelous views of the hills that surround the villagers make up for the lack of the good things that we consider necessities?

Chapter 21

British India: The Raj and the Rajahs

W oodstock School is to some extent set apart and above the Indian scene, but both the shadow and the dazzle of the British Raj have reached it.

We heard a nostalgia for the Raj when we listened to old men and women compare the then and now. We saw vestiges of it in the architecture, the names of buildings and businesses, the churches, and people, both British and Anglo-Indian. We enjoyed the achievements of the Raj when we rode the railroad, and, though we took it for granted, we benefited from its language when we could get along almost anywhere in India with our American-English tongues. We missed the heyday of the Raj by about a century.

For most of the sixteenth century the Portuguese controlled what commerce there was with India, with the Dutch making persistent inroads. When the Dutch raised the price of pepper by five shillings a pound in 1599, a group of English traders with a charter from Queen Elizabeth I formed the East India Company to find another source. It was the Mogul emperor Jehangir in Agra who in 1609 gave Captain William Hawkins permission to buy land and operate factories. The English ships carried spices, gum, sugar, raw silk, and cotton back to England and returned with English goods eagerly sought by the growing number of colonials and by prodigal Indian princes. The East India Company owners did very well.

(It may puzzle modern cooks why spices played such an important role in the history of two nations. In Elizabethan times, cattle had to be slaughtered each fall since there was no method to feed them over the winter. Spices were necessary to act as preservatives as well as disguise the taste of tainted meat.)

The British went to India as traders, not as conquerors. But as the British extended their activities, they found resistance from the troublesome Indian rulers who owned the property on which they operated. The British defended their interests by military strength. Governors-general, almost inadvertently, extended political authority state by state and petty kingdom by petty kingdom. Some governors misused their positions to build fortunes.

The administration of Lord William Bentinck (1828-1835) was one of reform and peace. The benefits to the Indians were imitations of the British legal, administrative, and educational systems; the railroads and canals; and the English language. The British Raj brought stability but not prosperity to India. Lord Dalhousie continued Bentinck's reforms with a public works that built a telegraph and postal network and roads, including the famous Grand Trunk Highway from northwest India to Calcutta that Kipling used so graphically in his stories.

In spite of British achievements, revolution was brewing, and it culminated in the Mutiny of 1857, the massacre of hundreds of British subjects by Indian soldiers. Because of the loyalty of a few of the important maharajahs, the English were able to crush the uprising. The Mutiny marked the end of the Honorable East India Company. In 1858, Queen Victoria became responsible for the 300 million Indians.

The golden age of the Raj, the four decades following the Mutiny, saw the refinement of the legal system, a system of self-government, and a system for coping with the periodic famines. These reforms, while they increased the bureaucracy, did not prepare the Indians for self-rule, although the intention even of the East India Company had been to relinquish domination eventually.[48]

We will skip to the Independence of 1947 with only a few comments. Collins and Lapierre suggest that one of the causes of the decline of British interest in India was the decimation of young Englishmen in World War I. Those who survived the war were not interested in careers in India, and Indians came to be accepted more readily in the ranks of the Indian Civil Service and the Indian army officer corps.[49]

"The hundred and eighty years of British rule in India were just one of the unhappy interludes in her long story; she would find herself again," Jawaharlal Nehru wrote in 1946.[50]

The departure of the British left India with problems that had little to do with the British presence: the tyranny of the money lender, the repressive caste system, the corruption in the bureaucracy, unchecked population growth, and uneven distribution of wealth.

At this point the reader is invited to read long or short histories of India. We, however, will go on to more entertaining details of the British Raj, some of which relate at least marginally to life in a hill station.

What was life like for these often reluctant conquerors, particularly for the women? If your husband enjoyed a high level of responsibility, you would find yourself supplied with servants, entertained or entertaining non-stop, and often bored to exhaustion. One of the continuing themes of the poetry of the Raj was of exile: a terrible nostalgia for the green fields, the simple flowers, and the soft rains of home.[51] Taking an interest in India was not fashionable. Social service was not an option unless the reigning burra memsahib approved.

Another difficulty was educating the children. Very young children were sent "home" to live at boarding schools that catered especially to colonial "orphans." Raleigh Trevelyan wrote, "To me the whole experience of my life between the ages of eight and fourteen seems now to be summed up by a sentence that I was supposed not to have overheard: 'It's your turn to have Raleigh for Christmas.'"[52]

Lady Canning, wife of Viceroy Charles Canning, appreciated the advent of American traders, finding them "valuable creatures" for bringing ice, apples, and novels, items otherwise not available.[53] As the hot season approached, wives and children moved to hill stations, where social life took on an often frantic pace.

A number of Victorian women left records of their years in India.

The Honorable Emily Eden, sister and hostess of Lord Auckland, governor-general from 1836 to 1842, came reluctantly and remained unenchanted. She could not understand why anyone would want to come to India when they could stay home, even to take in washing, in a comfortable attic room with a fireplace and a wooden floor.[54] With her sister Fanny, she arrived in India on her thirty-ninth birthday and never ceased wanting to go home again. Although she was an unwilling traveler, she accompanied her brother on his tours, one of which was eighteen months. She sketched ruins and held court with her brother, gathering material for her book *Up the Country*, published in 1866.

Fanny Parks came to India in 1822 as the wife of a customs collector in the East India Company's service. She lived there for more than twenty years and wrote *Wanderings of a Pilgrim in Search of the Picturesque*, published in 1850. The book had a small edition and should be reprinted. She wrote with humor and flair.[55] Fanny was not the conventional memsahib in that she seemed to enjoy every aspect of the Indian experience, from hog hunting to climbing the Himalayas. For a time, she joined the Edens, undaunted by their rather cool reception.[56]

Lady Charlotte Canning was another of the reluctant ones who came out with her husband when he was appointed governor-general in 1856. On the list of governors-general and viceroys, Lord Canning was considered one of the more enlightened. Charlotte Canning had been lady-in-waiting to Queen Victoria, and she kept a lively correspondence with the Queen. Lady Canning, longing to return to England and to her relatives and her Queen, made a short tour to Darjeeling. She contracted the dreaded "remittent fever" and returned to Calcutta to die just before the Cannings' scheduled departure.

Flora Annie Steel learned Hindustani and enjoyed inspection tours with her husband. She was co-author of *The Complete Indian Housekeeper and Cook*, dedicated to and much appreciated by "English girls to whom Fate may assign the task of being Housemothers in our Eastern Empire." The book includes everything every woman in India wanted to know, including such esoteric information as the best way of making snipe pudding, how much cornmeal to give to the hens per day, and how to cure the squeak in a punkah. Most of this advice was intended for the women at lonely stations who, unlike Lady Canning, had to cope with everyday problems of existence. Her most useful advice went unheeded: the memsahib should learn Hindustani.[57]

From this digression of the British Raj as it was lived on the plains, and before returning to our Mussoorie hill station, I will insert a note about Simla, that most glamorous of hill stations.

Although 1,170 miles from Calcutta, Simla was the official capital of
the British Raj and the Punjab government. Most British wives were
revived by its pleasant air and whirl of dinners, dances, and garden
parties. Emily Eden considered it the only place in India really worth
all the trouble of getting there. She did complain about the fleas and
the monkeys in the bazaar. While his sister was being "uncommon-
ly gay," Lord Auckland, was agonizing over whether or not to invade
Afghanistan.[58]

Lady Canning did not like Simla but thought the deodars were
fine. To her artistic eye there were not enough straight lines and no
level spots for houses. "Here if one sees ten yards level, one screams
out, 'What a site for a house.'"[59]

We make our transition to the Mussoorie of the Raj with Lady
Canning as she rode horseback to Mussoorie via the Tibetan trade
route. When her husband had to "fly" back to Calcutta, she was
seduced by a plan that was adventuresome and almost foolhardy. She
left Simla with her escorts to go to Mussoorie by way of Chini, a
mountain pass on the border of Tibet. Lady Canning wrote that she
did "rather wonder at people recommending me this tour," with a
road only six feet wide and sometimes only three feet. The trip took
thirty-one days. She recuperated for a week in Mussoorie, proud of
her accomplishment. Queen Victoria responded to her description
of the trip: "Intensely interesting, but *I* think much of it sounded
very dangerous." The Queen was given to underlining.[60]

Outside of observing that she found it to be a more humble ver-
sion of Simla, Lady Canning had little to say about Mussoorie. An
early writer thought the distant prospects were splendid. And the
variety of game was good, although the terrain made hunting a challenge. Other writers were impressed with Mussoorie's hazards,
which were much more in evidence in Victorian times. When the
Honorable Emily Eden visited in 1838, she wrote:

> The bearers are steady men, I have no doubt, but still I
> wish they would not race with each other; for at the sharp
> corners where they try to pass, the jonpaun hangs over the
> edge and I don't altogether like it. In the afternoon we
> took a beautiful ride up to Landour, but the paths are

much narrower on that side, and our courage somewhat
oozed out; and first we came to a place where they said,
"This was where poor Major Blundell and his pony fell
over, and they were both dashed to atoms."[61]

An engaged couple cantering along the path around Camel's
Back flushed a kastura. The bird frightened the pony of the young
woman so that it shied and backed dangerously near the edge of the
road. The young man dashed to her rescue and both hurtled down
the khud to their deaths.

The world of the rajahs and the maharajahs (kings and great
kings) was so self-contained and unflamboyant by the time we lived
in Mussoorie that we were hardly aware of the few who still lived
there. Nevertheless, the maharajahs have played a colorful role in the
history of Mussoorie, as well as in other hill stations. Supposedly
they chose not to build homes in Simla because the Viceroy and
other British nabobs established their summer residences there. The
hunting in the hills around Mussoorie was also an attraction to the
safari-loving princes.

The Nawab of Rampur owned a large property which is now a
school, and the Maharajah of Nabha's summer palace has been converted into a hotel. The palace of the Maharajah of Kapurthala is one
of the more prominent buildings on the hill beyond Library Bazaar.
Although it has its own spacious grounds near the Savoy Hotel, it is
crowded about nowadays by homes of much less dignity.

When I finished reading Collins and Lapierre's *Freedom at Midnight*, which was on the Indian and U.S. best-seller list at the time, I
was still curious about maharajahs, all 565 of them, and the Partition
of 1947. Dick Wechter arranged a meeting with the Secretary of the
Maharajah of Kapurthala. My intuition about maharajahs is that they
are entitled to their privacy, but Dick assumed that they would welcome a visit from Woodstock teachers. His interest in gardening
opened doors for him, and he genially forced his way into the hospitality of strangers, as he had with Mrs. Lal, the mushroom lady, by
bringing them a packet of flower seeds or tulip bulbs.

We found the house of Mr. Singh, the secretary, by the brass
plate on the door. After we had explained who we were and where

we were from, the gracious tradition of Indian hospitality prevailed, and the Secretary and his wife, whose tea we were interrupting, made us welcome.

The room was comfortably furnished in the style of the 1930s with brown velour overstuffed furniture. On the walls and tables were pictures of the Maharajah and his ancestors in full dress, usually displaying them as hunters admiring their kill, tigers and wild boars.

The princely state of Kapurthala, about half the size of Rhode Island, was in northwestern India. The city of that name was known as early as the eleventh century, but in 1948, after the Partition, Kapurthala was absorbed into the state of Punjab. Now the Maharajah has no kingdom.

The Secretary spoke about his employer in eloquent English. "The Maharajah has a summer home in Mussoorie. He is, unfortunately, not in residence right now. He is a colonel in the Indian army, as are many of the princes."

We asked for details about the palace.

"There are five acres around the house, policed by guards. Some years ago we had our own liveried rickshaws with the blue and white colors of the house, as was the custom. The Chateau de Kapurthala is the best and biggest of the residences in Mussoorie. The main palace in the city of Kapurthala was constructed as a replica of the palace at Versailles, although it was built by an Englishman. [The maharajah who built it considered himself to be the reincarnation of Louis XIV.]

"Kapurthala is a city of palaces and gardens. 'Once upon a time there was a Rajah' with one hundred elephants and a carriage drawn by six horses. No longer. I am sorry to see the grandeur of that time fade away, but we must go with the times. We have advanced much since Independence.

"The main palace is now a school. In 1949 the Indian princely states were integrated with the State. The princes were given privy purses, but when these were withdrawn a few years ago, most of the princes could not afford to maintain their palaces and have converted them into hotels or schools."

Concerning his own career, the Secretary said, "I have been with the Maharajah all my life, and I was with his father before him, and my father served the family before me. The family is pukka Sikh, as are all the retinue, and goes back for fifty generations, before the British came to India. The state of Kapurthala was about half Muslim and half Sikh."

"What happened in Kapurthala at the time of the Partition?"

"The Partition? Not a single person was stabbed or murdered. The Maharajah, the father of the present one, avoided the carnage that beset most of the area by organizing an orderly migration under the protection of his army. Of course, after they reached the state boundary, we couldn't know what happened."

We left with cordial regards and Dick's promise of flower seeds. On our way back to the bazaar, we took the high road that ran above the palace to look down at the many windows and at the two turrets with their inverted ice-cream-cone roofs, each turret flying the Kapurthala flag. The buff walls and red roofs gave the palace a picture-book charm. We passed the grilled gates of three-sided "garage" where the blue and white liveried rickshaw wallahs used to await their orders.

We knew that there were still those with the privileges of princes and princesses in the world; but we could not feel sorry for the loss of privileges of maharajahs as we passed the ill-fed, ill-clothed Indian laborers who were returning to their crumbling quarters within the shadow of the palace.

While most of us can take our maharajahs or leave them, some of us have a curious fascination about them. Legend and history tell us of their opulence, their sexual exploits, their fairy-tale world. Jewels, elephants, tiger hunts, and harems were a part of this world, much of it at the expense of the poor people of the villages.

Collins and Lapierre make the point that many of the princely states were well run, and only a small number of those rulers who had wealth were so self-indulgent as to try to make all their fantasies come true. Not surprisingly, it is the latter group that makes entertaining reading.

The opulence of the maharajahs developed without help from the British. In 1838 when Lord Auckland with his sisters, Emily and Fanny Eden, visited Ranjit Singh, the Maharajah staged a parade for the governor-general. Looking ahead, Emily thought she saw a long white wall capped with red tile. What she saw were thirty thousand soldiers, a line four and a half miles long.[62]

The Maharajah of Patiala bought twenty-seven Rolls Royces to go with his French Dion, the first automobile in India in 1892. A later ruler of Patiala had a harem of 350 women. After years of single-mindedly pursuing the pleasures of sex, "he died of boredom." The Maharajah of Alwar designed a car that perfectly reproduced the English coronation coach. Its powerful motor hurled all that weight over India's sorry roads at seventy miles an hour. The Nizam of Hyderabad once bought a store's entire stock of shoes so that he could choose a pair at his leisure. The Maharajah of Kapurthala displayed in his turban the largest topaz in the world, set off in a field of three thousand diamonds and pearls.

Even otherwise sensible administrators were prone to indulge in fantasies. The Maharajah of Gwalior owned a miniature electric train that ran on solid silver rails in the center of his banquet table. The cars could be filled with food on sidetracks that ran into the kitchen. The Maharajah sat at the control panel where he could deprive his guests of dessert by the flip of the switch. But once during an important dinner, the controls short-circuited and the train cars rampaged around the track, sloshing the food on the Maharajah's guests. "It was a catastrophe without parallel in the annals of railroading."[63]

Along with sex, many of the maharajahs were devoted to sport and games. The British encouraged their passion for hunting and were willing guests on safaris organized for their benefit. Over the years they nearly decimated the tiger population. The Indians introduced the British to polo, having learned to play using the skulls of enemies for polo balls. Even Mussoorie had its polo grounds, and Kashmir one of the most beautiful. From the British, Indians learned cricket and soccer. And some even took over the fox hunt, pursuing jackals rather than foxes.

Another import adopted by the Indians was the bagpipe. The Prince of Wales brought a piper with him in 1875. The Indian princes loved the bagpipe. It enchanted them. When one old Sikh chieftain heard the Viceroy's escort of Highlanders, he sighed, "This is indeed music! It is like that which we hear of in ancient story, which was so exquisite that the hearers became insensible." (Bagpipes were sometimes used at Mussoorie weddings.)

One maharajah had his Indian pipers adopt the kilt, wearing pink tights to hide their brown knees. While observing this spectacle, His Royal Highness, Prince of Wales, "wept from the pain of suppressed laughter."[64]

As I quoted Collins and Lapierre earlier, a good number of the princes ruled well. When Lady Canning visited the Begum of Bhopal, she was attracted to the Begum's unassuming ways. "She is a really clever, upright character and looks into the affairs of her country herself and rules it admirably." The Begum was invested by Lord Canning with the newly created Order of the Star of India for her loyalty to the Empire.[65]

A new generation of maharajahs lived less flamboyantly and brought education and reform to their states. The problems of the Indian working class did not disappear with the diminishing extravagance of the princes; there still remains the vast number of people who cannot rise beyond their lot of famine, poverty, and a fatalistic religion.

"Why is it called Library Bazaar?" I asked Muriel Powell, one of the unofficial historians of Mussoorie. "I can't find a library there."

"Of course there is a library! It is above the shops at the west end of the square. It has been there since the early days of the British Raj."

Vera Marley, who had lived in Mussoorie for over sixty years, said, "My dear child, certainly there is a library. A sign by the stairs says, 'No dogs or Indians.' You will probably find *Wanderings of a Pilgrim*, by Fanny Parks about her visit to the area in 1838. A delightful book."

I found the building and the stairs and I ascended to a broad glass-enclosed verandah furnished with wicker chairs and a view of the bazaar below. People-watching must always have had a place in hill-station life. I looked in vain for Fanny Parks' book. The young man who seemed to be in charge helped me look through the rows and rows of books that were kept locked in glass-fronted cases, arranged alphabetically by the most important word in the title. I must have seemed very persistent. "Surely you have the book. It is about Mussoorie's early history."

"No, Madam, we have nothing about Mussoorie," he assured me.

Mr. Abhinandan remembered Mussoorie during the latter days of the Raj.

"Were you born here? Where is your family home?"

"I was born in Mussoorie in 1920. My father was an accountant with British people and he worked at the Exchange Building for Trevelyan and Clarke, a large British department store. It was the largest in Mussoorie, selling clothes, shoes, everything. We were six brothers."

I asked about the Castle Hill Estate with its gate guarded by soldiers. "Is there something behind those walls?"

"The Castle Hill Estate? There is nothing special to see there, but I will tell you something interesting about it. It used to belong to the bank agent, a British man. My grandfather was an accountant for his bank in Mussoorie. One night the bank was broken into. The agent held the key and he was responsible, but he declared that he had given the key to my grandfather. In the court case that followed, the bank officials asked my grandfather to say in court that he had that night left the bank unlocked; in other words perjure himself and take the blame. He would have to spend a few years in jail. But for doing this, the bank would give him the Castle Hill Estate, which was a very valuable property.

"My grandfather refused to do this. He turned down the opportunity for wealth and so he left his good name untarnished to be passed on to this children. That was the moral code for that time, not for today. The German lawyer representing the bank received the estate as a fee for his work. It is now owned by the Survey of India."

"Was business better in Mussoorie in the days of the Raj?"

"No, because population was less. Except before 1947 the rajahs came to Mussoorie in the summertime and spent their money here."

"Was the British Raj a better time than the time after Independence?"

"I can't say. In those times you didn't see Ambassadors or Marutis or tourists and all the people who come here. It is interesting now. People who say the British rule was better are narrow-minded. They know their world is only in Mussoorie. They are homesick for the way things used to be. How many years have passed since the United States got independence? Two hundred? So you see our country is a young country, twenty-eight years only."

We left Mr. Abhinandan to walk back to Woodstock School, past all those houses scattered along Tehri Road that were named by homesick Englishmen for places of their youth. Their ghosts sit on verandahs overlooking the Doon Valley. They hear the music from transistor radios of pedestrians who never give a thought to the Raj, its accomplishments or its atrocities.

Chapter 22

The Wider World

A number of holy cows lived in the Landour Bazaar. They were healthy animals, harmless to people as they nuzzled the piles of grain in the shops and were shooed away with good-natured swats. Dehra Dun had a few more that lived on the garbage in the streets. In Benares we saw herds of dairy cows stabled in the inner city. One of the most widely known facts about India is that it is the country where the expressions "holy cow" and "sacred cow" are used literally.

The veneration of the cow probably dates back 3,000 years. But there was a time in the Veda period (2000 to 1000 B.C.), according to Nirad C. Chaudhuri, when people did kill cows for food. The *Mahabharata* mentions, without thinking it necessary to add an excuse, that a very hospitable king used to have 220,100 cattle slaughtered every day for his guests. But sacred law evolved so that slaughter of cattle for food was forbidden. The custom may have been at one time a practical measure to protect the supply of milk, butter, and ghee (butter oil), staples for good Indian cooks. Their dung is used for fuel and fertilizer. It is mixed with mud for building material and thinned to be used as a glaze for dirt floors. Some Hindus think that drinking cow urine will purify the body and the soul. "Cow power" is still used for ploughing. Over the centuries, cherishing the cow became a religious tradition. When we visited our mission at Champa in central India, we learned that the city had a retirement home for old cows but none for people.

Why the buffalo is not in the same category as the cow is puzzling. The buffalo, too, is the wet nurse of Indian humanity, but it is not holy. Chaudhuri's explanation is that the buffalo is a native stock, while the humpbacked cow was brought from the Middle East by the Aryans who gave it extra care to insure its survival.[66]

Begging has the sanction of Hinduism, but we saw little interest by Hindus in giving to institutions, such as homes for lepers or beggars or crippled children, because Hindus prefer to personalize their giving and thus receive merit. Usually we averted our eyes from the ragged mother or misshapen child and passed on, for we had heard all about the profession of begging and knew also that Prime Minister Gandhi had declared begging illegal. In our earlier years in India, we could believe that the poor had already inherited the earth, but in later years we saw fewer beggars. Mrs. Gandhi's law prohibiting begging had had some effect.

The real poverty of India is in those villages where many people live on the fine line of survival, where the failure of a monsoon or the death of a bullock can mean hunger and hardship. Poverty on our hillside was evident in the bazaar when we caught glimpses of it in the living areas behind the shops; where some of the people would like to get from one meal a day to two meals.

One wonders if those glorious years that are described in the *Vedas* were not just the dream of the poet. It is easier to believe that India has always been poor. Mahatma Gandhi, by deploring the emphasis on heavy industry, had given poverty some respect along with the simple life and *khadi* (homespun) cloth. Mrs. Gandhi promised in 1971 to remove poverty. Prime Minister Morarji Desai and the Janata Party promised in 1977 to eliminate poverty in ten years. Up until then, Indians had assumed that poverty was life, that one depended on the gods for enough rain for a crop, and that one starved if the gods were not benevolently inclined.

The newcomer to India who strays beyond the modern streets of the city is appalled by the filth. The streets are littered, but usually the homes are clean, and the daily bath is part of the Hindu ritual. Americans keep clean because of the barrage of advertising that tells them to use this toothpaste or that bath soap. The Indian brushes his teeth and takes a bath because it is his religious duty.

People power was very visible at the building site of the barrage (dam) at Korba. We looked out from the mission garden to see lines of trucks crossing the sand river, and when we went to the work site we found brigades of men and women swarming up and down bamboo ladders, moving dirt and gravel and mortar from head to head. Of course such use of human power is unprogressive. A large earth-moving machine could have done the job with less effort. Having more time than money, India was spending money on people rather than on machinery. The money stays in India rather than going to more industrialized nations, such as the U.S. or Russia. On the other hand, the dam will be used for a very modern purpose: to generate electricity for the highly industrialized area, as well as for remote village television sets. The curse of Korba is the pollution caused by the burning of coal for the generators.

The idea of an industrialized India gave Gandhi nightmares. He wanted a middle ground between poverty and affluence, a classless society where all labor, physical or intellectual, would offer the same reward.[67]

After the British departure from India, many small manufacturers went into business. A Sunday afternoon Rotary picnic in Landour ended with a visit to a nearby thermometer factory which we had not known existed. Both industrial and small instruments were being manufactured. We were impressed by the technical expertise displayed by the 80 or more people employed in that small building. Small scale industries account for a major portion of India's manufacturing production, such as pencil sharpeners, toys, irons, ovens, heaters, and hot plates.

Note an ad in the newspaper: "Start your own profitable small scale industry for blouse hooks, pins, curtain hooks, flush chains [for toilets], eyelets, bob pins." I had never thought about there being money in flush chains.

The author of an article in *Forbes* was optimistic about the economic future of India with its 900 million people. He encouraged foreign investment. "You can look at India and see terrible poverty and overpopulation. Or you can focus on its potential for becoming one of the world's most powerful economies. 'We're like an elephant,' one Indian businessman said proudly. 'We're moving slowly but once we are on the move we'll come crashing through the jungle.'"[68]

An American girl in my English class at Woodstock wrote her term paper on astrology, quoting only authorities who lived by the stars. She cited famous leaders, including Congressmen in India, who made decisions by astrology. When she presented her paper to the class, I questioned her sources. I was surprised at the defensive response of the students for her uncritical approach.

Chaudhuri in his *Autobiography of an Unknown Indian* tells the story of his grandfather whose horoscope predicted that he would meet death by being eaten by a crocodile. His grandfather simply avoided places where crocodiles might be and took his daily bath at home. He died a natural death, and Chauduri said that he himself lost his faith in horoscopes.

But Indian literature, past and current, is filled with examples of important decisions made by the stars.

The subject of caste is probably as much discussed as the sacred cow when problems of India are listed. And although discrimination of castes has been outlawed, it has not been eliminated. The Hindus and the British could understand each other on the subject of caste and classes and the fine distinctions that separated one level from another. The system of caste had its uses. It defined one's place in society. Every detail of life was prescribed, when bowels were to be moved, when baths were to be taken, what one's occupation was to be. Some of the aspects of the system were defended by Chaudhuri. It organized Hindu "racial, social, cultural, and economic diversities" as one wave of barbarians after another flowed in from the north. The caste system made it possible for each new culture to organize its anarchy. It was also the Aryan way of escaping from being absorbed by the native Darks. But Chaudhuri saw the caste system as flexible, evolving; he saw India as a "warehouse of civilizations."

Caste and family, the shapers of the Indian life and tradition, are most apparent at the village level where the family is made up of grandparents, numerous brothers and their wives, and all the children. Ninety-nine percent of the eligible males and females marry at least once in their lifetimes, for it is the religious duty of Hindus to procreate. In the joint family, early marriage is made easy because the young couple need not be economically independent, nor do they set up their own households. Population control is difficult in a society that puts a high premium on sons. Couples persevere until they have the number of sons they desire, sons who will look after them in their old age, continue the family line, and perform religious rites at the time of the parents' deaths. This situation is changing slowly, faster in urban than in rural areas. The birth of a daughter is not considered the calamity it once was. Even so, Walt received condolences when he confessed that he had begotten only daughters.

Arranged marriages are intended to preserve caste. Although the more educated young people may break tradition, there is not the rebellion against the tradition of arranged marriages that one might expect. Even the missionaries saw advantages of such marriages, which often became love matches.

Foreigners are amused by marriage advertisements in Indian papers. The *Times of India* not only ran several full pages of matrimonial columns in the Sunday edition, it also ran ads for the ads: "Nice grooms were difficult to find until I advertised in *Times* classifieds," with a picture of the handsome, happy family with two children.

> Wanted homely [a good homemaker], educated and pretty bride for a tall handsome 31-year-old Punjabi Brahmin army major. Caste no bar.
> Suitable Bengali match for Kashyap Brahmin, fair, accomplished girl, B.A. teacher in Convent School, height 1.63 meters, 26 years.
> Wanted compassionate groom for a very beautiful accomplished intelligent Brahmin girl. Has small white spots on feet not apparent.

"Fair, smart, attractive, homely, handsome." So what about the girl who is not so beautiful and the groom who is not so handsome? After the sex of the newborn baby has been determined, the second question asked is whether the baby is fair or dark. A little girl with dark complexion is a source of worry to the parents. Who will marry her? But the dark boys and girls also have to be married. So the society reminds itself that Lord Krishna was dark, the color of dusk, and the offending color will be balanced by other considerations. But there is a limit to acceptable fairness. When the British came, their light hair and pink skins were disdained. "They look boiled rather than roasted."

An advertisement was submitted for (not by) a Woodstock teacher. She was a young, attractive piano instructor from Kansas.

Ajit Singh was the teacher of Indian music, and without consulting her he put an ad in the matrimonial column of a Delhi paper: "Young American, interested in marriage with young Indian man; she has a substantial private income of her own," etc. Barbara received 750 replies from every part of the country, of every age from a sixteen-year-old who wanted to get out of a bad home situation to a widow-er who wrote for his son but said he was also available. Ajit (nor Barbara) answered none of them, although he received many a follow-up letter pressing for a reply.

Mr. Abhinandan thanked Walt for supplying the school jeep for his daughter's wedding.

"Was it an arranged marriage?" I asked.

"It was an arranged marriage. Some of my friends introduced me to the family and I found the boy to be all right. He came for tea, sitting with my daughter at this table, and he approved the girl and they were married in four weeks. The wedding was in Dehra Dun because my son-in-law said he could not come up to Mussoorie in the cold weather."

"Are they happy?"

"They are both happy. They are happy, I am happy. She comes for a month or so in June and for another visit in October."

Mr. Abhinandan was at one time concerned about his two fatherless nieces for whom he had to find husbands. He had been try-ing for three years, but their dowry was not enough to attract hus-bands. He thought that in ten years, dowry might not matter so much. He did eventually find grooms for them.

But the current scandal in the newspapers has to do with mid-dle-class brides who were "accidentally" burned to death a year or so after their marriage. The husband's family would hope to receive more dowry in a second marriage, such as VCR's or motorcycles.

Muriel Powell said, "Our postman can't get his pension because he does not have Rs.200 to pay someone to see about it."

Bribes are paid to get a ration card, a driver's license, a building permit, or a gas cylinder. Delhi students nearly rioted one year when the clerk demanded payment before he gave them the roll numbers for their annual examinations.

One example of bribery: Susan wrote from home asking for a police clearance for good conduct of her time in India so that she could get a living permit for Belgium. We applied for it, and the official said it would be "swiftly forthcoming." It never came. In the meantime, Susan managed to get her permit without the document. Months later after we had forgotten the request, a visitor came to Walt's office saying he had something very important that Walt would be very pleased to have. If Walt would give him a certain amount of money, he could have Susan's police clearance. The official was crestfallen to learn that that piece of red tape had already been cut, that the document was no longer needed.

Usually we stood on principle and would not give a bribe, deciding instead to wait out the impasse. But when time was squeezing us and we needed clearance to catch a plane home, we authorized our intermediary to negotiate.

Many good Indian citizens feel trapped in a life of boring survival. The husband may have a low-level office job without a future. If he has no connections, no relatives in high places, no opportunity or inclination for bribery, he may see himself in his rut forever. He may dream of an education in a Western country which would open all doors, but the first door has to be opened with a bribe.

Prime Minister Indira Gandhi was assassinated by her Sikh bodyguards on Wednesday, October 31, 1984. The nation was stunned and grief-stricken, as well as uncertain about what could happen next. Hindus were angry. We at Woodstock, both Indians and expatriates, felt the same shock and disbelief. Added to these feelings was concern about the safety of our students in grades six through twelve who were out of Woodstock for Activity Week. Telephone lines to Delhi were jammed, so we were unable to contact the staff sponsors of groups there.

The bazaar closed from Wednesday evening through the following Sunday. Thursday began quietly enough, but by afternoon we could see smoke rising from the area of Library Bazaar. The rumor was that some Sikhs were celebrating Mrs. Gandhi's death and had distributed confections. Hindu hooligans started burning the homes and shops of Sikhs. They looted the photography and radio shop of good-hearted and gentle Mr. Thukral and smashed the photocopier. A mob headed for Landour, but was stopped by the police at the Clock Tower.

Greater rioting and destruction was taking place in Delhi and other large cities, Hindus against Sikhs. Many stories were told in the days following of the mad violence of some Hindus and courage of others who defended Sikh neighbors. The death toll in Delhi was over five hundred and in Dehra Dun several people were killed. Our own students told of their bus being stopped, but the Sikh student had been hidden under a seat and was not found.

On Saturday we went to Brij and Viola Lal's to watch the funeral on television. We saw Rajiv Gandhi perform the ceremonies of lighting the pyre. Then and later he spoke out against violence and revenge. Sadly, he too would meet death by assassination in May 1991.

United States and Indian relations were at a high point during the Kennedy administration. Then India was soured by Lyndon Johnson's stingy help with food supplies during the famine years (a revenge for India's criticism of his Vietnam policy) and by Nixon's support of Pakistan and rapprochement with China. On the other hand, the U.S. was offended by India's policy of non-alignment. When Ranjit Dass gave the world news to the student assembly one Friday, reporting that "The U.S. Congress handed President Reagan a stunning defeat by overriding his veto," the students applauded, reflecting Reagan's lack of popularity in India. Even though we read about all this in the daily papers, we never became very knowledgeable about the politics of India or comfortable with the bias against the U.S. in the news. We knew that we as Westerners were welcomed in the bazaar except on rare occasions when the U.S. had favored Pakistan to the disadvantage of India.

Chapter 23

Religions of the Hill Station

Percival Spear wrote: "There is no end to the study of Hinduism and no statement about it which cannot be contradicted." Further he says, "No one can be sure that he has fully penetrated its mystery. Veil screens veil, and when, drawing all aside, we believe we have penetrated to the innermost sanctuary, we are uncertain whether we have reached the All, or the nothing."[69]

Hinduism is essentially monotheistic, the gods being the many facets of the personality of the Supreme Being. Their triumvirate includes Brahma, the lord of all creation; Vishnu, the lord of preservation; and Shiva, the god of destruction and recreation, for the two ideas must go together to form the endless cycle. And then come layers of reincarnations of gods and goddesses.

Hinduism is thought to be the world's oldest religion. Once upon a time the people of the Ganges Valley lived comfortably on the food and shelter provided by nature. They had the *Vedas*, transmitted through oral tradition, and the worship of nature, with sacrifices to appease the gods of natural disasters. But after awhile, this philosophy was not enough to answer their questions of how the universe began and how it would end. The *Upanishads* evolved, giving answers to questions about suffering and inequality. The Creator, all powerful and always merciful, was not to be held responsible for death and hunger. Men were responsible for their own suffering because of their own evil deeds. They developed the ideas of *dharma*, one's duty, and *karma*, one's destiny. The *Bhagavad Gita*, a religious classic which is part of the epic *Mahabharata*, says, "It is better to do one's own duty badly than to do another's duty well."[70] There can be no end to life. Existence is like the turn of a wheel that takes countless years for one revolution and then it starts over.

The idea of nothingness, or zero, dawned first on the Hindu mind in connection with his religion. We Westerners say, "In the beginning was the Word." Hindus say, "In the beginning was silence."[71] The repetition of the sound of OM is the most direct access to God-Consciousness. "God is the sound and silence. His name is OM," say the *Upanishads*.

In the novel, *The Gift of the Cow, (Godaan)*, by Premchand, the main character is beaten down by the poisoning of his beautiful cow, the abuse from his son, the failure of his crops, the oppression by his landlord and the village rulers. "Fight back," we cry. But it is his dharma to obey and his karma to die of exhaustion. His security lies in abjectness. The story is depressing. For many Hindus, life is full of suffering, and their ambition is to escape from this world. We might expect a high incidence of suicide in such a society, but suicide is not considered the way out. It would not end his life, and it might even prolong his cycle of rebirth after rebirth. He can only endure. If he does his duty, he will have a good karma and be reborn into a better life next time. Ultimately, ultimately, he will be absorbed into the Divine Essence. He knows the Biblical maxim, "Whatever a man soweth that will he also reap." For him, there is no forgiveness in the reaping.

But Hinduism is not the same for everyone who says he is a Hindu. The villager finds color and drama in his local gods for his otherwise drab life. Bradford Smith wrote,

> At the village level there is a confused mingling of primitive animism, superstition and belief in magic mixed together with the worship of local as well as the major gods. The better educated reject the magic, the anthropomorphic conceptions, the superstition, and concentrate upon devotional exercises of prayer and meditation.[72]

Hinduism has a history of toleration for other religions, with the belief that God is the center of a circle and that there are a million ways to him. Hindus cannot understand the arrogance of a religion that thinks it has the only way or that a leader would claim divinity. Shridharani contends that making a Hindu into a Christian and a Christian into a Hindu is often a mere change of labels and seldom a spiritual experience.[73]

Coming from a denomination that believes in nonviolence, we were particularly interested in aspects of nonviolence in Hinduism. Bradford Smith traces the roots of India's nonviolent philosophy back to the forest sages of the Himalayas, perhaps as long ago as 2000 B.C. From there it has made its convoluted way to other continents and then back to the country of origin with an influence that has changed history. The Buddha adopted nonviolence, and his disciples spread the ideas through Asia. The scholars of the British Raj discovered the idea of nonviolence, *ahimsa*, in the religious books of India. Translated into English, these books found their way into the Harvard College Library to be read by Henry David Thoreau. In 1849 he wrote his famous essay on "The Virtue of Civil Disobedience." In 1908 Mohandas Karamchand Gandhi found a copy of Thoreau's essay in a South African jail and returned to India with the idea of starting the nonviolent movement toward independence.[74] Gandhi was also impressed by the writing of Leo Tolstoy. Martin Luther King, Jr., acknowledged his debt to Gandhi for the success of the civil rights movement.

Dehra Dun is not far from the holy cities of Rishikesh and Hardwar; it is on the route to the source of the Ganges, so we saw many pilgrims as well as resident holy men. They were dressed in saffron cotton robes, reminding us of gladiolus among more soberly dressed citizens.

Traveling by train, we watched with lowered eyes as a saintly-looking Hindu woman performed her morning devotions. From a small suitcase she removed a book about the size of *Webster's Unabridged Dictionary*. Sitting cross-legged on the seat opposite us, she quietly read and prayed from her own scriptures, drawing a cloak of meditation around herself, undisturbed by the bustle of the other passengers.

Khushwant Singh, journalist, was cynical about Indian spirituality. "There is more talk about money and material things in India than in the so-called materialistic societies. Nevertheless, religion and ritual pervade the lives of Indians more than they do the lives of most other people."[76]

About holy men, Singh comments, "Sadhus go to the extreme of concerning themselves solely with achieving peace of mind. They cannot be disturbed by floods, epidemics, earthquakes, droughts, and famines. Rarely does one see a saffron-clad volunteer in any relief camp. The privilege of service is left to Christian organizations."[77]

Although their number is small, we could not ignore the Muslims in Mussoorie. By way of amplified speakers in the bazaar, we were called to prayers from sunrise to sunset. Islam came to India in the late twelfth century when the Turks invaded North India. Today Muslims make up 11 percent of the population as compared with Hindus of 85 percent. A greater number are in Pakistan, where Islam is the national religion. Because Muslim states are often making news, we Westerners probably know more about this religion than about other Eastern religions.

Islam was begun by Muhammad, a camel driver who lived from 570 to 632. His visions are recorded in the holy book, the *Koran*, which is the absolute authority for Muslims. Their religion of one God abhors the Trinity. The moral code is based on the Jewish religion of the time of Muhammad. One might think that with the *Koran* telling the believer exactly what is right and wrong, peace and harmony would reign among Muslims, but Islam has proliferated into many sects who defend their own interpretations.[78] On this point, it has a trait in common with Christianity.

In the history of India, great thinkers have come forward to begin reform movements within Hinduism, seeking to escape from the treadmill of reincarnation. Sikhism is one of these movements. All Sikhs are named Singh, but not all Singhs are Sikhs, pronounced *sing* and *seek*. (We had a dozen Singhs on the Woodstock payroll and only one or two of them were Sikhs. By translation, every Singh is a lion.)

On Sunday morning in the bazaar, the day off from work, the Sikhs stroll about with their children, the men in white pyjamas, their long black hair just washed and hanging down their backs. After their hair has dried, they pile it under turbans the colors of sweet peas. Their black, ferocious beards are usually rolled neatly into little nets and tucked under the turban. The young boys at school wear their hair in topknots tied into white handkerchiefs.

The founder of the Sikhs was Guru Nanak, a gentle Hindu (1469-1538) who set out to reform Hinduism during the time that North India was being ruled by the Muslims. He taught that there was one God for all men and for all religions; he wanted to abolish caste. By the seventeenth century when they were threatened by Muslim rulers, Sikhs became militant in an effort to retain their religion. They extended political power over northwestern India. With the advent of the British, they became even more militant. Although Sikhs make up only two percent of the population in India, their influence and importance are far greater than their numbers would indicate. A group of them are determined to establish their own state of Khalistan and are a persistent problem for the government.

Sikhs come from the Punjab, our neighboring state to the northwest. We saw them as taxi drivers, carpenters at the school, merchants in the bazaar, journalists, truck drivers, mechanics, farmers, and soldiers. Taller and huskier than most other Indians, the men were conspicuous at sporting events.

Also highly visible in the bazaar were Americans from California and British Columbia, converts to Sikhism who came to teach at the Guru Nanak School on the west side of Mussoorie. Their blonde children, dressed in Indian clothes, acted so breezily American that we had to stop to stare as they skate-boarded through the bazaar.

After a visit to Kashmir, we returned to the warmth of early June while the world of the monsoon waited breathlessly for rain. We arrived by plane in Amritsar, the Rome of the Sikh religion, in 107 degree heat. A kindly hotel manager let us use a room with a fan while we waited for our train. We asked ourselves what we could do to improve the hours. Walt and I wanted to see the Golden Temple, but the girls preferred inertia.

"When you've seen one Golden Temple you've seen them all," Susan said as she flopped down under the ceiling fan, unwilling to see even the one and only.

Being in Amritsar without seeing the Golden Temple is like being in London and not visiting Westminster Abbey. Walt and I gathered every scrap of energy to hire a bicycle rickshaw. We were taken to what seemed the middle of town, then down a narrow alley which opened into the tiled plaza that fronted on the pool in which this marvel of Sikhism floats. (Amritsar means "tank of nectar.") A marble causeway leads to the white marble temple with its dome of glittering gold leaf. A cleansing process is required before one can enter the holy area. Leaving our shoes on the plaza, we stepped into the wash water and then crossed over the hot tiles to the causeway.

At the time of the Partition in 1947, the Sikhs let themselves be led by a fanatic who had lost members of his family in a riot that he had himself provoked. The Golden Temple has a museum showing this torture of Sikhs by Muslims. But the Temple has many beautiful and gentle aspects. The Holy Book is wrapped in silk and covered with fresh flowers daily. We listened to the reading of the scriptures which goes on continuously and is completed once every forty-eight hours. Musicians also sing and play around the clock. The sweeper was using a peacock feather broom to clean the marble floors.

Even before the assassination of Prime Minister Indira Gandhi, the Punjab was divided by religious and political factions. The Temple became the scene of violence and was closed to visitors. Economic and cultural differences continue to keep Sikhs separated from Muslims, and today Sikhs are just as much separated from Hindus. Officially, India is a secular state, but religious factions continue to war with each other. However, at this writing, tourists are again allowed to visit the Golden Temple.

We learned about the Jains from Mr. Abhinandan, the cloth merchant. Jainism was also a reform movement of Hinduism. Although it does not have the visibility of the other Indian religions, only one-half of one percent of the population, it has two million adherents who make their religion known by their sometimes fanatic "right-to-life" beliefs. The monastic will sweep the path before him to avoid injuring living things, or refuse to eat after sundown for fear of imbibing an insect. Jains are strict vegetarians, as we learned at Mr. Abhinandan's table.

The founder of Jainism was Mahavira, born about 540 B.C., probably a contemporary of Buddha. Mahavira was a non-Aryan noble who believed that everything has a spirit; animals and insects, stones and trees, each has a separate soul. These ideas resulted in a philosophy of nonviolence, ahimsa, that became a part of Hindu philosophy. Without Mahavira there might not have been a Gandhi. "We would rather die than kill," the Jain replies when asked what he would do if his life was threatened.

Jains do not deny the existence of the gods, but they do not give them a place as personal interveners. The world functions according to universal law and not according to whims of the gods. Jains use memorized prayers and read from prayer books and scriptures. The Landour temple runs an eye hospital, an information center, and a holiday house for low-income Jains who come from Delhi.

Mr. Abhinandan spoke of his respect for Christians. He deplored the lack of character in people nowadays. "I think the Lord Christ said, 'Always try to give, don't expect to receive.' I love those lines." He commended villagers who were satisfied with what they had and were not always striving for more.

Our contact with Buddhism came with our visits to the Tibetan School located in Happy Valley on the west side of Mussoorie. There we toured the *Gompa*, the Buddhist temple. The use of rainbow reds, greens, and yellows and lots of gold is gaudy but pleasing, and the dragons are ferocious but harmless. Always, when we visited, a tiny old woman was circling the temple spinning a prayer wheel by which the text of the written prayer inside the wheel drifted up to heaven.

We were told of the Middle Way, a theology that avoids extremes and cleaves to the Eight-fold Path: right views, right resolves, right speech, right action, right living, right effort, right recollectedness, and right meditation. As in any religion, there is a discrepancy between the ideal of the theology and the way it is practiced. Although India is the birthplace of Buddha, few Indians are Buddhists.

The Dalai Lama is the god-king, the reincarnation of Chenresi, the Buddha of Compassion. When the Communists gained control of China in 1949, they promised to liberate Tibet from the imperialists, the Americans and British. (It was said that at the time the total of such imperialists in Tibet was five.) Coercion increased to the point that the Dalai Lama was in danger, and he escaped to India in 1959. Mussoorie was one of the hill towns where he and his people were welcomed as refugees. They are still waiting to return to Tibet.

We were returning from the bazaar one Saturday afternoon when we heard the music of an approaching procession. By flattening ourselves to the side of the building, we made room for the procession to pass in the narrow street. Riding on a cart following the band were several actors costumed and made up for the *Ramlila*

drama that would be performed over a period of ten to twenty days during the Hindu Dusserha festival. The *Ramlila* is real folk drama that depicts the story of the *Ramayana*. Rama fights with the demon Ravana and then returns after fourteen years of exile. The final celebration, Diwali, is the festival of lights marking the victory of Rama and his return and enthronement. The battle between good and evil results in the triumph of good.

Diwali, in September or October, has a touch of Christmas about it. Everyone who possibly can goes home for Diwali to receive the blessings of the goddess Lakshmi. Earthenware cups are sold in the bazaar to be filled with mustard oil and a cotton wick. Thousands of these luminaries (more lately with strings of electric lights) outline steps, roof tops, windows, and shelves. Prayers are offered, gifts given, special sweets eaten to the accompaniment of fireworks. Diwali also has the aspect of New Year's Day, for it closes the Hindu fiscal calendar. Businessmen take inventory and count their money. Lakshmi is the goddess of both beauty and wealth.

We were well aware of Holi, the spring holiday most like the medieval Feast of Fools. Everyone has license to throw colored powder or water. Like most holidays it is based on a myth, probably the story of Krishna's frolic with the milkmaids, but no one can trace its origin precisely. The general hilarity, abandoned morals, and ribaldry reminded us of Mardi Gras, and during Holi we avoided the bazaar and its firecrackers and drunken revelers.

Elton Trueblood writes that other religions contain insights and truths which the Christians must accept, even while they maintain that "whatever is true in all religions is genuinely consummated in Christ."[79] I am inclined to agree with Trueblood. But Shridharani considers this a mischievous attitude which makes unequal comparisons of the Hindu and Christian religions.

The last word has not been said, or the last judgment made on world religions. I have to think of how much we learned from our friends in India. They helped us in our own spiritual growth.

I like this story told by Margaret Parton, a journalist based in

New Delhi. For Christmas she put out her creche and told her servants and their children the story of the birth of Jesus and why Christians celebrated Christmas. Later she found that they thought she was telling the story of the birth of the Lord Krishna. "They were so delighted that we should be celebrating the birth of one of the Hindu gods that I hadn't the heart to disillusion them."[80]

Chapter 24

Missionary Life and Good Times

In the 1960s and 1970s, many of the faculty and staff and a majority of the students had some connection to the missionary communities in India. Like us, many of the teachers and dorm parents were supported by religious denominations, and the students came from central and northern India "mission stations." (Missionaries from South India had their own international school at Kodaikanal near Madras.) In the 1960s, Mennonite and affiliated missions had over 40 students at Woodstock. During the bleak winter break, staff, whether mission connected or not, received invitations to the homes of students and alumni in various parts of India.

The books about mission work include delightful pictures of missionaries traveling. We see the missionary pioneers atop bullock carts and elephants, sitting in country longboats, crowded into buffalo tongas, standing beside bicycles and Model T Fords. The men are dressed in dark suits that absorbed the Indian sun and the women in long dust-catching skirts. Both men and women wear the white topis, those pith helmets that were the colonial badge of Western civilization, intended to keep the Indian sun from cooking their brains.

We had it easier. Our family Going-down Day for the Christmas holiday was a gala occasion. Weather was always pleasant. The December days were mild and sunny, but we knew that nights on the train would be cold. To be properly equipped for traveling, we hired one derzi to make Walt a shirt, another to make suitcase covers for our better pieces, and a third to make Punjabi outfits for the girls and me. This trouser-dress combination is recommended

The Mission bungalow at Jagdeeshpur

for train travel which requires climbing into those upper second-class bunks.

In our time, there was no way to leave Mussoorie undetected. The trip started at two in the afternoon with the usual walk through the bazaar, following the coolies who insisted on carrying everything. With all our baskets, tin trunks, and sleeping bags we looked like any traveling Indian family. The shopkeepers asked anxiously when we would be back. We usually resolved to go to Dehra Dun by economical bus, but a taxi driver would soon talk us into leaving immediately rather than waiting for a bus and then not getting the less nauseous front seat. The driver sped down the hill and delivered us to the Dehra Dun train station with a squeal of brakes and plenty of time to spare. We arrived in Delhi the next morning and then boarded the evening train for a long ride through one-third of India. At Nagpur we changed trains to travel east to Raipur in Madhya Pradesh. We were usually met by someone from our Jagdeeshpur mission field and with them we took a bicycle rickshaw to Gass Memorial. Named for an early missionary, Gass Memorial is a no-frills hostelry with plain concrete floors, sturdy bolts on the doors, and mosquito nets on the beds. After a satisfying breakfast, we caught the early morning bus for the 90 miles to Jagdeeshpur. Or we paid to have the mission car meet us in Raipur. So much for spartan intentions.

We always arrived at the mission exhausted. One or more of us spent the first day recovering from something. But then we were ready for holiday activities: Christmas services, reading in the sun, picnics, wedding khannas, sight-seeing tours to other stations, and sometimes helping with mission projects. Each of the stations taught us something about India: at Jagdeeshpur, rural village life; at Champa the brass and silk industries; at Korba the influence of the East with its Russian-built power plants, generators, coal mines, barrages, and machine shops, all built on a scale to match the vastness of Indian needs.

Nothing in our life on the Hillside had prepared us for our first experience on a mission compound. I had been misled by my preconceptions of "bungalow," "compound," and "station." Most surprising was the bungalow. I had a picture in my mind of a certain peaked roof and a small front porch, a snug little house. The mission car approached the village of Jagdeeshpur, turned a corner and stopped before a rambling, red brick structure with wide verandahs and brick pillars. The house was shaded by ancient trees, and the grounds extended for several acres. The other bungalows housed the doctor and the hospital administrator. We were impressed not only by the size of the bungalows but also by their setting. Roselle, papayas, pomeloes, and oranges were doing well, and the garden vegetables were just coming on. Bougainvillea and poinsettia bushes to us Kansans seem extravagant. And every verandah had its potted geraniums lining the steps like something out of *Better Homes and Gardens*. Every garden was a picture. When we returned to Mussoorie, we took back a pomelo in our duffel bag, lemons stuck here and there in our luggage, and all the roselle I could stow away for the making of red gelatin desserts.

Inside the bungalow we found spacious rooms. Whitewashed walls and concrete floors created a monastic effect, reminding us of Shaker simplicity. We had little difficulty feeling at home as we traveled from one mission setting to another, or even to those of other denominations. The furniture was of the same style, built for hot weather, or rainy weather, no overstuffed sofas. Each bedroom had an adjoining bath with water piped into a tank from which we dipped the water we needed. We were relieved to find Western style toilets.

The early missionaries were not being frivolous when they built those bungalows. They were designed after the pattern the British used in an attempt to make the climate endurable. The brick and cement were from local materials and did not dissolve in the rains.

They proclaimed to the Indians whom they hoped to convert, "We are here to stay."

The visitor to a mission station may have been surprised by, impressed with, critical of the program. Surprised that it was so extensive, so self-contained, so well-organized; impressed with the variety of work going on, and critical of the difference in standard of living between the missionary and the villagers, or of programs that seemed too sophisticated for the village being served.

I once heard the grandson of a missionary say: "I had always been critical of the mission program, wondering if people would not be just as well off without our interference. But when I visited the places in India where my grandparents had spent their working years, met the people, and saw the work of the church that they helped to plant, I changed my mind. I was impressed."

The Jansen Memorial School at Jagdeeshpur had earned a high reputation in the state. When we were there, all of the graduating students had passed their exams, while the average for India was 35 percent.pass. Edward Burkhalter, missionary in charge of schools, gave credit to the excellent Indian staff and in particular to its Indian principals, including Samuel Stephen and Willie Walter.

The boarding students live in dormitories, empty buildings with space for students to roll out their bed mats and find a place for their tin trunks. Walt had some envy of the administrators. A school can be run inexpensively when furniture, food, heating, and cooling are that simple. Woodstock School, minimal as its facilities were, had many more administrative concerns as it operated within the framework set by its competition.

The mission program at Jagdeeshpur included the distribution of relief goods. Central India was suffering from famine, and the mission had received a shipment of wheat from Church World Service. Wheat was to be exchanged for work by both Hindus and Christians. Those who were able-bodied dug a tank, a large pond that would fill with monsoon rain and provide drinking water and a place to bathe for both people and buffaloes. Other men and women worked at building a road. (During the Depression of the 1930s, the U.S. had a similar program called Works Progress Administration, the WPA.)

The workers felt some discontent about the program, and one morning they threatened to strike. We felt critical of the workers for biting the hand that was feeding them. In the giving of alms we expect the recipient to be grateful. The problem in this case was not one of ingratitude so much as the haves dealing with the have nots. Hungry people do not understand our method of limited help. They wonder why we cannot feed them until both we and they are destitute, for that is the way they manage in their extended families. We are stingy, they think. But we, "having done our part," think of ourselves as generous. They must trust God for the rest, we tell them. Their experience with Hinduism tells them that this is one more suffering to endure before their next reincarnation. Margaret Parton wrote,

> [Indians] loathe the American demand for gratitude. I wish that we could act with direct simplicity—with the same simplicity with which a woman gives a glass of milk to a hungry child, not asking anything in return, but rather hoping the child will mind his manners after he's been fed. But even that hope is unimportant; the important thing is hunger and therefore food.[81]

The mission administered schools and a hospital at Jagdeeshpur. An outstation at Saraipali, a town to the east, included work with women, brides' schools, and pastors' retreats. The missionaries there also supervised a weavers' cooperative and worked with farmers to improve crop production.

The Champa station, about forty miles north of Jagdeeshpur, was the first to be established by the General Conference Mennonites, along with the Janjgir station west across the Hasdeo River. One year when the bridge over the Mahanadi River was still out, we were driven by way of country roads to the river, where we waded out from the rocky shore to knee-deep water and then poured ourselves into the country longboat. We joined the village people who were crossing the river with their bicycles, poultry, and sacks of whatever. On the far side we waded in to the sandy shore where a jeep from Champa met us. (Now there is a proper bridge that does not wash out with the monsoon.)

The country longboat

The mission at Champa operated a leprosy home and hospital as well as a general hospital. An extensive agricultural program supported the leprosy home. We especially liked the architecture of the church for this community. The building was open and airy, with unglazed windows and Gothic arches. It was large enough to hold eight hundred people who sat on low benches, women on one side and men on the other. At the moving communion service, we saw the victims of Hansen's disease receive the bread in their deformed hands. The elements were a piece of chappati and a sip of raisin juice.

At Champa we were shown a storeroom full of relief supplies. During that year of famine, various relief agencies had sent clothing.

"What will you do with this stack of fur coats?" we asked.

Missionary Aron Jantzen, too, was baffled as to how to use them. "A fur coat is not a high priority item here," he admitted.

A major food distributor in the U. S. had donated canned sandwich spread. In spite of the famine, Indian villagers were not fond of it, and would eat almost anything else first. Other donations from well-known corporations were highly appreciated, especially the hospital equipment and medical supplies.

In Champa we toured the streets where the smiths were hammering out brass plates and bowls, using simple tools. We followed the process from the time the brass sheet was shaped to the polishing and engraving. Weavers worked with raw silk thread stretched into 27-yard lengths to form the warp, throwing the shuttle in and out. I watched a pretty teenager twirl her distaff and roll the emerging raw silk on her bare thigh to form the thread. The day was warm. The smell of urine in the open trench and the sight of the six-inch callous on her thigh made me feel ill, and I left ahead of the party.

We visited the shop where shining lengths of silk saris, one after another, were flung out on the sheeted floor so that Paula could chose one for her graduation sari. She selected one in a natural tan with a woven border of gold and bright blue. Champa sends tons of its finished silk to other countries, especially to Germany. The weight varies from heavy for upholstery to light for silk shirts.

The missionaries at Champa attended the Indian church service on Sunday mornings and met together in the evenings for an English meditation followed by a time of socializing. To climax one evening when we visited, Arthur Thiessen with his cello and Joe Duerksen with his violin were the guest performers with the New York Philharmonic. They followed the scores, playing first chair of their respective sections. It was quite some Haydn.

Korba is 25 miles north of Champa, by mission car if it happened to be going, or by bus. One bus trip took us five hours. In 1914, P.A. Penner, P.J. Wiens, and C.H. Suckau made a trip to Korba to select a site for the mission station. The trip was made atop a Champa elephant. They might have made the trip in less time than we did, for elephants travel six miles an hour. On the way back, the missionaries were in danger of drowning when their elephant was almost swept away in a flooded stream.

Paula's teenage dream was to ride from Champa to Korba with the other missionary kids on an all-night oxcart trip. An oxcart travels four miles an hour, two miles in a caravan. This journey remains one of Paula's unfulfilled fantasies.

Korba was once a small village of two thousand where the rajah and the missionary owned the largest houses. Now tiers of modern apartments are available for the managers and workers in the coal and bauxite mines, the machine shops, the fertilizer and the hydro-electric plants. We visited the long established mission church as well as a number of house churches in different areas of Korba. Near the mission bungalow and church is the grade and high school which uses Hindi as the teaching medium. Across town, Beacon School, using the English medium, brings together children from different parts of India as well as from other countries, giving them the opportunity to study in a common language. The Hindi school has been turned over to the government, but Beacon School is a thriving, self-supported private school.

In Korba we were more aware of the "cow-dust hour" than we were in other towns. The hundreds of evening cooking fires produced a gray-blue haze as Indian mothers prepared a meal over *chulhas* fired with cow patties, and as the cows and goats were herded back to home corrals. The evening was pleasant with the familiar smell and the muted sounds of the Indian village drifting over to us as we sat on the verandah of the mission bungalow. One night we were awakened by raucous laughter on the road, as though a gang of teenagers was carousing through the area. Next morning we learned that we had heard a pack of jackals. By the 1980s, the cow dust had changed to the ever-present pollutants from smokestacks. The jackals have disappeared as the town has spread over the plain.

I will make an observation: Missionaries like to tell jokes. That statement applies ecumenically. Missionaries even like to tell jokes on themselves, about the difficulties with the new language, hunting exploits, traveling experiences, fleecings by shrewd taxi drivers who take advantage of their lambish naivete'. Experiences which may have been frightening at one time become part of the missionary legend. Probably some of the tales become embroidered. Jake Giesbrecht tells of killing three wolves with one bullet, a story I didn't believe, but his cohorts verified that one.

Missionaries are adept at making do, fixing up, and doing without. There is the story of P.A. Penner, who arrived in India in 1900, having trouble with his Ford. Like a good missionary he tried to solve the problem himself, but after several days he gave up and, at considerable expense, called in a mechanic from Raipur. The mechanic asked why he was using molasses rather than oil in the crankcase. It developed that Martha had received a gallon of molasses in a carefully cleaned oil tin and put it on her pantry shelf, where P.A. had found it.

Many of the activities of mission work included the handling of cash. When we visited, each mission bookkeeper asked us to help set up a better system for keeping track of it. The mission policy was that anyone, Indian or Western, had to pay out of his own pocket for any cash shortage when he turned the books over to someone else.

As we audited, we received an education. "Expenditure, Rs. 2 for killing python." The mission schools were glad to pay for snakes killed on the campus. Or "Rs. 3 for rescuing Eliah from the well." A receipt had the notation, "Left thumb print of Tilaso Bai." We did not verify the thumb prints, but we could have if there had been a question of fraud. We did learn to read Hindi numbers on invoices, a confusing process because of the similarity of some Hindi numbers to English numbers not equivalent. Banking was done in Raipur, and reconciling bank statements was difficult. The early missionaries had banked in Calcutta, five hundred miles away. To be sure that their deposits arrived safely by mail, they had been encouraged to cut their bills in two and mail half at a time.

The mission always, from the beginning, had the objective of turning the management of churches, schools, and hospitals over to the national church. In the 1970s this was the trend of all the denominations. Permission to stay in India was being refused by the government for most missionaries whose work was to plant churches.. In 1976 a plan for turning over the program by the Mennonites was speeded up when many of our workers were sent home by the government. Our last missionary couple returned to the States in 1989, after a long process of turning over property, some to the church and some to interdenominational trusts.

Early missionaries had a willingness to sacrifice along with a pronounced spirit of adventure. They suffered from loneliness, harsh climate, and unheard of diseases. Some of them felt that they single-handedly had to bring in the Kingdom of Heaven, and tended to exhaust themselves trying. Many of them were "characters." Although they were all human enough to own flaws (some of them were difficult to live with), many of them were saintly. They deserve our admiration.

Mennonite students and staff in 1966; Ruth and Walt Unrau on the left, Paula second from right standing in the front row, Susan hidden in the back; Photo from Mennonite Library and Archives, Bethel College, North Newton, KS

Missionaries, along with statesmen, soldiers, and businessmen, must take credit and blame for the Westernizing of India. The evangelical movement in Britain in the early 1800s sent pioneers to India like Baptist William Carey and Anglican Henry Martyn. Medical work, schools, and colleges, while not converting many Hindus to Christianity, influenced their thought. Christlieb told of a conversation with a Hindu friend in the 1920s:

> "Perhaps what is wanted in this country is a little more Christianity?" I ventured. "I am a Hindu," he replied, "and may have different views on that subject. I must admit we need the Christian standards. I am a Christian College man myself, and I confess it has altered my standards for my whole life. There is this about Christianity. It is so plain—it teaches something to simple people.
>
> "A little while ago I had to do with coolies. I had to classify them, so I asked of each what religion he was. One coolie woman said she was a Christian, and I asked her what she meant by that. I confess I asked just to make fun of her, for I saw she was quite uneducated and poor. To my surprise she answered at once, 'We must not steal, we must not tell lies, we must be kind, we must serve God.' She had some idea, she knew something!
>
> If I asked a Hindu coolie woman what she meant by being a Hindu, she would not be able to say anything. Yes, we need the Christian standards! The absence of them makes work in the villages most difficult."[82]

Chapter 25

Going Places

> Arrived here. These words sound simple enough but cover a multitude of complications . . . . The unkind fates are piling it on too much. If two or three things go wrong, and mean to discourage me, all right. I'll be discouraged. But when every mortal thing that can go wrong does go wrong, I will not oblige any longer.[83]

For some of us, along with our love of India is a love of travel, and India offers such diverse and inexpensive opportunities that when we return home we can dine out on our travel stories for at least a year. As we travel vertically and horizontally, we discover a different India at every stop-off. And there is enough of risk to make every venture exciting, although for us Unraus, none of our escapes was truly narrow.

Early in her missionary career Marie Luise Christlieb, quoted above, discovered Murphy's Law: anything that can go wrong will. This is a fatalistic philosophy to which I do not subscribe, but it was often quoted as we patched together our travel plans. The second most popular saying was "*Kya kare?* What to do? Not to worry."

Murphy's second law is that nature always sides with the hidden defect. This law is illustrated by the number of taxis we hired that had some major disease that did not reveal itself until we were well on the way. People who travel in India should be Talented Travelers, who have Inner Resources that they can call on to entertain the children and have the Patience of Job while they wait for those trains, planes, and bullock carts; while they are stranded by monsoons, wars, and landslides.

Anyone who has traveled beyond the city limits becomes a story teller. The melancholy fact is that our friends are willing to sit still only for our disaster stories. "You missed your train in that remote village and another didn't go for a week?" Although at the time of the disaster, our courage drains from every pore, in the telling we rise above the situation and remember that we met it with aplomb.

We have a disaster story for every trip we made to India, but I will tell only one. The second time we went we had suitcase trouble. We were Talented Travelers by that time and had purchased the lightest of suitcases and had purified our luggage so that we were carrying exactly our allowed weight limit. (Fortunately, bouffant skirts had gone out of style since our first trip.) The four of us had eight pieces of luggage besides our carry-ons. My particular responsibility was a heavy gear for the Woodstock jeep. In addition I had my electric hair curlers and a large box of Tootsie Rolls entrusted to me at the airport by a friend of the mission children of Woodstock.

The suitcase trouble started in Japan. First the handle came off Paula's new economy model; then the handle came off Susan's Deluxe Graduation Special. Then as we were strolling around the Osaka airport, luggage all checked through and sent on its way to the plane, I stumbled across a red suitcase in the middle of the lobby.

I said, "Someone else must have bought luggage at Kmart."

Paula said, "This is my suitcase."

Walt said, "It couldn't be. I just checked in eight pieces, and I have eight tags to show for it."

Susan said, "Someone who probably wants to go to Detroit has a piece of luggage going to Delhi."

The young Japanese woman at the desk said, "I think you had nine luggages."

She called the luggage back from the runway to count it, and even in Japanese she could count only seven pieces. She gave us another tag for our "ninth" piece and sent it all back to the plane.

Walt turned to the matter of having our tickets checked so that we could go to the departure lounge. He gave them to the clerk, and while she was in the process of checking them, a party of thirty American chiropractors interrupted her. Evidently she had instructions to take care of large parties before small parties. When she returned to Walt, she handed him only three tickets. His was missing. He protested, having expected to accompany us on the next leg of the journey. She insisted that he had given her only three. She wanted us to look through all our pockets and purses; she called back our luggage a second time and asked us to look through it for that fourth ticket.

The time of departure was drawing closer, and we felt lonely in that empty lobby, all other passengers having been checked through to the boarding area. In desperation, Walt buttonholed a man who looked official and explained our predicament. Walt asked the official, who understood English, to have the other passengers look through their ticket envelopes to see if they might find an extra ticket. The official explained that this would be a breach of Japanese courtesy. Then reluctantly, with many apologies, he made the announcement of the lost ticket to the other travelers. The ticket was found in the pocket of one of the chiropractors.

The desk clerk apologized with large tears, and we ran for our plane. Walt, a thorough person, happened to look back and saw our luggage standing in splendid isolation. He raised an alarm and got our bags on the same plane with us.

There is more to our story, for this was a long journey. We were to change planes in Hong Kong and then proceed immediately to Delhi. At the Hong Kong airport, BOAC sent their prettiest Chinese stewardess to tell us that we were to stay overnight in Hong Kong, courtesy of the company, because of a strike of BOAC mechanics. Rather than putting us on another airline, BOAC insisted that we should have this experience of a night at the Miramar Hotel. This turn of events made it necessary for us to go through customs. When Paula unzipped her suitcase for inspection, the zipper caught in her nylon nightgown and broke. The customs official gave us jute twine to hold our belongings together. By that time, the straps on my purse had let go, the jeep part having proved too heavy for the plastic.

We were an inelegant, dispirited, rag-tag of gypsies that arrived on the doorstep of the luxurious Miramar. "Luxurious," in fact, understates the Miramar. It was rife with leather-padded walls, push-button drapes, a phone in the marble bath, Oriental rugs, crystal chandeliers, and pillows filled with cement. Walt and Susan went out into the sinister Hong Kong night (well, actually, the place was still well lighted and jumping at ten o'clock) to find two new suitcases. When they returned, we relaxed enough to enjoy the elegant surroundings and bring Paula back into favor. She needed sympathy, for she was developing a painful infection on her cheek.

We made it to Delhi without further incident, unless you consider the mid-morning snack of dainty sandwiches an incident. It was to be our only meal until midnight. We arrived half a day late to be challenged by another traveling snafu already described.

I forget who said, "If I had a dollar for every hour I have spent in airports, I could buy the Eiffel Tower." Hawaii, Singapore, Frankfort, Hong Kong, Bangkok, Delhi—airports tend to resemble each other, although for elegance my favorite is Singapore. I have a bit of advice which may be worth the price of this book. Don't let your children spend all their souvenir money in airport shops before they get to their destination.

"But Daddy, we'll never be in Singapore again and I'll regret all my life that I didn't buy this jade ring."

How does a sixteen-year-old know that she will never be in Singapore again? And is she really in Singapore if she is in the airport, waiting for the plane to be swept out?

It is hardly possible to travel by train in India without using the services of the coolies. In the first place, you have more luggage than one person can manage. And then there are so many coolies, thousands of them trying to make a living carrying people's belongings. Once they get the situation sorted out, they load each other. One will pile three of our suitcases on the head of another and then hang baskets and sea bags on his arms. They run off with our precious belongings, expecting us to follow. Coolies often have the information you need about trains and tracks and boogies, and you do well to take their advice. When it comes to paying them, there was a time when you asked what the charge was, and the coolie replied, "Whatever you think." When you gave him what you thought, he would demand more, even throwing your money at your feet in a display of pique. Now there are definite rates per piece of luggage, but you are still expected to add a little *baksheesh*, a tip.

People in India often travel with all their belongings. They brought bed rolls, tiffin baskets and eating utensils, tin trunks of clothing, a sack of rice, and everything essential for remaining alive away from home. But Indians don't mind if there is no space on the floor for their feet. They will sit cross-legged on the seat, or stretch out to sleep on top of the luggage.

The second-class sleeper will sleep six in a compartment at night and seat sixteen or any number by day. First class is more comfortable. The seats are reserved and well padded and the compartment has a door that can be locked. The best of all possible classes is first air-conditioned, but now second class AC is very good, although it does not have as much privacy since it has only a curtain rather than a door. No matter if you come to India intending to "go village," sooner or later you realize that you were not brought up "village" and are not village conditioned. When the temperature reaches 117 degrees Fahrenheit, you decide to blow your savings and go comfortably. Restrooms on any class of train are efficient but spartan, often grimy with dust. The toilet is a hole in the floor and a faucet for flushing, with a circular view of the roadbed below. One of our mission children managed to lose his glasses down the toilet hole.

Train travel provides the best way of seeing India, getting a perspective on its geographical vastness, its antiquity, its villages, and its cities.

Every so often the train stops at a little station. Children come crowding outside our window. "Baksheesh, memsahib, baksheesh, sahib," they repeat over and over. Taught to beg, they join their hands together, roll their huge brown, black-fringed, innocent eyes, their beautiful young faces smiling. Only the train moving on brings a halt to their incessant prayers.

Enroute to Delhi we awakened during the night when the train stopped for long layovers. We soon accustomed ourselves to the noise and singsong of the wallahs' *gharram chai* (hot tea) and went back to sleep. We awoke about six, when the boogie came alive as we anticipated arriving at the Delhi station and prepared to join the grand explosion when we would all detrain. Then we settled ourselves at the window for a quiet half-hour's leisurely ride through the fields—green, flooded, or dry depending on the season—and then through the *bustees* (slums). We watched India waking up.

The first time we made this trip, I was surprised to see all those people with their little brass containers strolling through the fields, squatting leisurely besides the tracks and in the middle of the fields. When I became more knowledgeable, I averted my eyes, realizing that they were making their first trip to the toilet, a religious duty. In many parts of India, this is a communal act. The villagers share this togetherness with the people who ride the trains.

The atmosphere of the Old Delhi train station makes one think that war has just been declared and everyone is rushing to the front. People seem to be living at the station. Families stake out a claim and settle down with their baggage. The average village family, we were told, does not inquire beforehand when a train is due in. They just go to the station, and if they have to wait a day or two for a train, never mind.

A tiffin basket of bread, cheese, peanut butter, hardboiled eggs is less dreary than a tray ordered ahead, which arrives uncovered at the next large station. The station meals are more appetizing. For breakfast we favored the onion omelets. Even though the toast might be cold, the tea was hot and strong. The nicest eating experience while traveling happened when we bought a basket of oranges, four or five dozen, from a wallah who came through the boogie. We ate as many as we wanted and arrived at the mission station surfeited with oranges.

We survived all of our travels without succumbing to dysentery, due to the fabulous Unrau luck, I suppose, for people more deserving of good health than we were not so fortunate.

Our visits to some of India's tourist centers gave us kaleidoscopic views of the country.

The city we visited most often was just down the hill. Dehra Dun is known by its admirers as the garden city of India, with little white cottages set in gardens "where the bulbul sings love songs in Persian." Almost like home in England and a wonderful place for retirement. The shops are diverse, those around the clock tower catering to the middle-class and well-to-do shopper. To us, the town was a confusion of streets, but the many small bazaars scattered throughout the town supply the needs of the general population. Walt ordered furniture and could have watched it being built on the pavement in front of the store. The pharmacy advertised in its windows the merits of its birth control plans by way of pictures of attractive families with two children.

We stopped at Kwality's or Nepoli's for cool, never cold, limeade. When we asked euphemistically for the washroom, we were shown the open sink and spigot. But on our last visit we had a meal at Chugh's new restaurant adjacent to his modern hotel. Chugh was also our travel agent.

Six kilometers from the town center is the famous Forest Research Institute, its imposing brick buildings set in a tea garden.

Street scene in a town on the way to Delhi. Photo by Vic Reimer

The head office of the Survey of India is now located in Dehra Dun, and India's second satellite earth station is nearby, with links to France, Japan, and Britain.

When we rode by taxi from Dehra Dun to Delhi, we knew that we were inside the population explosion, perhaps at its very eye. As we passed through towns, we were mesmerized by a blur of people walking, fanning out in front of the taxi. Every driver and every pedestrian seemed casually intent on leaving this life and entering into his next reincarnation.

Still, the ones that really own the road are the lorry drivers. Tata-Mercedes-Benz lorries have printed on their tailboards HORN PLEASE, but that is useless etiquette. When vehicles meet on a one-lane road, they play chicken, waiting until the last possible moment to take to the shoulder. The common saying is that a lorry will move off the road for no one, not even for another lorry. This is not quite true: they give way to India's 15 million bullock carts. We admired the lorries for their decorations of flowers and curlicues in rainbow colors.

We did little sight-seeing in Delhi, keeping close to Connaught Circle and the YMCA or International YWCA. We did even less shopping, but a little inquiry would reveal that someplace in Delhi, on some twisting lane, anything could be found.

On one visit we combined a celebration of our wedding anniversary which coincided with Paula's seventeenth birthday, and saying goodbye to Susan and her husband as they left for Africa. It seemed fitting to use our anniversary gift from Walt's relatives to eat at the coffee shop of the Oberoi, that shining splendor of marble, glass, red velvet, gleaming brass, and air-conditioning. Paula blew her share of the gift on a tall glass of orange juice, and I ordered that rarity in India, iced tea. We all ordered other marvels such as steak (beef from a real cow), tossed salads, and baked potatoes. We were puzzled by the fried egg on each steak. Fried eggs we had plenty of at Woodstock.

In Delhi, we neglected our inhibitions. Students and staff on October break headed for the American Embassy pool and ordered hamburgers, cokes, and french fries. When we returned to Woodstock, we mourned for those who thought such luxuries were necessities, who drew extra pay for living in Delhi because it was a "hardship area," who couldn't walk to where they had to go.

We did the tourist route when we accompanied the Hindi Club to Lucknow, the city of palaces. We dutifully visited the historical palaces of the Muslim *nawabs*, but the most memorable part of the city for us was the Residency where the Mutiny of 1857 was focused. The siege lasted six months and was the most desperate of the battles. Of the 3,000 British and Indians who sought refuge in the Residency on June 29, only 1,000 marched out on November 8. The attractions for the students were the art school where Woodstock's art instructor, Frank Wesley, had studied, the Indian music college, and the bazaars. The bazaars were famous for chikan embroidery work and perfumes. The girls bought vials of earth, cucumber, and onion, as well as more exotic scents. What we remembered of our two-day look at Lucknow was the vitality of the people we talked with. Their spirit was in contrast to the crumbling opulence of the palaces and the history of decadence. Lucknow citizens probably don't think much about the nawabs except at Mohorram, an Islamic holy day when all the chandeliers in all those palaces are set ablaze to celebrate the new year.

The Taj Mahal

Of course we went to Agra to visit the Taj Mahal. Everybody does.

With your first look you are left without words. "Exquisite," "femininity in stone," "a poem of masonry," "a jewel in India's architectural diadem" are some of the expressions you read. We were impressed by the *jalis* (screens of marble lace work) and the flower inlays of semi-precious jewels in the marble walls. One small flower may have sixty different inlays, so smoothly embedded that the joinings are scarcely revealed by a microscope. Along with the Taj, the tourist visits other beautiful mosques and the old town of Fatehpur Sikri, Akbar's folly. His new capital which he moved from Agra was abandoned after fifteen years for reasons unknown. One theory is that the river changed its course, leaving the large court without adequate water.

We visited Varanasi (Benares) where life focuses on the burning ghats along the Ganges. We took rickshaws from our hotel in the not so early morning to pay our way onto one of the old wooden boats that tourists take to watch the rituals on the ghats (steps down to the river). The late December morning was cloudy with a drizzle, but worshippers were undaunted. On a bad day, one could see parts of bodies floating down the river. A scarcity of wood might mean that a body had not been entirely consumed by cremation.

Near Varanasi is the deer park where Buddha preached his first sermon to his five disciples. Sarnath is a pleasant place of ruined monasteries, mango trees, images of Buddha, and grassy knolls. We mingled with Japanese tourists and a young man from Yugoslavia who had high praises for his now chaotic country.

Benares silk and glowing carpets are the temptations of the bazaars. An excursion included a visit to a sari and cloth shop, forced on us by the rickshaw wallah.

"We will not buy."

"Only look."

Half an hour later: "We will each buy one piece."

It was in Calcutta that we were closest to the poor of India: the children sifting through garbage heaps for something salable; the street people camping on the sidewalk under plastic sheets attached at the top to the brick fence around the park. We saw many enterprising, cheerful people trying to sell a little something on the sidewalk, cakes of fuel made of dung and coal dust, a few pieces of fruit, flowers, rags, bottles.

Calcutta makes history easy with so many prominent visual aids. One morning we visited the Park Street Cemetery. The first undertaker in Calcutta was Mr. Oldham, probably also in the monument business. He had urged his mourners to erect conspicuous and ornate monuments. They certainly did. It is "a small cramped town of domed temples, pyramids, obelisks, urns, and broken columns." History is written in the inscriptions.[84]

The story of colonial India is also written in Calcutta's buildings, with their inscriptions to well-known Britishers like Thackeray, Dickens, Macauley, and others who slept there at least once.

Chapter 26

Other Hill Stations

Traveling for pleasure has not been part of the middle-class Indian tradition. Indians traveled to visit relatives, to make religious pilgrimages, to conduct business, or to escape the heat of the plains. Traveling for the well-to-do meant going to the capitals of Europe. But in more recent years, Indians have discovered their own country as a playground. Kashmir, even though remote, is a vacation land that is now attracting middle-class and wealthy Indian tourists. That is, when the political climate is agreeable.

We arrived at the Tourist Reception Center in Srinagar after a twenty-four hour trip by foot, bus, taxi, train, and plane. A horde of houseboat owners attacked us, and we were taken captive by one with whom we had had tentative correspondence. We thought his price was too steep, but he assured us that his was not just your average houseboat, and it was not on your average lake, such as Dal Lake. His boat flaunted flush toilets. His boat owned a European bathtub. His boat was on Nagin Lake. He urged us to "just come and see, come and see"; so we went by taxi to Nagin Lake and then by *shikara* (rowboat) and saw his houseboat. As he had predicted, we stayed.

For a week we owned a little front porch at which the shikara docked, a living room, a dining room, two bedrooms, and a bathroom. A stairway led to an upper deck where we were served afternoon tea under a canopy. The boat was fully outfitted with carpets, china, brassware, and framed pictures of tiger hunts. A sheaf of yellowed chits lay on the table for us to peruse so that we would know how highly regarded the host had been by past generations of guests. We were enchanted by our quiet watery front yard with its kingfishers and the ring of distant mountains. It would have been impossible to think of going back to Dal Lake with its prow-to-prow houseboats.

The owner and his family lived in a kitchen boat nearby which was joined to ours by a plank. They brought over our meals, skipping nimbly along the catwalk and into our little pantry. Two sons served as shikara paddlers, and members of the family cleaned and dusted. We saw one of them washing dishes in the lake which also received the drainage from our bathroom. None of us got sick. I don't know if our good health could be attributed to some germ-killing agent used in the rinsing (probably not) or the fact that Nagin Lake was filled with holy water. The owner acted as friend, tourist agent, guide, and bearer. On a cold, rainy morning he brought each of us a *kangri*, a pot of charcoal in a wicker basket. We warmed our hands and feet over the coals, but Kashmiris wear the pots under their robes against their stomachs.

On a sunny afternoon, we swam from the decks of the swimming boat nearby and watched other tourists water ski. Some of the women were skiing in their saris. The noise of the motor boats seemed out of place on our Mogul lake.

The saying is that it is impossible to be unhappy in Kashmir unless you happen to live there. The charm of the shikaras with their heart-shaped paddles contributed to the air of romance effected by history and scenery. The shikaras had ludicrous names like "Whoopie" and "Here I Am." The most pulling advertisement seemed to be that the boat boasted "spring seats," some of which were fully sprung. One was invited to lean back, half reclining under the decorative canopy, and enjoy the scenery.

Srinager is the Venice of India. Built beside the Jhelum River, its main streets are the lakes which are formed by run-offs from the glacier. The lakes reflect the clouds and trees, the tall, wooden-balconied houses, and even the mountains. The views of mysterious little waterways, keyholed by stone bridges, the gardens and factories, are a textbook for photographers. A woman reaches out of a houseboat window to dip water; a child gathers flowers to sell from a water garden; a merchant calls from shore to invite us to see his factory. Floating gardens of flowers, melons, and tomatoes are cultivated by families for the extensive tourist industry that devours food and flowers in season.

The charm of shikara travel can become an exasperation. As we drifted around the lake, other shikara wallahs approached us, urging us to buy their cigarettes, shawls, carpets, candy, and jewels. As we relaxed in our living room, shikaras came to our open windows with everything from toothpaste to expensive wood carvings. The flower shikara welcomed us with free roses, but after that he suggested that we were obliged to put in a standing order for a daily delivery.

The people have a Biblical look, as do their surroundings and their tasks. The children wear loose robes and little round velvet caps. The Kashmiri language sounds more of Central Asia than of any of the Indian languages, but our host could also speak Hindi and English. Although the summers are pleasant, the winters are harsh. The tourists go away and the tourist houseboats are closed. In their dark, small-windowed, tall houses and in their low-lying houseboats, the Kashmiris wrap themselves in their robes and blankets, hugging their charcoal kangris to their bodies.

The town was an hour's shikara ride away from our houseboat. Once in the city, we went from place to place by tonga, a high-wheeled conveyance from which you face backward and try not to fall forward out of. From the city we caught buses to other towns. One of our side trips was to the Shalimar Gardens. The gardens had been built by Shah Jehan for his beloved Mumtaz, for whom he later built the Taj Mahal. "Pale Hands I Love Beside the Shalimar" was a song from my high school chorus days, and I wondered whose hands those were in this color-conscious country. Those of Mumtaz, no doubt. But the words were written by a romantic English woman, Adela Florence Cory, who married Colonel Nicolson and followed him through India and Afghanistan disguised as a Pathan boy. The music was written by another English wife of a Bengal officer. So much for the pale hands of Mumtaz.[85]

One of the charms of the Kashmir Valley was the ring of snow-streaked mountains that enclosed us. We rode to the mountain village of Gulmarg on a bus that was piled on top with garden produce. At Tanmarg, a point below the resort, we transferred to ponies, each one accompanied by a *syce* who led the animal. My pony was named Bulbul, although he had few bird-like features. He wasn't even flighty. The path up was pleasantly shaded and smelled of hot pine needles and horses. Set on the edge of a saucer, Gulmarg (meadow of flowers) is a left-over from the British Raj. But what we saw of a golf course and a ghost town has now become a first-class tourist resort.

Our destination another day was Pahlgam, sixty miles up a mountain road lined with poplars, willows, and chenars. A scene photographed on our memories is of rice paddies as they rose on the hillside, jewel after jewel, small terraces enclosed by curved dikes. The water that flooded them seemed to flow uphill. Pahlgam is a one-street village, the starting place for treks into the mountains. Pilgrims assemble here for the climb to the cave of Amarath, another abode of Lord Shiva.

Susan and her husband came from Belgium to take a vacation with us. Where does a hill station dweller go for a June vacation? To another hill station, and we chose Kulu Valley.

Naturally we planned for an Early Start, which is always accompanied by irritation with someone who is not ready on time. Irritation is no respecter of places. When we went to Kulu Valley, it was imperative that we get there in one day, early enough to find our cabin and make supper before dark. We engaged a taxi to meet us at four in the morning at the Woodstock Gate. This was a fine plan and it lasted all the way from our house to the gate. After waiting for 20 minutes, Walt went up to the driver's house to arouse him. We arrived half an hour late in Dehra Dun where we met the long-distance taxi driver, who sulked for the first fifty miles. Kulu is about 125 air miles from Mussoorie, but 400 miles as we headed south, west, north, and east to get into the valley.

We drove through the states of Himachal Pradesh and Punjab, which is about the size of Kansas and known as India's breadbasket, with fields of wheat and sugar cane and sun. Most of the crops depend on irrigation from the "five rivers" from which it gets its name, Punjab. These farmers are rich by Indian standards. Most of them are Sikhs with fewer caste taboos and more openness to change than their Hindu cousins. The climate here is less enervating than that of the plains, and the Punjabi farmer seems more energetic and aggressive than the plains farmer.

By the middle of the afternoon we were climbing, glad to be out of the heat and to follow the Beas River as it rushed below us. Alexander the Great of Macedonia had slept somewhere in this area. He had conquered the Persian, Darius II, who had dominated northwest India in 327 B.C., but he could not force his homesick troops to go further than the Beas River. Some historians think that Alexander could have conquered India. He left reluctantly, but the invasion was important in that it opened routes that were followed by the next conquerors.[86]

We found our cabin in Manali by the light of the moon and settled in. We had brought a tin trunk of food and survived on rice with lots of different toppings. One meal we ate out. A sign advertised Indian meals at a "Johnson Guest House, 24 hours notice." So we gave notice and were served an excellent chicken curry meal. The English name made us curious, as did those on the gates of apple gardens. Banon and Johnson were descendants of British pioneers who had married hill princesses. Although the marriages were usually without benefit of an English magistrate, they resulted in stable families.

When efforts with tea gardens failed, the settlers turned to fruit and by the 1880 were producing thriving crops. The problem of transportation arose. Simla, a demanding market, was 140 miles and two formidable mountain ranges away. The growers found that coolies and pack animals were too costly. Then Captain Banon tried parcel post. Evidently the government subsidized the mails in that country, for mail runners made the venture profitable. Nowadays the fruit is delivered by lorry, and the Kulu fruit we bought in the Mussoorie bazaar often rivaled the more famous Kashmiri fruit and was less expensive.

Hippies were a part of the Manali scene. The town was suitable for their style, a place where the weather permitted them to sleep out and where food was available by begging. A group stopped us in the bazaar and asked in halting English for money. We gave them a few apples. One of them made a comment in French that was less than gracious, and Susan astonished him by answering in French. The young man had assumed that we were one-language Americans.

Manali advertises its good hunting and fishing, opportunities for trekking, and spiritual peace. This is a valley of a hundred temples and a thousand deities. Not far from our cabin was the temple of Devi Harimba, the most important goddess of the valley.

Our most ambitious trip was up to Rohtang Pass by bus. The pass divides India from the no-man's-land of Lahul, Spiti, and Ladakh, which forms a buffer zone between India and China. We stood at the pass, 13,400 feet up. Below us lay a thickly inhabited, fertile valley, heavily wooded. Turning, we faced the dirty snowfields of late June, a desolate, rocky, windswept moonscape. Penelope Chetwode wrote that the original name of Kulu Valley was Kulanthapitha, "the end of the habitable world." The name seemed apt as we looked into Lahul, but it did not explain the good blacktop road and the fact that this has long been the pass used by traders carrying salt and borax down to Kulu and returning with packs of rice for inhabitants of those mountains on the other side of the pass.

We turned our backs on the moonscape to look back toward the habitable world. Had this quiet valley been affected in any way by the Partition of 1947?

Again referring to Chetwode, we have the story of the Donald sisters, Hilary and Barbara, who farmed the ancestral estate in this valley. In 1947 they offered sanctuary to a number of Muslim refugees. When the Hindus started burning Muslim homes, the sisters were warned that the same fate would be theirs. To avoid retribution, the sisters penned a few calves in the bathroom because they knew the Hindus would not burn a house with cattle inside. This situation lasted for six days, and then the headman of the local village offered protection to the refugees. The Muslims were divided into two groups. One group went down the road to a remote village, but the Hindus had removed the braces from a pushta, and the Muslims fell to their deaths. The other group went up the valley to the district capital. The Hindu police who had been given rifles to protect the Muslims turned against them and picked them off one by one.[87]

That was history just twenty-five years before our visit. Terrorism continues as a means of venting hopelessness and anger.

Our taxi driver came back for us a week later as he had promised. Soon we were descending from the mists of the mountains into the hot winds of the Punjab. We stopped in Chandigarh for a Kwality lunch and were indeed grateful for the restaurant's air-conditioned gloom. We had read of Le Corbusier's Chandigarh, a newly created city built to be the capital of the state of Punjab and Hariana. "Le Corbusier fans will go wild over the architecture and highly original layout," says *India on $5 and $10 a Day*. We did not give the city a chance to drive us wild. It seemed eerily deserted in the midday heat. We drove around a few dusty streets, shielded our eyes from the reflections off the white, sharp-angled buildings and left. We expect Indian buildings to be towered, domed, latticed, inlaid, or decorated. Someday we should go back, preferably in December, to see what the guidebook was talking about.

In the Almora hills

Saroj Kapadia, who taught Hindi at Woodstock, had often spoken of her family in Almora and her childhood memories of those hills. When we learned that we could not go to Nepal for our winter vacation, Walt, Paula, and I decided to spend a few days in Almora while Ron and Saroj were there.

As the crow flies, Almora is about 120 miles east and a little south from Dehra Dun. As the train creeps, it is more than three hundred miles. We took the night train to Barielly and then a narrow gauge railroad north to the railhead, Kotgodam. There we decided against a taxi in favor of a four-hour bus ride to Almora. It was a diesel-scented climb, and the bus made a good deal of fuss about it. But the driver nursed the vehicle along with the skill of a racing car driver. The rider sits up straight on those buses, or slanted if the seat is broken. You don't read and you don't sleep. You just stare at your watch, which seems not to tick as fast as it should, and wonder if you deserve such imaginative torture. But the fare was Rs.11 rather than Rs.60 for the taxi. En route we decided to return by taxi.

Almora lies in the curve between Tibet and Nepal with a population of about twenty thousand. Although it is, like Mussoorie, a hill station, it has a very different character. Almora claims to be a purely

India station in contrast to Anglicized hill stations like Simla and Mussoorie. It existed before the arrival of the British, having been founded by Rajah Kalyan Singh about 1560. A hare he was chasing turned into a tiger, and he considered such a marvel a good omen for founding the town there. The people are handsome and sturdy with a Mongolian look. Except for a few hippies living up in the old Methodist mission bungalow, we seemed to be the only Westerners in town.

We found our way to the residence of the principal of the Adams Girls College, who was on leave. Her cook hosted us and saw to it that we were well fed and had plenty of blankets and hot water bottles.

While touring the town with the Kapadias, we asked about the prevalence of the Wheeler name over garages and other businesses. We were told that in the early 1900s an English colonel had visited the area, found it to his liking, bought a couple of mountains, and settled there, leaving his progeny to carry on his name. He must have been the original Wheeler-dealer.

The Methodists brought Christianity to Almora. Besides the Adams Girls College, we saw the school for boys, the hospital for lepers, and at least two churches. The work has all been turned over to the Indian people. Saroj's father had preached in the church on the hospital grounds; her brother at that time was manager of the hospital. Her mother had died when Saroj was a child, and the children had been raised back in the hills by their grandparents. When we visited the brother's family in Almora, the grandmother was there, a tiny woman in her white sari, bent with her hundred and more years, creeping around to find the warmest sun. Her grandchildren referred to her lovingly, remembering her past kindness to their motherless family.

A jeep trip out into the mountains gave us a view unlike our Tehri Hills. These were much more thickly populated, with many more terraced acres and substantial houses with slate roofs. The mountains were closer and more snow covered than those we saw from Mussoorie. Nanda Devi, which we could sometimes glimpse from the top of our own hill, in Almora seemed within arm's reach, not more than thirty miles away. Nanda Devi rises as a snow-covered cone to 25,646 feet, twentieth on the list of the world's highest mountains. Here is another abode of Shiva, where he sat with the rivers flowing from his hair. Hindus refer to the eternal snows of the Himalayas as the piled-up laughter of Shiva. The treasure of Almora is its view of the snows. I have never heard anyone say about mountain views, as they say about cathedrals or Muslim temples, "When

Students at the Woodstock gate prepared for a hike. Photo by Nathan Dick

The Unraus, Ruth, Walt, Paula, and Susan

you've seen one, you've seen them all." Every mountain view is different. Every mountain is a challenge, even though we know we will never climb it.

There are many Indias: the India of the Raj and the maharajah, the India of Forster's *Passage to India*, Mahatma Gandhi's India of civil disobedience, Lord Mountbatten's India of the violence of the Partition. This is Unraus' India, marked by all of the above. Those who know another India may not recognize this one. And this world was true for us only during one short period in one small place with a limited number of people. Did we find the "real India"? The real India, we are told, is in the villages, but we thought we saw it in the cities, in the resorts, and on treks into the mountains.

Many Britishers went in search of Rudyard Kipling's India, looking for the romance and adventure portrayed in his stories about the Raj. Many of them found it and couldn't get it out of their systems. In North Newton we belong to a group of India wallahs who get together three or four times a year to eat Indian food and to meet a visiting Indian colleague or a returning missionary. Our India family grows to fifty or sixty when we gather with all those in the area who have taught or been students, or parents, at Woodstock. Then we reminisce, sometimes hear reports from the visiting principal of the school, and savor the Indian khanna, which always includes rice and curry. Missionaries and their children want to go back again, and then again. We can't get India out of our systems. (I should modify that statement somewhat. Unfortunately, sometimes those who have heard the siren call of India are married to spouses who have not.)

But for most of us, whether it is the smell of the cow-dung cooking fires, the first rain of the monsoon, or spices in the bazaar; or the sound of mule bells, the Indian cuckoo, or the twang of the cotton fluffer; or the Doon Valley at night; or the gentleness of the people, something about the country has hooked us.

Bradford Smith said, "No life is complete without India in it."

End Notes

1. *A Mussoorie Miscellany* by "The Rambler" of the *Mussoorie Times* (Mussoorie: Mafasilite Press, n.d.)

2. Margaret MacMillan *Women of the Raj* (New York: Thames and Hudson, 1988), p. 182.

3. Major H.P.S. Ahluvalia, *Eternal Himalaya* (New Delhi: Interprint, 1982), p. 113.

4. *Mussoorie Miscellany*, pp. 47-48.

5. T. Walter Wallbank, *A Short History of India and Pakistan* (New York; New American Library, 1958), p. 35.

6. MacMillan, p. 184.

7. Ramesh Berry, *The Story of the Doon Valley*, (Dehra Dun: Jugal Kishore and Co., 1970).

8. *Asian Student*, April 22, 1978.

9. *The Quadrangle* (Woodstock School, Mussoorie, U.P., India, 1977), pp. 2-4.

10. Charles Allen, *Raj, a Scrapbook of British India* (New Delhi and London: India Book Company, Andre Deutsch, 1977), p.131.

11. Larry Collins and Dominque Lapierre, *Freedom at Midnight* (New York: Avon Books, 1975), p. 20.

12. Theon Wilkinson, *Two Monsoons* (London: Duckworth, 1976), p. 1.

13. *The Quadrangle*, 1977 p. 4.

14. *Ibid.*, p. 6.

15. Read Paul Scott's, *Staying On*, a novel about this group of expatriates.

16. Charles Allen, *Plain Tales from the Raj* (London: Futura Macdonald & Co., 1975), p. 105.

17. H.S. Bhatia, editor, *European Women in India* (New Delhi: Deep & Deep Publications, 1979), p. 92.

18. Geoffrey Moorhouse, *India Britannica* (London: Paladin Books, 1984), p. 136. One of the immediate causes of the Mutiny was the objection of the Indian soldiers to the beef tallow used on the bullets, which they had to bite.

19. Stephen Alter, a Woodstock alumnus, writes with understanding of Anglo-Indians in his first novel, *Neglected Lives*.

20. *The Quadrangle*, July 1910, p. 7.

21. *Ibid.*, November 1978, p. 2.

22. John Kenneth Galbraith, *Ambassador's Journal* (Boston: Houghton Mifflin, 1969), p. 214.

23. Edith Jones and others, *Woodstock School, the First Century 1854-1954* (Mussoorie: Woodstock School, 1954), pp. vi, 13. Vol. 2 by Ruth Hilliard continues from 1954 to 1983, a detailed and very readable history.

24. *The Quadrangle*, November 1961, p. 16.

25. Allen, Plain Tales, p. 125

26. Jones, p. 2.

27. *Ibid.*, p. 94.

28. *Ibid.*, p. viii. Another source claims that the house was built by or for Sir George Everest, and perhaps he built the present structure.

29. "Cricket Tales from the Hills," *Debonair*, April 1987, pp. 31-33.

30. Jones, p. 86.

31. Sandord Yoder, *Eastward to the Sun* (Scottdale, Pennsylvania: Herald Press, 1953), p. 121.

32. Krishnalal Shridharani, *My India, My America* (New York: Duell, Sloan and Pearce, 1941) p. 81.

33. Jones, pp. 27-28.

34. R.K. Narayan, *Waiting for the Mahatma* (Lansing: Michigan State Univeristy Press, 1955), p. 183.

35. Charles Allen, *A Glimpse of the Burning Plain: Leaves from the Indian Journals of Charlotte Canning* (London: Michael Joseph, 1986), p. 167.

36. Shridharani, p. 53.

37. Jones, p. 42.

38. Shridharani, pp. 161 ff.

39. Allen, *Plain Tales*, p. 261.

40. Francis Yeats-Brown, *Lancer at Large* (New York: The Viking Press, 1937), p. 37.

41. Jones, p. 29.

42. Idries Shah, *The Way of the Sufi*, (Penguin Books, 1968).

43. Prakash Tandon, *Punjabi Century 1857-1947* (London: Chatto & Windus, 1963), p. 56.

44. Shridharani, p. 207.

45. Gerald Berreman, *Hindus of the Himalayas* (Berkeley, California: University of California Press, 1972).

46. Robert Alter, *The Quadrangle*, 1983 pp. 2-3.

47. *The Quadrangle*, Winter 1984, p. 2

48. Wallbank, p. 35.

49. Collins and Lapierre, p. 22.

50. Quoted in *Far Eastern Economic Review*, "Independent Ways" (August 20, 1987), p. 32.

51. Michael Edwardes, *Bound to Exile: The Victorians in India* (London: Sidgwick and Jackson, 1969), p. 69.

52. Raleigh Trevelyan, *The Golden Oriole* (New York: Viking, 1987), p. 1.

53. *Ibid.*, p. 273.

54. Wilkinson, p. 8.

55. Charles Allen, *Raj*, pp. 158 f.

56. Pat Barr, *The Memsahibs: the Women of Victorian India* (London: Secker & Warburg, 1976), pp. 24 ff.

57. *Ibid.*, pp. 152-153.

58. Trevelyan, p. 151.

59. Macmillan, p. 182.

60. Charles Allen, *A Glimpse of the Burning Plain*, pp. 136-137.

61. Jones, p. vi, quoting from *Up the Country* by Lady Emily Eden.

62. John Lord, *The Maharajahs* (New York: Random House, 1971), pp. 156 ff.

63. Collins and Lapierre, p. 160.

64. Lord, p. 66.

65. Allen, *Raj*, p. 149.

66. Nirad C. Chaudhuri, *The Continent of Circe* (Bombay: Jaico Publishing Co., 1965), pp. 197 ff.

67. Collins and Lapierre, p. 230.

68. James W. Michaels, "The Elephant Stirs," *Forbes* (April 24, 1995), pp. 158-159.

69. Percival Spear, *India* (Ann Arbor, Michigan: The University of Michigan Press, 1961), p. 50.

70. Lucille Schulberg, *Historic India* (New York: Time-Life Books, 1968), p. 136.

71. Shridharani, p. 250.

72. Bradford Smith, *Portrait of India* (New York: J.B. Lippincott Co., 1962), p. 143.

73. Shridharani, pp. 339-341.

74. Smith, p. 210.

75. Norman Cousins, ed., *Profiles of Gandhi* (Delhi: Indian Book Company, 1969), p. 193.

76. *Khushwant Singh's View of India* (Bombay: India Book House, 1974), p. 13.

77. *Khushwant Singh's India* (Bombay: India Book House, 1967), p. 116.

78. Spear, p. 47.

79. Elton Trueblood, *The Validity of the Christian Mission* (New York: Harper and Row, 1972), pp. 174.

80. Parton, p. 7.

81. *Ibid.*, p. 219.

82. Marie Luise Christlieb, *An Uphill Road in India* (London: George Allen & Unwin Ltd., 1927), pp. 174.

83. *Ibid.*, pp. 68, 118.

84. *India* (New York: Time, Inc. 1964), p. 133.

85. MacMillan, pp. 206-207.

86. Robin Lane Fox, *Alexander the Great* (New York: Dial Press, 1974), pp. 368 ff.

87. Penelope Chetwode, *Kulu, the End of the Habitable World* (London: John Murray, 1972), pp. 129 ff.